PENGUIN BOOKS

MINDPOWER

Nona Coxhead has been interested in 'mind-science' and allied subjects for over twenty years. She is a very experienced writer, having produced six novels – *Though They Go Wandering; House of Mirrors; The Heart Has Reasons; Simon West; The Monkey-Puzzle Tree; The Richest Girl in the World, an American Odyssey* – and many short stories. She has also written two biographies, *Amelia Erhart* and *Greta Garbo*, and in non-fiction, *The Awakened Mind: Biofeedback and the Development of Higher States of Awareness* (with C. Maxwell Cade).

NONA COXHEAD

Mindpower

*

PENGUIN BOOKS

Penguin Books Ltd, Harmondsworth, Middlesex, England
Penguin Books, 625 Madison Avenue, New York, New York 10022, U.S.A.
Penguin Books Australia Ltd, Ringwood, Victoria, Australia
Penguin Books Canada Ltd, 2801 John Street, Markham, Ontario, Canada L3R 1B4
Penguin Books (N.Z.) Ltd, 182–190 Wairau Road, Auckland 10, New Zealand

First published in Great Britain by William Heinemann Ltd 1976
First published in the United States of America by St Martin's Press, Inc., 1977
Published in Penguin Books 1979

Made and printed in Great Britain by
C. Nicholls & Company Ltd
Set in Monotype Times

For Judith Skutch

While the over-all theme of this book represents the author's viewpoint, its spectrum of fact, information and theory is not based on her personal opinion.

Contents

Introduction   9
Acknowledgements   14
Abbreviations   15

**1 Psychic phenomena, old and new, under scientific
scrutiny**   17

  A. The march of experiments   26
  B. New dimensions for parapsychology   35
  C. Current trends of experiments   62
  D. The world of psi education   70

**2 A tidal wave of mind control and mind expansion
techniques**   76

  A. New methods of mind control through biofeedback
    training   97
  B. Mind-suggestion takes new directions   108
  C. Science looks at mind travel and mind sight   116

3 Expanding horizons for non-medical healing   129

  A. Science looks at healing power   138
  B. An ancient healing technique bridges east and west 154
  C. Medical and non-medical healing combine in new
    techniques   168
  D. Science investigates a far-flung shore of non-medical
    healing   181

**4 The moving together of metaphysics and physics, of
science and religion**   190

  A. Parascience and the study of consciousness: a bridge of
    theories and philosophies   202
  B. Science reaches into religion and mystical experience 218
  C. The explosion of research for a science of mind, spirit
    and consciousness   225

5 **The burgeoning inquiry into extended ranges and reaches of the mind**   229

6 **The pattern that emerges**   236

Bibliography   243

Organizations and centres concerned with mindpower research   257

Index   263

Introduction

THIS is an extraordinary time to be alive. Despite the very apparent failures and disillusionments of our twentieth-century world, as it moves into its last quarter excitement is gathering for a source of expansion, change and progress never before so extensively and scientifically explored – MIND; mind in man, mind as the primary mover and essence of life.

Evidence of this may not be immediately obvious to those without access to pertinent information, or a global perspective on the intercommunication of ideas that is weaving man into a network of self and cosmic inquiry – but once these are provided, awareness becomes irreversible, the implications accumulative and compelling.

Which brings me to the reason for writing this book. I feel that many of the specific ways in which this common inquiry is being conducted should be pointed up, recorded, laid out as a spectrum for general consideration. For if they are as significant in outcome as they are in promise, they will constitute unique history, as well as a timely preparation for the profoundest evolutionary advance man has so far experienced.

Apart from this, I hope to awaken or deepen interest in those who have just begun to think about the until-recently periphery and muted realms of mind, and link up the widely scattered action and research for those involved in a particular aspect and perhaps lacking time or opportunity for the broader view that could extend and enrich their own.

This action and research taking place in nearly all parts of the world, ranges from mystical belief in mind as an omnipotent, omniscient and omnipresent intelligence to methodical scientific deduction of how and why mind works in relation to individual and collective man (and perhaps interplanetary beings).

In many areas of the world, non-physical, or psychic phenomena are being re-examined, re-evaluated, re-classified and tested anew in relation to present-day concepts of science. Mainly labelled 'Parapsychology', the subject covers a wide variety of interconnected, often interfused experiments and systematic investigations of phenomena such as clairvoyance, telepathy, precognition, psychokinesis, out-of-the-body experiences, out-of-the-body perceptions, and many others.

A once suspect area of human speculation, parapsychology was in 1969 taken under the wing of the American Association for the Advancement of Science, and in America today parapsychology courses are taught in well over a hundred colleges and universities, at least seventy-five of the courses accredited.

In Russia, investigation of extrasensory perception subjects has become a government-sponsored science, its priority being to anticipate the indicated western trend, both as a safeguard and possible means of scientific supremacy, and as a means of scientific progress in general

Conversely, perhaps partially as a result, organizations for the purpose of parapsychology research and experimentation are multiplying rapidly in a number of other countries, and conferences and symposia, allied with medicine, psychology and psychiatry, anthropology, physics and religion are everywhere attended by hundreds vitally interested, including eminent doctors, engineers, professors and scientists in many fields.

Books and journals on the subject, spurred by the general public as well as specialized demand, have become a substantial area of publishing, and articles appear with increasing frequency in mass-circulation media. Television and radio programmes dealing with ESP and related subjects have increased from the occasional to the frequent and regular.

Methods of non-medical healing are gaining steady ground in many countries east and west. Patients are surging ahead of the medical profession in application of the various techniques, which, though differing in theory, are commonly based on an invisible, mentally-conceived source of power. Doctors are beginning to follow in slow caution, primarily as a last resource, but increasingly in private acknowledgement of its mysterious effectiveness.

Spiritual, or faith healing is being revived by many orthodox churches, some applying it through widespread multiple splinter groups providing individuals with present or absent healing, and newer, metaphysical beliefs make it their underlying principle. In vast halls and auditoria people like Kathryn Kuhlman in America and Harry Edwards in England (and many others) are gathering increasing thousands of believers and practise public healing. (Kathryn Kuhlman and Harry Edwards have both recently died.) In Britain, there is a federation of some 9,000 members many of whom receive special training, and in 1,500 or so British hospitals healers are legally allowed to administer to certain patients in cooperation with the medical staff.

Many thousands of ailing people from all over the world have journeyed to Brazil or the Philippines to undergo operations by 'psychic surgeons', closely scrutinized by disbelieving doctors, and, to the doctors' puzzlement (and persisting disbelief), have appeared to recover from sometimes lifelong complaints in statistically impressive numbers.

Biofeedback, or electronic measurement of brainwave frequencies, is an advancing frontier of possibilities for self-regulation of physiological processes through voluntary (mental) control, as is mind expansion, with its techniques for producing visionary experiences without drugs. Hypnosis, dream states and many other 'altered states of consciousness' including meditation are explored in new and experimental ways that often overlap with ESP.

Arising out of the ultimately dead-end road of drug use and addiction, disillusionment with materialism, established education and dogmatic theology, the youth of today has gone searching for new answers and goals and found them within age-old spiritual concepts of the East. The way of the mystics, of transcendence of self to cosmic consciousness, has brought hundreds of thousands of young people into new awareness of the self-revelations that lie veiled, yet apparently reliably available in the mind. Many forms of meditation – among them Yoga, Zen, Transcendental – have replaced their drug-induced inner experiences with those of more intense beauty, genuine upliftment and salutary counter-effect on their health and daily lives.

Intrigued by the success where all other curative methods had failed, Science has looked into the meditative state and found in it significant physiological support. Studies conducted in several universities and laboratories show that there is a marked decrease in the work-load of the heart during meditation, and that when practised consistently there is definite emotional and physical benefit.

These measurable quotients, together with the development of more sensitive instruments that have been able to measure the electro-dynamic force-fields shaping and controlling all living things, have brought science and physics into closer discourse. Research into invisible energy systems is on the increase; Auras, Radiation Photography, Bio-electronics, Bio-magnetics, are some of the categories that are bringing the 'etheric body' of mysticism and the 'plasma' of science into the same arena of hypothesis and study.

Beyond all this explosion of speculation and evidence, the objective knowledge and methodology of science is being brought to bear on increasingly far-reaching prospects of mindpower. In Exobiology, theories of the possibility of extraterrestrial life are being explored on an international basis. Already there have been conferences and symposia to consider its main concerns: how life on earth might have originated, the origin and evolution of intelligence, the search for other forms of life and possible interplanetary systems. More powerful radio telescopes are being developed for observation, and concurrently ESP is being considered as possibly the chief means of communication, thereby intensifying telepathic experimentation.

And, to sound out the planet Earth's bemusement with mind, theories also abound that move out beyond all these speculative and evidential vistas of mind, leading where only mathematical and scientific pioneers can range: a quantum mechanical hypothesis of consciousness to explain mind itself, Hypernumbers, Resonance, Psycholinguistics . . .

Who knows what these far-flung postulates may bring back for us by way of near-conclusions – one cannot expect conclusions, for surely the ultimate mystery of mind must be bounded by our finite degree of perception.

So finally what does this crescendo of investigation and testimony add up to – what does it reveal and portend? Many years of immersion in a particular metaphysical philosophy has given me a point of view, but only that; the answer may be a different one for every reader, or it may emerge one and the same for all – different only in name.

Acknowledgements

THE author wishes to express her appreciation to Sybil Harper for her research and help in preparing the book; to Maxwell Cade, Alan Mayne and Fred Alan Wolf for their helpful comments on the manuscript; to G. McManus and K. Mundin for valuable support of the project; to Gilbert Anderson, David Bohm, John Hasted, Benson Herbert, Charles Honorton and Stanley Krippner of the Dream Laboratory of Maimonides Medical Center, Marcus McCausland, John Pierrakos, Rex Stanford and William Tiller for permission to quote from their papers; to Julian Press and Calder & Boyars for permission to quote from *Center of the Cyclone* by J. C. Lilly; to Viking Press and Macmillan for permission to quote from *Superminds* by J. Taylor; to Hutchinson for permission to quote from *The Challenge of Chance* by A. Hardy, R. Harvie and A. Koestler; to the Academy of Parapsychology and Medicine for permission to quote from their symposia transcripts; to Avon/Discus for permission to quote passages from *Consciousness and Reality* edited by Charles Musès and Arthur Young; to the Viking Press and Turnstone Press for permission to quote from *Mind Games* by R. E. L. Masters and J. Houston and *The Medium, the Mystic and the Physicist* by L. LeShan; to Doubleday and Hodder & Stoughton for permission to quote from *The Cosmic Connection* by C. Sagan; to Russell Targ and Harold Puthoff of the Stanford Research Institute for permission to quote from their *Final Report*; also appreciative thanks to the editors of *Psychic, Parapsychology Review, MIU Press, Science of Mind,* the *ASPR Newsletter,* the *Journal for the Study of Consciousness* and the *Journal of Paraphysics.*

Abbreviations

AAAS	American Association for the Advancement of Science
ARE	Association of Research and Enlightenment
ASC	altered states of consciousness
DNA	deoxyribonucleic acid
DPR	deep psychophysiological relaxation
EEG	electroencephalograph
EPI	Eysenck Personality Inventory
ESP	extrasensory perception
ESR	electrical skin resistance
FRNM	Foundation for Research into the Nature of Man
GSR	galvanic skin response
HSP	higher sense perception
OOBE	out-of-body experience
OOBP	out-of-body perception
PA	Parapsychological Association
PK	psychokinesis
PMIR	psi-mediated instrumental response
psi	extrasensory abilities and psychokinesis
QSC	quasi-sensory communication
REM	rapid-eye-movement
RERU	Religious Experience Research Unit
SFF	Spiritual Frontiers Fellowship
SPR	Society of Psychical Research
TM	transcendental meditation
UCLA	University of California, Los Angeles

We believe the consciousness of man has an energy available to it that has control over matter, that can move matter, that can change matter.

EDGAR MITCHELL (*astronaut and sixth man to set foot on the moon, now Head of the Institute of Noetic Sciences, a research organization for the study of consciousness*)

1

Psychic phenomena, old and new, under scientific scrutiny

UNTIL we put men on the moon and brought them safely back to earth, it was as if the achievements of science were products of a purely physical and mathematical universe, somehow unrelated to the mind of man himself.

It was probably this feat that made us aware that the saying 'What mind can conceive, man can achieve' was not total hyperbole. Awesome as it might seem, we began to realize that mind had first to ideate and develop the sophisticated machinery, to initiate its motion; the elements of the cosmos had not combined without us. We had wanted to go to the moon, conceived the means of getting there, and we had engineered and carried it out.

The mind of man had come into focus.

For thousands of years we applied mainly philosophical definitions to man's mental processes, but in the eighteenth and nineteenth centuries led by Mesmer's almost accidental discovery of the power of mental suggestion, by Freud's recognition of the importance of the unconscious aspect to mind and the subsequent development of these perceptions by others, the study of mind was defined as a branch of science.

To this postulate we put up protracted resistance. While acknowledging that psychology revealed the machinations of human nature, that it helped us understand each other and ourselves a little better, and that in its deeper application it could turn out the basement of our inner lives with therapeutic results, we could not believe that either the area of man's functioning or the observer's success were the reliable ground of science.

When, however, psychology combined with medicine to become psychiatry, we were less sceptical; this seemed to offer a more practical approach to human behaviour and human ills. When the many mental casualties of World War I provided psychiatry with an opportunity for wide-scale practice, we were further persuaded of the logic and necessity for 'doctors of the mind'.

Since then, almost unnoticed, we have accepted the concept of a science of human nature, both in its superficial application to our behaviour – 'it's psychological', 'an inferiority complex', 'neurotic', are current language – and in its deeper functions with the mentally disturbed – where 'nervous breakdown', 'psychotic' and even more technically 'schizophrenic' are common usage.

And among those who might still reject the validity or desirability of mind-science, there are few who would not seek help from its practitioners for cases of mental derangement.

The investigation of much less explainable manifestations of mind, 'psychic phenomena', have been even longer and harder resisted as an inclusion of science. Until ninety or so years ago the study of how we communicate without visible means (telepathy), know an event will take place before it does (precognition), influence objects without touching them (psychokinesis), see without eyes (clairvoyance) was regarded with extreme scepticism.

Then, in 1882, some eminent British scholars and scientists founded the Society for Psychical Research in London and began to keep records of and to classify reported happenings of a psychic nature, particularly ghosts and apparitions and various forms of evidence, through mediums in trance, of survival after death. An American counterpart, the American Society for Psychical Research, was established in 1884 (later to become an independent Society).

The early research of the two societies ran into many thousands of reports and studies of the experiments conducted under close supervision by members of indisputable integrity whose attitude was neither bias nor scepticism, but an openness to conviction.

Despite many promising demonstrations of spirit-survival, of voice-communication, of ectoplasm (foam-like substance supposedly taking the shape of a discarnate person), and other mediumistic effects, the experiments were not sufficiently cautious to preclude fraud or unconscious cooperation, to convince all of us. This, together with techniques of optical illusion, and stratagems in darkened rooms which became so expert and rife early in this century, tended to confirm our general conviction that psychic phenomena was no province of hard science requiring empirical verification.

Forty-five years later, in 1927, William McDougall, a former professor of psychology at Harvard, but now Professor of Psychology at Duke University in North Carolina and a leading authority on psychic matters, started a laboratory for research on the non-physical nature of man as part of the psychology department under the guidance of Joseph Banks Rhine, whose own degree was in biological science.

Dr Rhine's initial work was the study of clairvoyance by means of the written records of so-called spirit communication and of mediums themselves, including the famous medium Eileen J. Garrett[44] (who was later to establish the Parapsychology Foundation in New York). He hoped to find some common element that confirmed the existence of discarnate spirits and to settle the then so-much-emphasized question of survival after death.

By 1934, despite exhaustive trance-sitting in the laboratory under strictly controlled (every precaution that could be thought of) conditions, Dr Rhine and his wife Louisa who was similarly grounded in biology and worked with him, did not consider they had found irrefutable evidence of survival. They did, however, establish a system of card-guessing with Zener cards, a pack of twenty-five cards marked with five different designs, a square, a star, waves, a circle, and a cross – and gradually, through thousands of repeated tests, discovered that there were people who could guess them correctly without seeing them, with a consistency that was mathematically improbable.

They extended these tests to cover many different conditions, and distances between cards and percipient; the results continued to support the existence of an ability by some people to perceive beyond the normally accepted range of sense. This perception, the Rhines felt, covered both clairvoyance, a term borrowed from the French, and 'thought-transference', now renamed telepathy, and grouped together as 'Extrasensory Perception'.

Encouraged to present his tests and his case for the existence of ESP before the public, Dr Rhine composed a monograph which the Boston Society for Psychic Research published as a book called *Extrasensory Perception* (1934).[126] It aroused such widespread public interest that it antagonized the academic community and evoked a broadside of criticism for both the mathematical validity of the tests and their basic assumption.

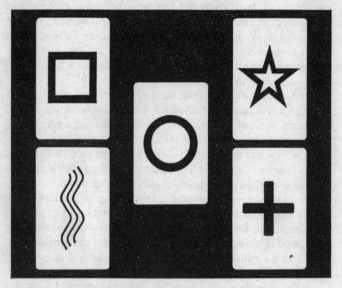

Figure 1 The Zener cards used by Dr Rhine and his associates in numerous experiments over the years to gather data and evidence for proving the existence of ESP.

Dr Rhine was not discouraged, but he tightened the control of his experiments to exclude chance, coincidence and other possible explanations of his evidence for ESP. His large-scale, mechanized tests of card-guessing and dice-throwing attempted unqualified statistical proof based on the law of large numbers. The ratio of correct guesses of his so-far successful subjects mounted astronomically against their incorrect ones, with odds over chance expectation, which were five out of twenty-five, sometimes as high as a million to one or more.

In 1937, Dr Rhine wrote another book, *New Frontiers of the Mind*,[126] and this one became a best-seller and Book-of-the-

Month choice. Interest in his research resulted in an excess of publicity and more criticism, some of which now reflected on the Psychology Department of Duke. To offset this, he separated his work with the distinguishing title of 'Parapsychological Laboratory', thus establishing a new label for modern research in psychic phenomena in America.

This helped his colleagues and his own cause, and when the President of the American Institute for Mathematical Statistics, after a hard assessment of his mathematical procedures, stated: 'If the Rhine investigation is to be fairly attacked it must be on other than mathematical grounds', it appeared that the door he had opened for ESP to become a science would not close. The year 1938 brought another 'trial by fire' when the American Psychological Association questioned his right of association, but again Dr Rhine's work failed to be voted out, and he carried on.

In 1940, Dr Rhine and colleagues wrote *Extrasensory Perception after Sixty Years*,[126] a summary of ESP evidence. It aroused little if any opposition. In fact, a certain pall had fallen over the subject due to the dryness and tedium of the statistical method. It did not seem to be leading anywhere, and it bored the percipients themselves to the point where they often seemed to lose their initial psychic ability altogether, and scored with equal extremity on the 'miss' side, with less than chance results.

This strange occurrence was to be a major discovery and turning point in Dr Rhine's investigations. More than the huge numbers of 'hits' this lapse to the other extreme proved some extrasensory element at work. During the forties he gave up experiments with emphasis on proving ESP existed, in favour of those that would try to reveal what it was and why it worked. The hidden variables of ESP performance were not found, a repeatable demonstration of its existence was unlikely, and it was this only, it now seemed, that could overcome our scepticism and the rejection by science.

The tests continued unremittingly, the conditions now designed to pinpoint the *mood* of the subjects when achieving both high and low scores of guessing against the odds of chance. Circumstances, environment and many other effects on the subjects' psychic responses were closely studied and computed.

Dr Rhine's standard experiments were duplicated by other people in the US and in other countries, and there were several important variations and developments of his statistical approach to extrasensory perception. In England, for instance, in 1941, a long series of tests were carried out by Dr S. G. Soal,[144] a lecturer in mathematics at the University College, London, with a subject named Basil Shackleton, a consistently high scorer who achieved odds against chance in card-guessing (carrying coloured pictures of five animals instead of the Zener cards) that ran into billions to one.

Of this statistical result of a strictly supervised and sharply observed experiment, Professor C. D. Broad, Professor of Philosophy at Cambridge, wrote:

'There can be no doubt that the events described happened and were correctly reported; that the odds against chance coincidence piled up billions to one; and that the nature of the events which involved both telepathy and precognition, conflicts with one or more of the basic limiting principles (of physical science).'

The significant contribution was not merely the statistics, however, but the revelation that Shackleton's guesses of cards in a different room from the experimenter, randomly selected in a system which precluded the experimenter himself knowing the card to be guessed, consistently guessed not the card turned up but the next one just ahead. He did this approximately four thousand times, and with several different experimenters. (Soal's work has been questioned from time to time, but not disproved.)

Another kind of experiment along the lines of Dr Rhine's new work was carried out by Dr Gertrude Schmeidler,[134] Professor of Psychology at the City College, New York, who made a comparison between the scores of those who believed in the existence, or at least the possibility of ESP, and those who did not; she called the believers 'sheep' and the sceptics 'goats'. The intriguing result was that the sheep scored higher than the goats. Dr Schmeidler tested this fact further under a variety of conditions and with large numbers of people. In experimental work between 1945 and 1951 with over a thousand people Dr Schmeidler found that the sheep scored correctly by 0·4 per cent more than chance expectation while the goats consistently scored 0·3 per cent less than chance. The mind-factor, personality and emotional quotients of ESP response and abilities was substantially confirmed, if not explained.

In the 1950s 'Experimental Parapsychology' expanded in scope and became more organized. J. B. Rhine's laboratory was separated from the Parapsychology Department of Duke to form an independent unit, and in the United States the Parapsychology Association, an organization for professional psychic researchers, was established.

The early 1960s brought more specialized and sophisticated experiments and the increased use of electronic instruments for randomizing and computing the test material. In 1962, Dr Rhine detached himself completely from Duke University and established the Foundation for Research into the Nature of Man (FRNM), and the Institute of Parapsychology as the research unit. Here, he intended to broaden his range of inquiries into mind and consciousness.

Other research units had by now been established, and many universities in America and some in Europe had parapsychology divisions and in Russia, some extensive and startling experiments in telepathy under hypnosis conducted by Leonid Vasiliev,[165] Professor of Physiology at Leningrad University, had initiated sudden interest in ESP, and government support for research.

Parapsychology was encroaching on scientific territory in many directions, but in the West its gains were still unofficial. Even some parapsychologists agreed that the study of psi phenomena could not be made to fit science unless science itself changed. But others could see no difference between their systematic inquiry into an unknown that must be some part of nature, and that of the scientist, who must also start with a hypothesis at the non-material level and seek to prove it empirically.

On this premise, the Parapsychological Association had in three different years tried to achieve affiliation with the American Association for the Advancement of Science, the most august scientific body in the country, whose recognition would go far to decide the issue.

Although on each occasion the stringent terms of the application were exhaustively met – and these consisted of a massive assemblage of research papers, answers to procedural questions and supporting data (including the facts that two thirds of PA members held Ph.Ds and had been granted fifty or more Masters' and Ph.D. degrees for research in parapsychology by universities in most parts of the world) submitted to each of twelve scientists composing the AAAS Committee on Council Affairs – they were opposed on the grounds that parapsychology was not a true science.

In 1969, the PA made a decision to try once more. It was an expensive and time-consuming labour, requiring great determination and conviction, and at last, in November, the combined efforts of a past president, E. Douglas Dean, and other eminent members succeeded – the application was passed. Now there remained only the final vote of the AAAS Council, to win affiliation.

At an AAAS meeting held on December 30 in the ballroom of the Statler-Hilton Hotel in Boston, the crucial moment arrived. Following the announcement of the PA's application, there were two dissenting commentaries.

Then, as E. Douglas Dean has related,[35] the chairman said: 'The Committee on Council affairs considered the PA's work for a very long time. The Committee came to the conclusion that it is an association investigating controversial or non-existent phenomena. However, it is open in membership to critics and agnostics, and they were satisfied that it uses scientific methods of inquiry – thus, that investigation can be regarded as scientific.'

Now, Dr Margaret Mead, the famous American anthropologist spoke. 'For the last ten years,' she said, 'we have been arguing about what constitutes science and the scientific method, and what societies use it. The PA uses statistics and blinds, placebos, double-blinds and other standard scientific devices.' In a forceful pronouncement, she concluded, 'The whole history of scientific advance is full of scientists investigating phenomena that the establishment did not believe were there. I submit that we vote in favour of this Association's work!'

For parapsychologists the next moments were tense. The chairman said: 'The question of a vote is raised. Because of the controversial nature of this motion, we should have a show of hands. Please raise your hands, those Council members in favour of the motion.'

Approximately 170 hands went up.

'Those against?'

About 30 went up.

'It seems,' the chairman said, 'that the Motion is carried. If anyone desires a count of the hands I will ask for the vote to be repeated.'

There was silence.

'The Motion is carried,' the chairman announced.

Finally – parapsychology had become a member of the Scientific Establishment.

The fact that the Parapsychological Association was one of three hundred or so affiliated societies in the fields of science, medicine and engineering was a turning point in its history – not, perhaps as decisive as might have been anticipated or hoped, for there remained the uninformed, the unimpressed, the downright sceptical – but consideration and respect for parapsychology as serious and valid exploration of the nature of man was undeniably reinforced.

As parapsychology entered the seventies, it had dug in, and the boundaries between it and other sciences were becoming less definable.

1A THE MARCH OF EXPERIMENTS

In the last decade most of the emphasis has shifted from gathering data proving the existence of psi phenomena into research on how they work. Just getting information that there is such a thing is old-fashioned now.

CHARLES T. TART

(*Professor of humanistic and experimental psychology at University of California, Davis, formerly Instructor in Psychiatry at the University of Virginia Medical School and Lecturer in Psychology at Stanford University.*)

J. B. RHINE, like Freud had travelled a long nebulous road beset with opposition, had satisfied some of his enemies, if not by any means all, and established the study of another intangible area of mind as a science.

No one denied that Dr Rhine was the patriarch of para-psychology, but now it was out in the open for continued exploration by others as well as himself, and the key word was methodology.

None of the tedium receded. Experiments concentrating on discovering the nature of 'psi' capacity (psi had become the inclusive term for extrasensory abilities and psychokinesis) were still primarily based on the correct and incorrect guessing of long runs of cards, the faces of dice or the blind-matching of concealed simple line-drawings.

Those who felt that the parapsychologists laboured mightily to bring forth a mouse, which spontaneous psychic phenomena had ages ago proved beyond doubt, were upheld in part by the work of Dr Louisa Rhine,[127] who in 1951 had begun making a collection of psychic anecdotes and reports of precognition with the purpose of using them as suggestions for models of experiments. Later, in the *Journal of Parapsychology*, she advocated research into the degree of *conviction* as a factor in the outcome of pre-cognitive dreams.

But apart from this nod to the past, the amassing of statistics proceeded under every variable condition that could conceivably lend itself to producing another piece of the whole puzzle. Among the questions now to be asked were: When does psi function – under what particular circumstances does it respond, can it be evoked? Can it be induced – or is it inevitably an unconscious process? What are its common manifestations? What, among so many subtle derivations, causes it to 'decline' ('decline effect') after an initial significance? What causes the 'long-period decline' when the heretofore high-scoring subjects seem to have lost their ability permanently, etc., etc. . . ?

As the years between the 1950s and 1970s progressed, the list of questions became longer and longer, and the experiments evolved accordingly. Some of the answers were found, more bits of the puzzle emerged, creating others.

In the 1960s a Czechoslovakian physicist, biochemist and parapsychologist, Dr Milan Ryzl,[131] experimented with various ways of developing ESP in certain people by hypnosis. He succeeded in formulating a method that worked promisingly well, and began training a simple, good-natured young man called Pavel Stepanek, who did not claim to be psychic and had only volunteered out of curiosity.

When Dr Ryzl was able to hypnotize Pavel with ease, he led him on to guess the standard Zener cards which he held hidden behind a screen. The result was so remarkable, that Dr Ryzl quickly devised a more difficult experiment. Pavel was now asked to tell which side of a card, green or white, was on the 'up-side' within a totally opaque envelope.

Pavel's guesswork was consistently spectacular, but with scientific caution Dr Ryzl continued these experiments until Pavel had totted up 2,000 correct guesses, where 1,114 would have been a billion to one over chance expectation.

Many stricter experiments followed – with witnesses and visiting parapsychologists in attendance – with the same exhilarating effect. Soon, Dr Ryzl felt there was no necessity to hypnotize Pavel, and new experiments were designed to test his clairvoyance in a waking state. There was no change in his steady accumulation of correct guesses.

The reliability and repeatability of his performance brought several well-known Western parapsychologists to Prague, replete with challenging tests of their own, among them Dr J. Gaither Pratt, who had worked with Dr Rhine when he was at Duke University. Dr Pratt was astounded; Pavel was the first psychic he had encountered who could produce ESP 'on demand'. He invited him to come to America for further experiments at the University of Virginia, where he was now a professor of psychiatry.

Pavel's ESP, it transpired, was limited to this one kind of experiment and to 'favourite' cards, as if he could somehow identify certain cards no matter what kind of envelope was devised to conceal them, and sometimes there were as many as three different types of outer coverings. It seemed to prove that there could be such a thing as an extrasensory habit or rut, as well as a means of putting a 'psychic mark' on objects to identify them. Parapsychologists called this 'the focusing effect', and it became a new stimulus for research.

Pavel Stepanek continued to demonstrate his ability over the years, Dr Pratt (and others) sometimes travelling to Prague to test him, Pavel sometimes visiting America to undergo various rigid investigations (some of which are of sufficient official importance not to have been revealed).

Although no firm theory arose from all these experiments, Dr Ryzl, by means of Pavel, did establish that in some subjects ESP can be induced and developed under hypnosis, and that this ability can then be demonstrated under laboratory conditions.

In 1967, Dr Ryzl moved to America and continued his work at the Institute of Parapsychology of the Foundation for Research on the Nature of Man, and in 1971 he became associated with the San Jose State College in California, in the Division of Cybernetics. He lectured widely and wrote a book entitled *Parapsychology: a Scientific Approach*.[131]

Other means for searching out answers to the nature of ESP have been the comparison-experiments between the differing sets of conditions, or between two differing groups, in which the differences between the two sets of results are in various ways measured for significance. Loosely, these fall into the 'Sheep–Goat' category, in that they seek mainly to pinpoint the prevailing elements that seem most inducive and descriptive of ESP.

In these categories, experiments have been designed to measure differences in scoring between subjects who are familiar or unfamiliar with the testing material; between those who have been informed whether their guesses were correct ('feedback') or not informed, or even misinformed; between subjects in rapport, or ill-ease, with their experimenter; between those taking or not taking alcohol, or drugs, before the experiment; between those in or not in a state of meditation or other 'altered state of consciousness'.

Scoring statistics have also compared the ESP differences in males and females, in varying age-groups, in differing cultural and intellectual levels, between creative and non-creative subjects.

The importance of the emotional factor in ESP response has been of special interest to Dr Thelma Moss, Assistant Professor of Medical Psychology at the Neuropsychiatric Institute of the University of California, Los Angeles, and a leading parapsychologist. Perceiving the coincidence of psi experience with an emotionally-charged occurrence such as death, illness or grave danger, she and a colleague, Dr J. A. Gengerelli, also a psychology professor at UCLA, designed an experiment in 'emotional telepathy' by which they hoped to measure the differences between three groups – (a) ESP believers, (b) those with an open mind towards ESP, (c) those who did not believe it existed – in relation to target material with or without emotional content.[102]

A mixture of 144 males and females, ranging in age from 14 to 65, were divided into the three groups – 24 pairs in each group. One person of each pair in each group acted as the transmitter, and the other the receiver, and these sat in sound-proof rooms 20 feet apart, each room supervised by the experimenter who showed the transmitter lantern-slide pictures of a highly emotional nature accompanied by appropriate sounds through a set of earphones.

Absorbing the emotional effect of the picture and sounds, the transmitter attempted to convey it to the receiver, and the receiver was at the same time comparing the impressions received with various pictures to see which one most nearly corresponded. If it was found impossible to match any of the impressions with any of the pictures, the receiver was asked simply to make a guess. There were three trial runs to each experiment, and the results corroborated again the Sheep–Goat effect as well as confirming the significance of emotion to ESP – the group of ESP believers proved statistically correct in their matching to the sum of three thousand to one over mean chance expectation. Dr Moss and her colleague had made another contribution to the solution of the puzzle, and provided a model for further research along the same lines, which has been repeated many times since with other kinds of contrasting groups.

In England during the 1960s, John Randall, an instructor in biology at Leamington College in Warwickshire agreed with Dr Rhine and Dr Pratt (and other parapsychologists in Holland, France and America) that there was a fine potential source of group investigation of ESP in the classrooms of schools, despite some previous failure in England to produce much of significance in this area. In a series of experiments involving thirty-one Grammar-school boys of 14 or so,[124] in which he used his own form of personality questionnaire, and later, as well, the 'Junior Eysenck Personality Inventory' (EPI),* John Randall attempted to discover links between sufferers of certain types of illnesses, such as asthma, hay-fever, sleeplessness, depression, indigestion, persistent headaches, and ESP.

Using standard card-guessing procedures and several trial runs with himself as the experimenter, he found little evidence for ESP except in eight boys who suffered from hay-fever, and a group who fell into the EPI category of 'high-N' (neurotic) and 'high-E' (extrovert). Both these groups scored with outstanding significance; unspectacular but valuable clues, not far removed from those of ESP revealed to Freud in his patient-analysis, which prompted him in his latter years to say: 'If I had my life to live over again, I'd spend it in research of psychic phenomena rather than psychoanalysis'.

At Lund University in Sweden, from 1965 onwards, this kind of investigation was routine; all new psychology students being required to take part in ESP runs that provided information for advanced students taking psychology courses related to personality evaluation. These resulted in several experiments here with eminent visiting parapsychologists, such as Dr Gertrude

---

*EPI measure the two fundamental divisions of personality: extraversion and introversion.

Schmeidler of New York and Dr John Beloff of the University of Edinburgh.

Another form of test involving a large group took place in 1967 at Caxton Hall in London, England, where Sir Alister Hardy,[52] a marine biologist famous for his *The Living Stream* (and, most recently, *The Biology of God*),[51] head of the Religious Experience Research Unit at Oxford and parapsychologist by avocation, conducted a telepathy experiment with two hundred people. Based on 'blind-matching' of simple drawings (a test first organized by Malcolm Guthrie in the early days of the SPR for 'thought-transference'), it consisted of having twenty subjects seated in self-contained, light-proof cubicles arranged in four rows of five, supervised by experimenters, while randomized drawings were 'sent' to them by the other 128 members of the group who all concentrated on the same drawing shown on a screen. A buzzer would alert them to start 'sending', and the twenty percipients would attempt to receive and reproduce the drawing in black chalk on white paper.

The experiment was long and complicated and exhausted several means of exploring the transmitting power of massed senders, as opposed to the usual one, two or three.

In this respect, the results were not entirely beyond the bounds of coincidence, and were not statistically conclusive – but what did emerge was an unexpected similarity of ideas of percipients sitting near to each other in the booths. Here, the drawings matched uncannily. Was it chance? Coincidence? ESP? Sir Alister says: 'What do we really mean by chance and coincidence? It may be something even more remarkable than ESP, but something quite different', and certainly grounds for further exploration.

Confounding this close-proximity evidence, however, was the remarkable 'Long-Distance ESP' experiment carried out by Dr Thelma Moss and her colleagues in 1968,[103] in which the object was to further test the emotional factor in successful telepathic transmission.

In a room in Los Angeles, a group of twenty-two people (transmitters) all concentrated on slides showing emotional occurrences, with their atmosphere and mood intensified by appropriate sounds and music. In another room, in Los Angeles, was a group of twenty-eight receivers, in New York (3,000 miles away) a group of fifteen, and in the University of Sussex in England (about 5,500 miles away), a group of fourteen. Acting as 'control' in the experiment, was a supply of non-emotional target-material consisting of letters, numbers and short, variously-angled black lines, their order mechanically randomized.

The result was highly significant confirmation of the emotional effect: the targets of an emotional nature were not only received with a statistical score over chance of three thousand to one, but were most clearly received in Sussex, the furthest point. The impression often came through with poetical exactitude, and having also been asked to put down the possible matching thought-content of the transmitters, receivers gave amazingly close interpretations. The non-emotional material was received at only chance-expectation score.

Another piece of evidence had been established.

Experiments of a different kind had been throwing light on the nature of ESP in the context of Dream Telepathy. In 1962, Dr Montague Ullman,[160] a psychiatrist with interest in the ESP content of dreams and who was director of the Community Mental Health Center of Maimonides Medical Center in Brooklyn, with the practical help of Gardner Murphy, a leading proponent of parapsychology then Director of the Menninger Foundation, Topeka, Kansas, was able to establish a Dream Laboratory.

The Dream Laboratory at Maimonides was the first and only sleep laboratory devoted exclusively to parapsychological research. In 1964, Dr Stanley Krippner,[161] a psychologist, joined Dr Ullman as Director, and with the aid of colleagues began experiments of a sort to establish the transference of impressions from a sender to a dreamer.

Having established that 'rapid-eye-movements' of a sleeper indicated dreaming, and that a sleeper who was awakened the moment the REM (rapid-eye-movements) stopped, usually remembered clearly what he had been dreaming, experiments were devised whereby a carefully-chosen subject slept in a sound-isolated room, while his EEG (electroencephalograph) tracings of brainwaves were monitored by the experimenter in another room.

While the subject slept, the transmitter, variously-distanced in accoustically-isolated rooms, would attempt to transmit an art print randomly-chosen from a selection of vividly-coloured, emotionally-intense subjects, by concentrating on it most of the night at intervals indicated by the experimenter when the sleeper was dreaming, and writing down thoughts and feelings associated with the nature of the print.

When the sleeper was awakened to describe his (or her) dream, his report would be recorded on tape. Then the sleeper would go back to sleep. In the morning, the experimenter would review the night's dreams with the sleeper, now fully awake, and add any further associations he could think of. The dreams were then transcribed and, together with the collection of twelve prints, sent to three outside judges of parapsychological orientation who ranked the transcripts according to a set scale of correspondence.

These experiments were carried out under many varying conditions, using different kinds of subjects, sometimes psychologists or scientists, always adhering to the scientific method and repeated many times over. It was difficult to ascertain completely whether it was telepathy, precognition or clairvoyance at work, but decided evidence for extrasensory submission and reception during the dream state was repeatedly established at odds that scored with sufficient consistency over odds of chance expectation to prove definitively meaningful.

The Dream Laboratory amassed impeccable records that have been exhaustively investigated by sceptics and open-minded alike, and the fact that its failures were as meticulously recorded as its successes brought the Maimonides' Dream Telepathy experiment respect from the scientific establishment.

In the words of Dr Berthold Eric Schwarz, psychiatrist and consultant at the Brain Wave Laboratory of the Essex County Medical Center, Cedar Grove, New Jersey:

'Drs Ullman and Krippner have made a significant scientific contribution by their rigidly controlled, psychodynamically and instrumentally sophisticated dream and telepathy researches. Their at times, superficially inscrutable fragments of data and provocative interpretations should stimulate other research efforts both extensive and intensive. We are offered clues not only toward the understanding of telepathy and dreaming but also toward the unravelling of these relationships to dissociative reactions, everyday psychopathology, sleep disturbances, and behavioural and psychosomatic reactions. From their earliest publications to their current studies, Drs Ullman and Krippner have combined knowledge gleaned from clinical experiences with well worked out laboratory techniques from qualitatively and quantitatively exploring dreams.'

And, among many who have commented on the Maimonides's Dream Laboratory work, set out fully in the book *Dream Telepathy*,[160] by Dr Ullman and Dr Krippner with Alan Vaughan, editor of the well-known American publication, *Psychic*, Dr Ulric Neisser, professor of psychology at Cornell University, wrote:

'Ullman and Krippner are to be congratulated for the persistent and systematic way they have followed up their preliminary findings. By now they have built up a substantial body of positive results, which deserves further attention and replication. I would hope that every laboratory which is equipped to do dream research will give serious consideration to the possibility of carrying out such experiments.'

In April of 1973, the Dream Laboratory of the Maimonides Medical Center expanded into a new Division of Parapsychology and Psychophysics in the Department of Psychiatry. Objectives of the new Division include expansion of dream ESP studies, new studies of drug-induced states and ESP, studies of the effect of sensory-deprivation and sensory-overload on ESP, the effect of hypnosis on ESP, and inducing psi-favourable states with biofeedback (discussed in Chapter 2), the investigation of subjects with psychokinetic abilities, the development and training of young parapsychologists, collaborative ties with other centres, such as the Sleep and Dream Laboratory of the University of Virginia headed by Dr Robert Van de Castle (Professor of clinical psychology and a member of the AAAS), and generally maintaining scientific and professional integrity for parapsychological research in the face of ever-increasing public interest.

1B NEW DIMENSIONS FOR PARAPSYCHOLOGY

EXPERIMENTS in telepathy were not exclusive to the West. In 1960, Leonid L. Vasiliev, Chairman of Physiology at the University of Leningrad, a winner of the Lenin Prize and much-respected internationally in his field, addressed a meeting of leading Soviet scientists who had gathered to commemorate the invention of the radio.

To their amazement, Dr Vasiliev revealed that he had conducted experiments all through the Stalin regime on hypnotic suggestion by means of telepathy. Now, he felt, with the claim that the American Navy had been doing telepathy testing on the submarine *Nautilus*, it was time to report the nature of his work and imperative that the Soviet Union should emerge from its prejudice and false conceptions about the nature of telepathy (which, up to that time the Russians called 'biological radio' – if, in fact, its existence was even considered).

'The discovery of the energy underlying ESP,' he told them, 'will be equivalent to the discovery of atomic energy.'

In 1962, Dr Vasiliev's book, *Experiments in Mental Suggestion*,[165] written years earlier, was published. In 1963, the Kremlin bestowed top priority on the biological sciences, which included parapsychology. Not only did Dr Vasiliev have his own parapsychology Laboratory at the University of Leningrad, but by 1968 there were several important government-sponsored centres for the study of psi phenomena under scientific conditions, with ample budgets to allow for the development and introduction of sophisticated instrumentation for psi research.

Whether the *Nautilus* story was valid or not, the idea itself was the catalyst for a new era of psi research, for who could afford to fall behind Russia in such a potentially vital exploration! (In 1963 Dr Eugene B. Konecci, of NASA, the American National Aeronautics and Space Administration, confirmed at an International Astronautics Federation meeting in Paris, that NASA was also studying 'energy transfer', or 'psycho-physiological information transfer'.)

Soviet scientists who now entered the once-taboo arena of psi, did not stop to reaffirm its existence – there were sceptics in the USSR just as everywhere else, but they weren't worth convincing at this point; Dr Rhine's work was well known and considered of sufficient weight to provide a springboard for further inquiries. In what biological area of human existence did it belong? How could it be harnessed and put to use? What were its ramifications in terms of humanity, the planet, the cosmos? There were the questions of 'bioenergetics',* the Soviet term for ESP and PK.

Dr Vasiliev had exploded the old Soviet hypothesis of some form of 'mental radio', of radio-type electro-magnetic waves explaining telepathy, by repeating some of his 'tele-hypnosis' experiments in what was called the 'Faraday Chamber'. These were refrigerator-like chambers with metal screening; the hypnotist sat in one, and the subject in another. Telepathic communication still took place, proving that a new theory was needed.

Over the years, Dr Vasiliev had issued dozens of different thought-commands such as 'walk forward', 'raise your right hand', with impressive effect. Later, he had experimented with a paralysed patient in the Leningrad Hospital, commanding her to move her paralysed left arm. She had done so, and sensed who commanded her. Other hypnotists and doctors joined Dr Vasiliev in experimenting with the same 29-year-old woman, specifying particular nerves to be stimulated, and each time she responded, though ignorant of the technical name of the nerve used. Altogether, visiting doctors and professors conducted nineteen of these stimulus tests, resulting in only three failures.

In more recent years, new and bolder experiments were carried out by Dr Vasiliev, and when he died in 1966, his work was assumed by the modern school of Soviet researchers. Among their widely divergent approaches to telepathy experimentation was 'The Grand Moscow–Siberia Telepathy Test'[112], a milestone in scientific attempts at thought-transmission.

In 1966, at Academgorodok (Science City) in Novosibirsk in

---

*The term bioenergetics is also used in America by psychologists to denote a type of psychotherapy which deals with the physiology of the patient, e.g., posture, body-movement, etc.

Siberia, Karl Nikolaiev, a journalist, went into deep relaxation watched by a group of scientists, while in Moscow (approximately 1,860 miles away) Yuri Kamensky, a biophysicist, also relaxed deeply. At exactly eight o'clock, Moscow time, scientists began giving Yuri Kamensky objects in sealed envelopes (six altogether) one at a time. He opened each envelope, studied the object in it and imagined the face of Karl Nikolaiev, first in front of him, then as if he were peering over his shoulder looking at the object with the eyes of Karl Nikolaiev.

As this extreme concentration took place, Karl Nikolaiev felt something like a shock and began seeing the object as if it were real. In one case, it was a screwdriver; Karl Nikolaiev described it as 'long, thin, metal – plastic – black plastic', which was almost exact. With all six objects, Karl Nikolaiev's impressions were too close for any form of guesswork.

The tests were repeated on several nights with Karl Nikolaiev and other senders, but only with Yuri Kamensky was he faultlessly clear – Kamensky was trained in the art of sending – yet for the combined tests Karl Nikolaiev received more than half the transmitted images correctly, and at least six of these tests were 'sent' from Moscow.

Karl Nikolaiev was not himself surprised; he was certain that everyone who took the time and applied himself patiently could do the same. Nevertheless, his achievement caused a quickening of scientific interest, and together with Yuri Kamensky, he performed a variety of carefully monitored tests for many scientific groups.

One of these, conducted in Leningrad in 1967, consisted of attaching electrodes to his scalp while he sat in a sealed chamber and the graphs of his EEG were scrutinized by an electrophysiologist (Dr Lutsia Pavlova of the University of Leningrad) and a mathematician (Dr Genady Sergeyev, connected with a Soviet military laboratory), in a computer-humming laboratory. Nikolaiev was to squeeze his fist every time he felt the beginning of a transmission from Yuri Kamensky in Moscow. To the great excitement of the scientists, they found that changes in his brainwave activity coincided with the receiving of impressions from Kamensky.

This led to many more tests at different distances and more complicated mathematical analyses of the EEG tapes, as well as new exploration of the connection between brain activity and ESP – like all horizons, it receded at approach, but there was no question that another important part of the puzzle had been discovered.

The Soviet Union also turned a scientific spotlight on PK, with their discovery and meticulous testing of Madam Nelya Mikhailova (better known by her maiden name of Ninel Kulagina), who was able to move objects of various kinds by concentrating on them, without in any way touching them physically.

Madam Kulagina's PK was a far more dramatic demonstration of 'mind over matter' (in 1970, Dr Louisa Rhine wrote a book of that name on the subject of PK[127]) than the years of dice-throwing conducted by Dr Rhine and his colleagues. But again, what had been accomplished at Duke University Parapsychology Laboratory, like card-guessing, was carefully compiled statistical evidence for what Dr Rhine called psychokinesis (mind-movement).

Starting with laboratory-testing of the gambler's conviction that he knows what the fall of dice will be, several hazards to valid assessment of two main kinds of experiments – influencing the fall of the dice-face, or where the dice will land on a specially roughened surface – were gradually eliminated. The 'bias' of the dice themselves, the hollowing out of the pips, which made the higher numbers more likely to turn up, were overcome by alternating target-objectives (sometimes high, sometimes low numbers) as were possibilities that hand-written records could contain the unconscious bias of the experimenter.

Despite thousands upon thousands of throws in which hits so far exceeded mean chance expectation, that even human errors were irrelevant, the results were treated with caution. Parapsychologists devised many differing situations, in which calls were made by someone uninformed of the intended target, by instrumental recording, or coins or other two-sided objects used instead of dice, or dice of different materials, some light, some heavier.

In 1951 another form of testing had been introduced by W. E. Cox (now a member of the research staff of the Institute of

Parapsychology, FRNM), called the 'placement' technique. In one of these, cubes or spheres were released to run down a wooden chute towards 'hit' or 'miss' sections, with chance expectation being one in two. Haakon Forwald, a Swedish engineer, took this 'placement' technique a step further with 'scaled placement', with cubes and calibrated surfaces, and W. E. Cox[31] in turn advanced this to the use of spheres and electromechanical devices.

And so PK experimentation had continued, its target material and concepts widening and broadening; if, as with card-guessing, dice-throwing or influencing still relied on the evidence of statistics, like the search for the nature of ESP it became more sophisticated and innovative.

With Madam Kulagina[112] in the Soviet Union, PK had taken a different, more sensational turn. Here PK needed no mathematical reinforcement to give it credence; it evidenced itself, and, it could be repeated at will under scientifically-imposed conditions. Madam Kulagina, an intelligent, attractive woman in her forties married to an engineer, by deep, intense concentration under the strict surveillance of the Soviet's foremost scientists, had moved a variety of objects, such as a compass, a small metal cylinder, fountain pen, boxes of matches, five cigarettes under a glass cover, without any form of actual physical contact.

In *Moscow Pravda*, in 1968, Dr Ya. Terletsky, Chairman of Theoretical Physics at Moscow University and a winner of the State Prize, stated with conviction: 'Mrs Mikhailova (her hopefully-protective pseudonym) displays a new and unknown form of energy'.

Despite some harsh and dismaying attacks from Russia's ultra-conservatives in the Press, together with the scepticism for PK fanned over the years by misreporting, over-credulous observers and highly-skilled magicians – this view was sustained by all who took part in serious investigations of her ability, and these included top physicists connected with the Joint Nuclear Research Institute at Dubna, the Mendeleyev Institute of Metrology, the Academy of Sciences of the USSR and many prominent scientists from other Communist countries who came to Leningrad to test her.

There have been perhaps sixty films made of Madam Kulagina

sitting at a table and moving assorted objects on it, sometimes by moving her hands in a circular fashion above them, sometimes by simply concentrating her gaze on them. Many tests were conducted under closed-circuit television, with reporters, film-crews, visiting parapsychologists and scientists bearing close witness. Since the force that Madam Kulagina exerts seldom fails her, the possibility of fraud seemed extremely remote.

Before demonstrations, Madam Kulagina was physically searched for hidden threads or other means of manipulating the objects, and X-rayed for magnets (though she also moved many non-magnetic items such as glass, wooden matches, eggs). Hypnosis of the viewers was carefully considered and ruled out. In her tests, such as one shown in a film where she caused a compass needle to spin and then the compass itself together with its case, as her hands circled over them and her body followed the motion, her strain was plainly visible; her face seemed sunken, her forehead was lined.

Scientists who worked closely with her observed that she might take as long as two to four hours to achieve the right state of energy-arousal for her feats, and those who have measured her physiologically at the time, such as Dr Genady Sergeyev, have found that her pulse-rate rose to 240 per minute, that she lost up to 4 pounds in weight in thirty minutes and showed the general effects of an organism under 'stress alarm reaction'. Afterwards she is usually exhausted, with the look of one who has undergone a tremendous physical ordeal; she had aches and pains in her legs, and on occasion has been temporarily blind.

Over the course of ten years or so, Madam Kulagina gradually moved so many diverse objects – cups, plates and bowls, china, glass, wood, plastic, metal – that there was no clue in the object itself, and since the table and chair, her position, what she wore and ate, as well as herself, physically, had been too thoroughly examined for remaining clues, the next logical step was to explore the force fields around her body for the nature of her power.

The Soviet scientists were not interested in Madam Kulagina's feats for their own sake, but for what significance might lie behind the law that was being used. If discovered, its potential could be compared to the discovery of electricity – a possibility many of them viewed with mixed feelings, for, if admitted, science might be looking to parapsychology for a new paradigm.

By now, Madam Kulagina had undergone laboratory tests in which she bristled with electrodes from head to foot, looking, in her sealed chamber, more like an astronaut about to take off for space than an ordinary woman making objects move jerkily towards or away from her. Dr Sergeyev, famous for his brain work in the Soviet Union, had found among the other physiological factors that, unlike most people who generated three or four times more electrical voltage from the back of the brain than from the front, Madam Kulagina's brain generated fifty times more voltage from the back of the head than the front.

Further to this, in part of his official report on her (translated in the *Journal of Paraphysics*, 1968, Vol. 2 No. 3), he stated: '... An analysis of the electrical signals on the skull surface indicated that the energy level of the signals was considerably lower than the energy level of electrostatic field fluctuations recorded from a distance. At the same time, however, there existed a significant correlation, within 5 per cent, between the parameters of the electrical bioturbulence and the electrostatic turbulence. It appeared that at the instant of PK phenomena, there was a marked correlation between these informational characteristics and at the same time there was a concentration of energy in the direction in which the subject's gaze was fixed. It was further found that the frequency of the heart pulse could be increased fourfold under these conditions. The modulation rhythm of the intermittent electrostatic field was associated in geometric ratio with heart and brain frequencies, suggesting the heart can influence the frequency-function of the space-field modulator.'

In the spring of 1973, Benson Herbert, an English physicist and director of the Paraphysical Laboratory, in Downton, Wiltshire, went for a second time to Leningrad with his colleague, Manfred Cassirer, to conduct tests of his own with Madam Kulagina.[55] His chief purpose was to be the first investigator from the West to measure directly her PK force.

On his previous visit in 1972 Benson Herbert had found that she could not only move objects at a distance, but could bring heat into either her left or right hand at will, and could produce

such heat in gripping the arm of another person that it caused
intolerable pain and left a burn mark that lasted for a considerable
time. On that occasion, she had not been well and explained that
she did not perform satisfactorily in the electrified atmosphere of
hot weather, that she did best when the temperature did not
exceed 18°C.

This time, Madam Kulagina was obviously exhausted, perhaps
from the over-use of her energies. But to Benson Herbert's relief
she later felt better and confronted his three tables full of apparatus for testing, showing special interest in the very instrument
he hoped to use for measuring her PK force.

This was a hydrometer floating upright in saturated saline
solution, protected by an earthed screen and monitored by an
electrostatic probe. He anticipated that this device would eliminate electrostatic forces and that Madam Kulagina would be able
to depress the hydrometer by a measurable amount, from which
the force could be calculated. The meter attached to the probe
would reveal any minute changes of field strength.

As Madam Kulagina voluntarily placed her hands in various
positions as if to attempt a demonstration, those with Benson
Herbert in the hotel room, among whom was Professor Sergeyev,
closed in with cameras. Benson Herbert scrutinized every detail
as she sat down and moved her chair to about one foot away from
the table and began to concentrate, and since they had all walked
between her and the chair a moment before, could see no possible
way that the threads or fibres would not have been destroyed.

Madam Kulagina slowly raised her arm until her palms faced
the testing instrument. After a while, it began to move away from
her in a straight line across the full diameter of the vessel, a
distance of $2\frac{1}{2}$ inches, and came to rest at the opposite side, the
transit occupying some 90 seconds.

With other tests, such as with two Crookes' radiometers, one
containing air at atmospheric pressure, the other rarefied, in
which, after circling her head counter-clockwise, both followed
suit, and another with a compass needle which swung to and fro,
Benson Herbert could not rule out to his own satisfaction the
possibility of vibration. But later, after he had done another
careful examination of her position, and even her shoes, he was

amazed to see the entire compass case turn round about 45° counterclockwise, then slide across the table in zig-zag fashion in jerks that took about one second to travel away nearly an inch, then to return 4 inches nearer to Kulagina than it had started.

Madam Kulagina breathed heavily throughout the demonstration but did not move. Benson Herbert had ample opportunity to pass 'fingernails under the edge of the table and around the corner and to slice with his hands through every inch of space around her'. Later, he and Dr Cassirer went over the whole area, floor, table, chair, the compass itself with a magnifying lens. Since he was expert at handling, detecting and trapping fine fibres, his own examination led to complete conviction that Madam Kulagina was 'capable of producing motion in objects at will, without the employment of any known force'. They found her co-operative, undergoing tests under their conditions, in their surroundings and with their equipment – extremely desirous of having scientists investigate her powers, and puzzled that no one else had been found who could do the same thing.

In analysing what the force is that they have measured, Benson Herbert has ruled out the possibility of supersonic vibration to reduce friction, magnetism, electrostatics and gravity. 'How she mobilizes the mitogenetic radiation of her own organic cells to yield these powerful effects, merely by mental concentration, remains at present a mystery still unsolved.' Theories are being pursued, but whatever the answer may turn out to be, it is Madam Kulagina's mental concentration that is causing something physical to happen – mind commanding matter.

Another form of PK (coupled with telepathic powers) came to the attention of science in 1971, with the discovery of remarkable feats by a young Israeli named Uri Geller.

Uri Geller, born in Tel Aviv in 1946, apparently had always been able to read thoughts and bend and break objects made of metal, but not until 1969, when he demonstrated these abilities for a school audience, were they seriously considered as a possible breakthrough in mindpower.

To observe what Uri Geller could do, and to make up his own mind whether the young man was genuine or merely an extremely gifted magician, in 1971 Dr Andrija Puharich, a senior research scientist at the New York University Medical Center (later aligning himself totally with parapsychology research), went to Israel.

Here, among many other achievements, he saw Uri Geller snap the heads off metal spoons, bend knives and forks, break metal, heavy gold rings and chains, start and stop watches (also make them lose or gain time), all with the concentration of thought-energy. Dr Puharich also claims to have witnessed far more spectacular demonstrations, such as dematerialization and re-materialization of physical objects, and has accounts of these in his book *Uri*.[122]

Convinced that Uri Geller was gifted with special powers of the mind, Dr Puharich arranged for him to take part in scientific experiments in America.

Before doing so, Geller lent himself to scientific investigations in Germany. There, in 1972, completely blindfold, he drove a car through the Munich streets at night, stopped a modern cable car over a 140-metre drop in the mountains of Chiemgau, made it move forward and back several times to his silent 'wish' and startled many watchful sceptics by warping or snapping various pieces of their jewellery without a touch.

Summing up four days of Uri Geller's Munich feats, Dr Friedbert Karger of the Max Planck Institute for Plasma Physics said:

'The powers of this man are a phenomenon, which in theoretical physics cannot yet be explained. Science already knows of similar cases. It is like atomic science. At the turn of the century it was already known as a reality. It was just at that time one could not yet explain it in terms of physics.'

Arriving in America later in 1972, Uri Geller demonstrated his abilities on national television before a panel including scientists. He aroused a storm of mixed reactions and a great deal of excitement. The natural tendency of almost all who personally witnessed his feats hovered between total conviction and stubborn disbelief. Some claimed that any good magician could do what Uri Geller could do, although none proved the claim.

There was also the fact that Uri Geller could not always perform, that he needed to 'draw on the energy' of a sympathetic audience, was affected by an atmosphere of disbelief. However, his own delight when he was successful was as great as any of his witnesses, and he continued to astound and entertain, often converting thoroughgoing sceptics by bending their rigid door-keys while they held them, sometimes without touching them at all, and there was the percentage that bent in people's pockets or near by whenever he was present.

For scientists, the problem that emerged from the countless demonstrations he made in universities all over the country, was not so much one of credulity as of forming models of testing this unknown form of energy, of finding where it fitted into the laws of physics as presently assumed.

In 1973, in England, a group of Cambridge scientists started a search for conceptual models by asking questions that rattled the foundations of physics itself. Dr E. W. Bastin had watched Uri Geller 'perform' in America. Among a trayful of objects bent and broken by Uri Geller was a spoon that particularly impressed him: it had somehow been 'pinched', in a way no human hand could have been strong enough to achieve. Since '"forces" don't do these things', Dr Bastin felt that some kind of 'thought-form' must be involved.[6]

In a New York demonstration, Dr Bastin was carrying in his pocket a case of small jewellers' screwdrivers. When Uri Geller drew one of them, without even knowing it existed, he sketched it with a bent top. Dr Bastin was puzzled enough, but later found the whole case-full of screwdrivers bent and broken, still in his pocket. Since there were no fields (area over which force exerts influence) between Uri Geller and the object, he wondered if Uri Geller could be 'an intermediate case' (state)? 'Perhaps it all starts at the level of elementary particles?' Dr Bastin, still searching for theories, also observed that the physical objects (affected by Uri Geller) 'are altered as if a personality were at work rather than a law'. Speaking collectively for the trouble all the physicists have in defining what Uri Geller accomplishes, Dr Bastin commented that physics was 'back in a natural history stage trying to know where to go next'.

Meanwhile, Uri Geller himself, somewhat disappointed by the extremes of caution, the impasse created by the lack of scientific explanation, continued his limited miracles – he claimed no clairvoyant ability, had no desire to attempt healing – in the only way practical and expedient, as an entertainer.

He was still accused of trickery, of using a laser beam, of concealing chemicals or instruments, of superhuman strength in his hands, but even these could not explain PK accomplished in laboratory tests, his ability to locate concealed objects or duplicate drawings with consistency that sometimes achieved statistics over chance of a trillion to one.

At Stanford Research Institute in Menlo Park, California (an organization separate from Stanford University which does research work for the government), physicists Dr Harold Puthoff and Russell Targ conducted two series of strictly controlled experiments with Uri Geller,[151] some of which were filmed. In one, extending over six weeks in 1972, Geller made eight successful 'guesses' on the fall of a single dice inside a closed metal box, 'sensed' which one of ten small cylinders, randomly arranged, held a small metal ball, and in another ten which one held some water. He was able to repeat several tests of this sort. He also recognizably duplicated dozens of line drawings such as geometrical shapes and simple objects (he says he receives the impression on a kind of screen in his mind), and among tests specifically for psychokinesis, was able by passing his hands near it to effect a full-scale deflection of a gaussmeter (an instrument for measuring the magnetic field).

In 1973, in thirteen new experiments, even greater precautions were taken: Uri Geller was kept separated from the experimenters by distance (some of the target pictures were 3,000 miles away on the opposite coast) or in an electrically shielded room to eliminate 'all conventional information channels, overt or subliminal'.

In one of the tests, a drawing that had been based on a noun chosen at random from a dictionary was held outside the steel-walled room by the sender. In other tests, Uri Geller was on the outside of the shielded room, the experimenters inside. Out of fifteen drawings 'sent' to him in variations of these conditions, Uri Geller passed on four (not feeling the 'lift' of confidence he experiences before success), came moderately close on four others, and undeniably succeeded with seven. Of these, a seagull in flight and a bunch of grapes were remarkably accurate: in the case of the grapes, without knowing quite what he was drawing, he reproduced twenty-four circles exactly as depicted in the target, in almost identically-numbered rows and with a jutting line that precisely duplicated the stem and its direction.

The official report on this *Investigation of Psychoenergetic Phenomena*[151] proved difficult for the scientists involved. They could not entirely establish Uri Geller's metal-bending ability, but conceded that the guessing of the single dice correctly eight times out of ten (Uri Geller passed the last two falls), which had a probability of occurring by chance of approximately one in a million, and that the 'mentally'-received drawings could not be explained as other than paranormal. They summarized their work with these cautious words: 'We observe that in certain situations significant information transmission can take place under shielded conditions. Factors which appear to be important and therefore candidates for future investigation include whether the subject knows the set of targets in the target pool, the actual number of targets in the target pool at any given time, and whether the target is known by any experimenters.'

In other words, there does seem to be 'information transmission' but what it is and why and how it works must still be approached with more experiments: after all, science is reluctantly engaged with the paranormal, it must proceed with utmost care.

And there the matter of the 'Geller effect' seemed to rest, indicating an impasse, even a lapse of interest. Certainly it would be more convenient for science if this implied threat to current physics dissolved in mist. But this was not to be the case.

In November 1972, Uri Geller visited England when he agreed to appear on the David Dimbleby television programme. Here, unexpectedly for all concerned, the Geller effect was given a new impetus when, in front of a highly sceptical audience of millions and a scientist who had come to do a 'hatchet job', Uri Geller succeeded in making a fork collapse, guessing drawings correctly, distorting watch hands and warping David Dimbleby's own door key before his very eyes. As a result not only David Dimbleby and a great mass of the viewers were converted, or at least dumbfounded, but the scientist, John Taylor, Professor of Applied Mathematics at King's College, London, determined to try and find out for himself how this talent, particularly the metal-bending, could be fitted into science.

In February of 1974, Uri Geller agreed to do some tests for Professor Taylor at King's College,[153] with objects prepared by the metallurgical department. Directly or indirectly, Uri Geller succeeded at almost all the tasks. When he bent metal by stroking it, e.g. a teaspoon, it was apparent that the stem softened first, broke, then hardened again. A piece of single crystal of potassium bromide about 2 centimetres long split apart when he stroked it for approximately 10 seconds. Also, metal strips enclosed in glass tubes and a strip of aluminium inside a wire mesh tube with closed ends had been bent or curved without his touching them (he had had no effect on wood or plastic). He also caused considerable deflection in a Geiger counter (an instrument for detecting radioactivity). Holding the monitor in his hands, and with extreme concentration, he influenced the needle to a successive increase of counts from fifty to one thousand counts per second, of two-seconds duration. The sound of the amplified counts rose to a wail and finally a 'scream'.

Professor Taylor concluded that a wide range of effects had occurred, with more than one process involved, including Uri Geller's brain activity, which he had not measured. He was keen to experiment further.

Meanwhile, as a result of other Uri Geller broadcasts at least a hundred people came forward who had discovered they too had a metal-bending or watch-stopping and starting ability. Professor Taylor began a study of thirty-eight of them, one man, three women, fourteen boys and twenty girls.

Several of the children he worked with over the months showed undeniable ability that has stood up to vigorous testing and there were some, he found, that improved with practice. Indications were that children up to the age of 17 had more ability than adults. Some of them achieve results by gentle stroking, others by just staring at the object. Only half of his subjects would be suspected of using force, even if unconsciously, because many objects affected were too strong to yield to human pressure.

In his search for an explanation, Professor Taylor constructed tests to indicate the length of possible radiation wave lengths involved and found ordinary radio waves could be ruled out. He tried temperature tests but found no temperature differences. He tried tests for an electric current but found none. He tried ultra violet radiation, also ionizing radiation using an electroscope, with no unusual results. In an effort to duplicate the stroking effect, he and his colleagues built a machine to imitate the process: perhaps the stroking set up vibrations of a sort to bend metal. This did not turn out to be the case – again, no result.

Then, in June 1974, several more events led to what seemed at least a provisional clue – another visit by Uri Geller to Professor Taylor's laboratory, and the emergence of two new subjects, boys aged 10 and 16 respectively, both metal-benders who proved to have equal, if not surpassing powers. This time Uri Geller not only demonstrated even more impressive feats, such as causing the very device measuring his exerted pressure itself to crumble, but in some way influenced various testing objects to bend at a distance or to fly from one part of the room to an-other, one of them hitting Professor Taylor in the back of the leg as he and Uri Geller walked along a corridor, some 70 feet from the room.

Test followed test, all closely supervised and watched by Professor Taylor and various colleagues: more proof, yet more confusion. The 10-year-old boy could place a number of straightened paper clips into a cardboard box, 'think' about them getting all 'scrunched' up, and the result was an incredible scramble of folded-over metal. It was then found that the 16-year-old could also do this, and on the basis of Professor Taylor's hypothesis that metal bent at a point of 'internal stress', in another test he removed the stress from two of three straightened clips, leaving the third one untreated. The untreated one bent the most.

Other feats of the 10-year-old boy were 'metal sculptures' made by the winding movement of thin, mind-bent metal and an iron rod that curled around and around on itself as supple as a snake. But when the 16-year-old deflected the needle of a com-pass, repeatedly and at will, Professor Taylor considered that he had found a demonstrable test even more reliable than metal bending. He devised other tests involving rotation. Cylinders and iron rods were used, and again in these, internal stress was studied, to be confirmed as a factor in the mind-effect. The presence of a low frequency electric field during rotation was also verified, and the 'intention' of the subject appeared to be localized as an approximately 3-centimetre disc on the inner arm above the wrist. The 16-year-old boy actually being measured said he could feel the build-up of static electricity in his arm and would occasionally feel shock when he touched water.

The nature of these findings has finally led Professor Taylor to the conclusion that the answer to this mind-metal interaction is probably electromagnetic, transmitted by a combination of 'waves from the body controlled by the brain, so creating a direct interaction between mind and object, a field of "intentionality"'. The repeatability of these recent experiments has also brought a more open response from science.

There are theories that ESP comes more naturally to small children but disappears later on as the social conditioning intervenes. At the Department of Psychology, University of Surrey, in Guildford, Ernesto Spinelli has investigated telepathic ability in sixty-six children aged $2\frac{1}{2}$ to 4. Interestingly he found that quiet, introverted children were the best 'senders', while the extraverted ones were the best 'receivers', and that the very youngest children got the best results.

Meanwhile, in Japan, there have been more incredible discoveries of children with powers such as Uri Geller's, some far beyond. After a visit to Tokyo, where Uri Geller again displayed his extraordinary talents, thousands of Japanese children between 5 and 15 revealed that they were able to do the same things, and more besides.

In 1974 Dr Shigemi Sasaki, professor of psychology at Denki Tsushin University in Tokyo launched a study-project with fifteen researchers and eight children selected at random.[106] Two main forms of measurement of their PK abilities were used: a vertical motion measure and a 'Tensil Turn Indicator', a sensitive electronic meter for measuring the solid and physical state of a piece of metal.

With the first, children succeeded in bending glass-enclosed wire downward without touching it, and in the second caused thin strips of steel to twist and the meter to jump, merely by exerting their mental force. The scientists were even further mystified when one small 12-year-old boy holding three spoons at once, made them bend almost double, one snapping in half right in front of their eyes. The spoons, which had been measured beforehand, when measured again showed a 0·03 gram loss of metal. The same boy was also able to recharge radio batteries. An 8-year-old girl could not only bend metal but split it in two by throwing it over her shoulder, and a 5-year-old boy could cause heavy objects in the laboratory to move slowly from a distance of several feet by simply naming them.

Altogether, the scientists agreed that they would not have believed these things possible until they actually saw them happen. Since they also found some evidence of healing power in the hands of these children, they feel there is some connecting link to the mind-metal effect, a view that is shared by Professor Taylor, who considers this aspect in his book.

Since it is not only in England and Japan that hundreds of children have come forward to reveal similar and even more extensive talents after hearing Uri Geller's broadcasts, but in several other countries where he has appeared, Andrija Puharich and a group of professional colleagues including a physicist and two doctors, are travelling about the world interviewing many of these gifted children in an effort to discover any common aspects of their intelligence. Speculations are leading to some preliminary theories, but it is as yet too early for them to be publicly voiced.

In the meantime, Uri Geller himself has no such indetermination: he believes that at least his powers are derived from another form of more advanced intelligence and that devices still need to be invented to measure its 'energy waves'.

Sensible open-mindedness should not exclude the possibility. As Dr Henry Margenau, Professor of Physics and Natural Philosophy at Yale University, observed at the 1969 Address to the American Society for Psychical Research:

'Today we know that there are many phenomena on the fringe,

at the periphery of present-day science, which are not yet understood, which are still obscure, but which will nevertheless be encompassed by the scientific method and by scientific understanding in the future.'

The phenomenon of the *poltergeist* (meaning 'noisy and mischievous spirit'), a spontaneous form of PK observed and recorded for centuries and generally interpreted as some form of psychic aggression, was in 1967 with 'the Rosenheim case' investigated with the knowledge and instruments of science.

In the autumn of that year and for several months thereafter, the office of a lawyer, Sigmund Adam, in the Bavarian town of Rosenheim,[8] was the centre of many inexplicable events; first the telephone and switchboard system began to function erratically, calls were broken off or didn't go through, or all three telephones rang at once, and when the meters were read, it was found that great numbers of calls were registered that no one had made, as well as the speaking clock having been rung, several times a minute, without having been dialled.

Engineers suspected trouble in the mains feeding the office, and a new installation was made. The mysterious disturbances continued. Suspecting planned malice, Mr Adam called in the Criminal Investigation Department, considerably increasing the number of witnesses, but now, adding to the mystification, light bulbs were exploding, neon light tubes twisting in their sockets, fuses blowing without cause.

Further measures were taken by the engineers and technicians without avail, and eventually the lawyer's office was separated from the mains and connected to an emergency unit while they brought in electronic equipment to record the disturbances.

The poltergeist activities continued – pictures falling from the walls or rotating at extreme angles, heavy furniture moving without being touched – but for the first time were recorded on tape.

In addition to telephone and electrical engineers, and the CID witnesses, a leading parapsychologist came to study the situation. Dr Hans Bender of the Institute for Border Areas of Psychology and Mental Hygiene at the University of Freiburg soon confirmed what the others had found, that the baffling phenomena occurred only when an 18-year-old assistant secretary, Annemarie Schaberl, was near.

Two eminent physicists were summoned from Munich, Dr F. Karger of the Max Planck Institute and Dr G. Zicha of the Technische Universitat. Their lengthy report of the events, in terms of electrodynamics, described them as being outside the known laws of physics. They suggested that the movements gave the impression of being under intelligent control and that there might be an undiscovered principle of physics that worked through human faculties.

In personal interviews with Annemarie Schaberl, Dr Bender found that she suffered from intense frustration and pent-up hostility. This fitted with his theory that adolescents with repressed aggression focused some kind of eruptive energy, and underscored the physicist's hypothesis.

Other poltergeist phenomena in recent years have been studied scientifically by W. G. Roll[128] and colleagues of the Psychical Research Foundation in Durham, North Carolina. In one case, in Miami, Florida, in 1967, a controlled study was made at a wholesale novelty store where two hundred incidents of breakages and objects flung from shelves had taken place. It had soon seemed apparent that the phenomena occurred in the vicinity of a 19-year-old shipping clerk named Julio.

After interviewing many witnesses as to the strange trajectory of the flung objects, target objects in chosen areas were assigned for observation; but except for one or two instances, objects only fell in any one particular area when the witnesses' attention had turned to another one. Some movement was observed, however, in the proximity of Julio.

At Durham, Julio underwent further observation. His brain-waves were measured on the EEG and found normal, but psychological tests revealed hostile aggression towards his parents, which he had transferred to the owners of the store, still unable to express it openly. PK tests showed significant ability: not only did he successfully influence the fall of dice from an automatic dice holder, but the holder itself fell apart. Additionally, when Julio was standing with the parapsychologists, in a hallway a few feet away, a vase suddenly shattered.

In 1968, at the small home of the Callihan family in Olive Hill, Kentucky, W. G. Roll was able to observe poltergeist phenomena actually taking place. The elderly couple had had almost all their breakable possessions smashed to pieces and had moved to a new home, but the disturbances continued. J. P. Stump, who was assisting W. G. Roll, saw a bowl and cloth doily fall suddenly behind the television set. Plastic flowers that had been in the bowl, slowly followed. A clock, also on the set, flew off about 4 feet in the opposite direction.

When the investigator looked behind the television, the bowl was on the doily and the flowers in the bowl, just as they had been when on top of the set. On another occasion, W. G. Roll[128] saw a heavy kitchen table lift into the air and circle about at a 45 degree angle, then fall back onto the chairs which had stood near by.

Altogether, there were nearly two hundred incidents, all finally linked to the presence of a 12-year-old grandson; incidents increased in relation to nearness of the boy, as if his again-confirmed hostility had a range and motion of force.

The subject is, however, far from clear-cut, and all poltergeist phenomena are not attributable to children or young people. The psychokinetic effect may relate to other unknown forces under investigation.

Mind-energy was focused, literally, in the 1960s, when a former hotel worker from Chicago named Ted Serios was found to be able to transfer a mental image onto Polaroid film by working himself into a state of extreme concentration. Although 'psychic photography' was not an unknown phenomenon – strange effects having appeared on film but without means of verification – this was the first time anyone claimed to be able to 'think' a picture onto film, deliberately.

Ted Serios, a man in his fifties given to heavy drinking, found no one of substance impressed with his 'thoughtography' until 1964, when Dr Jule Eisenbud, Associate Clinical Professor of Psychiatry at the University of Colorado Medical School, provided him with the chance to demonstrate his ability before qualified researchers under laboratory conditions.

Many long, patiently monitored sessions followed in which cameras, film, position, the possibility of contrived light or lens effects, of conjuring or any other kind of fraud was laboriously checked, and Ted Serios himself became exhausted from the effort and repetition. His success was elusive and erratic, and he had to drink while concentrating in order to produce the 'right' state; nevertheless, Dr Eisenbud felt impelled to write a book about this potentially significant phenomenon (*The World of Ted Serios*[38]), and there were further experiments by other parapsychologists.

One of these, conducted in 1968 by Drs Ian Stevenson and J. G. Pratt at the University of Virginia,[147] consisted of four approximately three-hour sessions in which Polaroid cameras and film belonging to the Department of Psychiatry were used and fifty or more trials were made by Ted Serios each session. The procedure required almost agonizing effort for him, and more frequently than a thought-image, when, perspiring and strained he called 'Now!', indicating he was ready, the peeled-off print would be various impressions of his own contorted face.

But among all the failures, there appeared recognizable portions of a university building (which he had seen on a postcard under the glass bureau-top of his hotel room), a cage-like object with bars, the letters V–A as if seen reflected in a mirror, columns with a conical effect behind them, a desk that was a spatial match of one in the building, none of them explainable technically.

Altogether, there were twenty-six 'abnormal' prints, not a great number, and there were unanswered questions about the use of microfilm inside the 'gismo' (a tube made of rolled film-paper about 2 inches long) Ted Serios was in the habit of holding in his right hand. But substitution of their own 'gismos' and constant surveillance of his movements during and between sessions did not reveal any attempt at trickery.

The trials were not completed, but the conclusion of the two parapsychologists was:

'We remain fully aware that we have not been able to describe conditions and results which should remove all doubt that the Serios phenomenon is paranormal. But weighing the various features we have discussed, and considering again our failure to detect anything the least suspicious of conjuring, we think that our findings increase the importance of further research with Ted.'

Later in a German television documentary, Ted Serios demonstrated that he probably used a combination of PK and ESP, for not only did the television picture gradually darken with his intense effort of concentration, but a new image appeared that was recognizable – a target picture in a sealed envelope which he had never seen.

While Western experiments may have failed to reveal just how Ted Serios achieved these effects, Russian parapsychologists considered them significant enough to pursue their own investigation of 'psychic photography', the main difficulty being not the question of thought-transfer itself, but finding subjects with sufficient patience, will and power of concentration to evidence research material.

Perhaps the most sophisticated psi experiments were instigated by Dr Helmut Schmidt, a physicist at the Boeing Aircraft Research Laboratories and later Director of the Institute for Parapsychology, with his fully automated experiments in 1969.

Inspired by the pioneering work of Dr Rhine with the hypothesis that gamblers, when confident, could will the fall of the dice at odds higher than chance, Dr Schmidt set about constructing a machine that hopefully would provide electronic, therefore thoroughly scientific corroboration.[135]

The machine he devised had four coloured lamps which lighted in random sequence determined by a radioactive source. The task of the subject was to try to decide which of the four lamps would light up next and to press one of four keys corresponding to the chosen lamp.

The results of one intensive test brought Dr Rhine's statistical evidence to an apex; out of over 70,000 guesses there were hits with odds over chance expectation of roughly 2,000,000,000 to 1, and subsequent tests proved even more significant in ruling out the possibility of chance elements.

'Schmidt's machine' as the device became known, proved to be such a useful means of testing ESP in its various forms, that it was put to work in many parapsychological laboratories. Yet how it worked did not answer how the mental transfer took place; as Dr Schmidt himself commented: 'The subjects are mentally affecting the flow of electrons or some other part of the machine

. . . We don't know how, but the results disagree with generally assumed concepts of physics.'

In a later experiment this machine was developed to include an electronic device which flipped a coin in a random sequence of heads and tails. The device was connected to a circle of nine lamps, one of which would light up each time the coin fell, and the light would jump round in a clockwise or anti-clockwise direction whenever a head or a tail was produced. The coin flipper was set to make 128 decisions in about two minutes while the subject tried mentally to force the light to move more steps in a clockwise, rather than anti-clockwise direction; if successful this would mean that the subjects were compelling the coin-flipper to generate more heads than tails, even though they were concentrating on the lights and did not understand the coin-flipper mechanism.

The results were a little surprising as they showed a negative scoring tendency – the lights moved more often in the opposite direction to that which the subjects intended it to move. This kind of PK missing had been noticed in other experiments, especially if the subjects felt ill at ease in the situation, and in this case they were seated in a dark cubicle in front of the panel of lights. Since Dr Schmidt was interested in any observable PK effect, he reinforced the negative feelings by associating the experiment with a sense of failure. The result was a significantly negative PK effect with odds of more than 1,000 to 1 against chance.

However, an outstanding positive effect was obtained with one subject who said she felt herself to be psychic. Her positive scoring rate was 53·5 per cent in twenty-five test runs – chance being 50 per cent – which meant that the odds against chance were more than 1,000,000,000 to 1.

Reaching from past to future, by-passing countless forms of rigorous experimentation that seldom came to the attention of occult dabblers or the general public, but added steadily to the weight of scientific evidence over the years, was the famous Moon-Earth ESP experiment made by the astronaut Edgar Mitchell during the flight of Apollo 14 in 1971.

Edgar Mitchell,[97] sixth man to set foot on the moon, became interested in parapsychology several years before as a result of dissatisfaction with traditional concepts of and theologies for the purpose of man. He began delving into the paranormal, sceptically at first, but with growing interest that was not dismayed by its aura of charlatanism and perversion by fanatics. Despite his three doctorates in space science, he felt parapsychology held potential enlightenment that could extend man's horizons, give him a new frontier of 'inner space'.

It later occurred to him that his flight to the moon could be a unique opportunity to test telepathy at a distance. He enlisted four people to act as receivers on earth of his mental transmissions from space, and did several 'warm-up' sessions with them, using the standard Zener cards.

In the actual test, Captain Mitchell (who piloted the spacecraft) used random numbers from one to five set up in eight columns of twenty-five numbers each written on a sheet of paper. His object was to select six of the columns during the flight and to give each number an ESP symbol just before the transmission.

While a world generally unaware of this watched the miracle of the moon-shot itself and the three astronauts rocketing incredibly through space in the lunar module *Antares*, Captain Mitchell found time for four transmissions of his symbols, two on the way up and two on the way down (in his rest period).

Dr Rhine and Dr Karlis Osis of the ASPR who had offered to analyse the results found them significant in two ways: (1) they proved precognition rather than telepathy, because all but one transmission had been delayed by the delay in the craft's lift-off, and somehow the receivers had picked on the targets next in sequence; (2) they had a decidedly psi-missing score of three thousand to one below the expectation of chance.

'Apparently time is no obstacle to psi ability,' said Captain Mitchell. 'I can't explain it, but that's what the data indicate.'

Apart from this try-out of space ESP, Captain Mitchell had been profoundly affected by the perspective of our world in relation to the universe. 'It became absolutely clear to me that the universe and its harmonious functioning throughout is not solely the result of a cosmic accident based on chance and random processes . . . This view from space has shown me how limited a view man has of his own life and that of the planet.'

This inspired sense of transformation stayed with Captain Mitchell and led to his retirement from the Navy and space programme, and finally, in 1973, to the establishment of the Institute of Noetic Sciences in Palo Alto, California, and dedication to a new vision.

The Institute of Noetic Sciences was to have five main functions: to perform basic research in the nature of consciousness and the mind-body relationship; to offer educational activities to expand human awareness and release human potential; to inform society about activities, developments and trends in the areas of personal and cultural transformation; to advise and consult with governments, industry, science, education and other areas of society on planetary problems and their solution; and to consult, support and coordinate with those working for the transformation of human consciousness and culture.

Among the many projects already undertaken by the Institute and Edgar Mitchell by 1973, were two documentary films (made with Hartley Productions), one entitled *Inner Space* and the other *The Ultimate Mystery*. The films deal with a blend of subjects – psychic phenomena, consciousness research, and the nature of the universe – and include a psychic healing, business executives being tested for precognition ability, work in plant consciousness by Cleve Backster (*see* page 190) and forms of meditation as practised by Sufis, Tibetan lamas, yogis, and American Indians.

Rounding out this highly diverse but far from complete catalogue of psi experimentation is the work of The Psi Communication Project, which was started in 1962 at the Newark College of Engineering, in Newark, New Jersey, America, whose aims were to 'utilize scientific talent and methodology to investigate various aspects of ESP, and to utilize engineering talent and methodology to develop practical, beneficial applications of the Psi phenomenon'.

To this end an experiment was developed for a completely distinct precognition target; the percipients were asked to guess at a 100-digit number which did not yet exist. Later, a 100-digit number was generated by a computer, using the techniques of a

random number generator. Following this, the 100-digit number
guessed at by the percipients was checked with the computerized
100-digit number (also by computer). The results showed that
some of the guessers had scored well beyond chance, as high as
twenty-two when chance expectation was three – free of possible
signals picked up consciously or unconsciously, it seemed a
purely precognitive test had been found.

The test was given to people in a wide variety of age-groups
and occupations, proving useful in perceiving certain factors of
precognitive ability, such as that it related less to intelligence than
to dynamic personality, and was often correlated with high-level
executive ability.

Towards more effective decision-making and generation of
profitable ideas in big business, the Psi Communication Project
was given a grant to help the Rand Corporation (which had
devised the 'Delphi Method' based on use of the intuition of
individuals, as opposed to group-structured expertise) to 'pre-
select' superior executives through precognitive ability-testing.

In May 1972, 'ESP in Decision Making' was a subject of discussion at the eleventh annual US Army Operations Research
Symposium, the theme of which was 'Risk Analysis'. Partici-
pating in the session on ESP were Dr Rhine and John Mihalasky,[95] Professor of Industrial Engineering and Director of the
Psi Communication Project of the Newark College of Engineering.

'In solving problems, the engineer will have to delve into areas
beyond the confines of established technical knowledge,' said
Professor Mihalasky in a paper presented at the Design Engineering Conference earlier the same month. 'He has to consider
variability and uncertainty. In the area of Risk Decision Analysis,
the Department of Defense has studied the facets of uncertainty
into "known-unknowns" where you are aware of your areas of
uncertainty, and "unknown-unknowns" where you are not aware
of your areas of certainty.'

A book written by John Mihalasky and Douglas Dean,
Executive ESP,[35] gives an 'in-depth' study of the subject with the
details of controlled (IBM) computer testing of top executives,
both individually and in groups. The authors' conclusion was

that, while their figures do not prove that ESP-ability and profit-making are *always* related, they do show that the probability of an executive with precognitive ability also making more profit-making decisions is substantially demonstrated. Also, since nineteen out of twenty-five executives who scored above chance proved to be 'profit doublers', this precognitive, or ESP-ability test appeared superior to the standard psychological tests for the same purpose.

Perhaps the most eloquent summary of the long tortuous emergence of ESP from dim outer limits of credulity to the growing light of veridity, was the term 'quasi-sensory communication' (QSC) coined for it in 1970 by Professor William MacBain of the University of Hawaii. While the telepathy test he and a group of scientists conducted with twenty-two pairs of psychology students, in an attempt to achieve more definitive transmission than with standard chance guessing, provided further meaningful correlates of character and ESP ability, the greater significance may have been the milestone terminology. (Details of this test can be found in the 24 June 1971 issue of the *New Statesman*, London.)

In Russia, terminology for ESP had even another connotation. Called bioenergetics it was not to be considered as something supernatural but a form of energy to be studied as science. In Czechoslovakia it was called 'psychotronics'. Further, to describe its association with other life-systems, in the West the prefix 'para' was tacked on, creating 'paraphysics', 'parascience', 'para-medicine' and many others. The semantics of invisible forces, over the course of a hundred years, had the ring of a new language; made up of words, numbers, symbols and imagery of the senses, it was not just the tongue of a few metaphysicians – but as man had made basic words to speak of nature, of fire and water, of life, death, the hunting and killing for food, so he has begun to make mind-words, words to describe mind in motion, mind in expression, mind in the very awareness of being mind.

1C CURRENT TRENDS OF EXPERIMENTS

> We felt there was a higher proportion of scientists in the audience at this programme than at any previous PA–AAAS symposium, and the level and nature of the questioning indicated intelligent interest in the phenomena rather than either irrational scepticism or blind acceptance . . . persons were seemingly reacting to our presentations the same way they would react to presentation in other scientific areas.
>
> REX STANFORD
>
> (*President of the Parapsychological Association, in a report about the PA's participation in an American Association for the Advancement of Science symposium in December 1972.*)[115]

QUESTIONS, he said, had been 'forward-looking': in what direction was the research leading? To what degree were the findings linking up with other bodies of knowledge? There was little doubt that the tide of opinion among scientists was beginning to turn in their direction.

In three years since its acceptance by the AAAS, parapsychology had made decided progress.

At the Parapsychological Association Convention in 1973[115] in Charlottesville, Virginia, members presented forty-two papers. There were thirty-two experimental reports, five of spontaneous cases, and five methodological papers, in which several more correlates of the psi-personality-relationships were contributed. Animal choice-behaviour was further evidence though not yet categorized.

Ten papers dealt with 'free verbal response', three with 'emotional behaviour', and five with spontaneous cases, all of which came under the growing experimental area with ESP in altered states of consciousness (ASC), i.e. deep relaxation, suggestion, meditation, trance, modification of internal states, sense-deprivation, dreaming 'out-of-body experience' (*see* Chapter 2), perhaps close to thirty states all-told between waking and deep sleep, and premonitions (of impending death or disaster).

The other fifteen papers dealt with PK effects of various kinds, significant rise from previous years to almost one half of all the experimental papers.

The following chart (modified from the original) shows comparison of papers in each category over three different periods, indicating the shape and trend of modern psi research.

The changing emphasis in psi research

	1958–1960	1965–1966	1973
Experimental	40	64	32
Spontaneous	6	4	5
Methodology	12	8	8
Choice	31	40	8
Free response	1	14	10
Emotional response	1	3	3
PK	7	7	15
Zener cards	10	14	1
Dice	7	0	0
Stable system PK	0	1	8

Adapted from *Parapsychology Review* March–April 1973

Note here that the proportion of experimental, spontaneous and methodological papers have remained comparatively the same; that the emphasis on choice behaviour has declined; that free response papers are numerically increased; that there is a shift away from the 'classical image' of parapsychology (card-guessing, dice-throwing, etc.), and that among the PK papers, the preponderance had moved from reports on the influencing of targets to the moving of 'stable' objects, such as achieved by Madam Kulagina in Russia.

In America, another woman had shown the same ability and Charles Honorton, Researcher with the Maimonides Dream Laboratory in Brooklyn, showed a film of Felicia Parise (a Maimonides laboratory technician) mentally moving non-magnetic objects away from her, and another report gave evidence that she had moved a compass needle several degrees, and that the deviated needle did not return to its true position until 25 minutes later.

Professor Hal Puthoff of the Stanford Research Institute reported evidence that Uri Geller could 'induce displacements of up to 1·5 grams in a laboratory balance weighing a 1 gram weight, as well as affect the readings of a Bell gaussmeter up to 0·3 Gauss.

This sketchy survey of the advanced work of serious para-psychologists in many areas of experiment has not included some of their new suggestions for research, but, as Dr Robert Morris (Research Coordinator of the Physical Research Foundation, presently teaching parapsychology at the University of California, and representative of the Parapsychological Association to the American Academy of Arts and Sciences) wrote of the Convention, its emergent design was largely the result of 'increased technical sophistication'. He added that there was 'a renewed desire to learn something about the processes underlying the phenomena rather than just repetitive mathematical demonstration that there are phenomena to learn about, an increased feeling that for one reason or another the older techniques simply aren't telling us what we need to know, and a greater intellectual diversity among those willing to devote their energies to para-psychological topics'.

If research has formed a changing pattern of emphasis, so have the theories of ESP, of all that is termed 'paranormal'. Although to a considerable extent the public at large still leaves explanation (if they want it) in the realm of the supernatural, the 'unknow-able', this is most often because they have not been exposed to sources of information, to the parapsychological literature and work that is going on; they are no more informed than they would be, *en masse*, about the latest work in, say, quantum physics. The present trend in theories, therefore, may seem so far removed from those who are only just beginning to accept the possibility that ESP exists,* as to be incomprehensible jargon.

This does not preclude the innovative thinking that gropes

---

*In a survey published by the *New Scientist* in 1973, of 1,500 readers who completed a questionnaire on ESP (63 per cent had degrees, and of these 29 per cent had higher degrees and only 5 per cent had no schooling), 25 per cent of the total held ESP to be an established fact; 42 per cent thought it a 'likely possibility'; 3 per cent thought it an impossibility, and 12 per cent called it an 'unknown'. Since the majority of the readers were working scientists and technologists, it showed that even with caution a large number of serious scientists consider parapsychology to be a highly interesting, immensely significant branch of science.

towards hypotheses, attempts in differing fields to position ESP in universal and specific forms of life, if only to provide models for models, theories for more theories. Some are too scientific, particularly in terms of 'energy' for this chapter and are gone into later, or related to subjects of forthcoming chapters. Here, the few theories mentioned are in keeping with what has so far been presented.

From earlier research, Dr Robert H. Thouless,[155] then Professor of Psychology at Cambridge University and a one-time President of the SPR, and a colleague offered the suggestion that psi experiences were simply rare instances of normal processes of perception and motor activity. When an entity which they called 'shin', somewhat corresponding to 'soul', and what may be termed consciousness, sometimes communicates directly with the brain without the intervention of the nervous system, the result is sense perception in the form of a mental image.

Naturally, this leaves questions.

G. N. N. Tyrrell,[155] an English physicist who worked with Marconi to develop radio and President of the SPR in 1945, held that 'travelling clairvoyance was not actual travel as consciously conceived, but that two pictures or thought-forms, one the agent and the other the percipient, came together in 'an elaborate sensory construct created by mid-level elements of the personalities (of each) working together, and not a conscious or semi-conscious being'. He did not hold that subjective experience had spatial properties, but rather that 'Our perceptual consciousness has constructed for it an elaborate system of sense-data which gives it a picture of a spatial environment as seen from a particular standpoint, and gives it an irresistible feeling of being in that picture'.

More recently, yet to some extent in accord, is the ESP theory of A. M. Young[104] of the Foundation for the Study of Conciousness in Philadelphia, Pennsylvania (USA) and editor-contributor for *Journal for the Study of Consciousness*,[67] who says, in part '. . . The subjective states, feelings, emotions which constitute the most real part of our existence and are experienced directly, are not objects in space, as are atoms. . . . Attention, which is the true centre of being and enables it to experience one of a number of these states, is at a still "higher" level, doubly removed from the atoms, molecules, or organic entities (cells) which comprise the physical body. . . . It is reasonable, too, to say that the emotional states do not have location, another spatial attribute. It then follows that subjective states, not being spatial, need not follow spatial laws, and if this conclusion is really accepted, we can no longer, on categorical grounds, rule out their transmission.

'Following the thought a bit further, we might ask, have we any ground for isolating the subjective side of persons in the same way that we know their objective and physical bodies are isolated? Is your subjective spatially separate from my subjective? On the ground we have covered, I have to say that it is not.'

Haakon Forwald,[31] the Swedish engineer who had followed on with Dr Rhine's experiments, formed a theory from his own high-scoring experiments with PK (rolling cubes down an incline and himself attempting to influence their left or right direction as they reached a flat surface). After having tested for and finding no evidence of magnetic and electrostatic fields, he decided that a gravitational effect might be present – the needed energy being released from the cube material by a 'transformation' on the microphysical level, set off by the mind motion, the mental force.

Still vague, but perhaps suggesting areas for investigation of how psi interacts with matter. (Pierre Teilhard de Chardin,[154] the 'priest-palaeontologist', who wrote prolifically on such matters, had long-since postulated that consciousness was inseparable from matter, and that it was 'spirit' that influenced the specific patterning and/or action of matter. And this was echoed in the observations of two other scientists who left their theoretical mark: Sir Arthur Eddington who as early as 1928 said that 'The stuff of the world is mind-stuff,' and Sir James Jeans who in 1937 said that '. . . The stream of knowledge is heading towards a non-mechanical reality; the universe begins to look more like a great thought than like a great machine'.)

While the final answer may emerge from 'The New Physics' by the finding of a new paradigm of science in which the paranormal can be accommodated, a theory with a concrete everyday ring is that of Dr Rex Stanford, President of the PA, who won an ASPR award in 1973 for outstanding parapsychological work.

He believes that '. . . Psi plays a definite, but subtle and largely unrecognized or unconscious role in our life experience. Often we experience odd or even weird "coincidences" which, while seemingly meaningful, are usually dismissed as "mere coincidence".[146]

'. . . A surprising number of experiments, as well as psychoanalytic observations, suggest a rather powerful, unconscious function of psi in the service of the individual's needs. These experiments and observations led me to develop a conceptual model of psi in everyday life. This model, though specifically concerned with ESP, can be extended to include PK and the conjoint use of ESP and PK.

'*The psi-mediated instrumental response (PMIR) model*

'The organism uses psi to scan its environment for need-relevant objects and events and for information crucially related to these. This scanning is more or less constant depending on the constancy or critical character of the needs of the organism. When extrasensory information is thus obtained about need-relevant objects or events, a disposition towards PMIR arises; that is, the organism then tends to act in ways which are instrumental in satisfying needs in relation to the object or event. Production of or preparation for PMIR often involves such changes as motivational or emotional arousal (e.g. restlessness), attention-focusing responses (i.e. starting to notice certain things around you which you have not been noticing), and other preparations for response.

'The strength of the disposition towards PMIR is, all else being equal, directly and positively related to the importance or strength of the needs in question, to the degree of need-relevance of the object or event, and to the closeness in time of the potential encounter with the need-relevant circumstances. The needs subserved by PMIR are strongly related to individual factors related to need arousal and to the interaction of these two.

'PMIR can occur without a conscious effort to use psi, without a conscious effort to fulfil the need subserved by PMIR, without prior sensory knowledge even that the need-relevant circumstance exists, and without the development of conscious perceptions (e.g. mental images) or ideas concerning this circumstance. Complete PMIR can occur without the person's being aware that anything extraordinary is happening.

'Here are some of the many subtle ways in which PMIR can be accomplished: (1) an *unconscious timing mechanism* which allows one unexpectedly to be at the appropriate time to encounter a favorable event or to avoid an unfavorable one, or which causes him to perform a preplanned action at a time when the act has definite, logically unforeseen, favorable consequences; (2) *forgetting or remembering* (e.g. forgetting to go by the grocery store on the unanticipated occasion of a wild shooting spree outside the store by a berserk person); (3) *mistakes* which work out, surprisingly, to one's advantage and which seem based upon extrasensory information; (4) *associations* (e.g. PMIR occasioned by the mere thought of a friend which results in dropping in on him when he has something interesting to tell you, but of which you had no sensory knowledge); (5) *numerous other possibilities*, including the perhaps overemphasized conscious psi-mediated cognitions (i.e. definite psi-mediated perception or ideas of the need-relevant circumstances). PMIR may often occur through psi-mediated release or triggering of otherwise "ready" responses, thoughts, memories, etc. PMIR tends to be accomplished in the most "economical" way possible; e.g. a full-blown conscious (psi-mediated) idea about or perception of the need-relevant event will not occur if PMIR can be accomplished in some simpler, less disruptive way.

'This model, though it suggests that PMIR is more frequent than could ever be apparent from simple observation, must also, if it is to be realistic, provide for definite limitations on, or "misuse of", PMIR. Many *limitations* are situational. The ones we shall specifically consider here are psychological, such as: (1) behavioral rigidity (e.g. preplanning of one's daily schedule or regimen and permitting little or no deviation from it), behavioral stereotype (i.e. tending to repeat an act or action sequence in exactly the same way it has been done before), and response chaining (i.e. when a given act tends always to follow another particular act); (2) psychological conflicts preventing the expression of some need. "*Misuses*" include: (1) PMIR used to validate a negative self-concept rather than to produce adaptive response (e.g. a person who thinks of himself as "incompetent" may use PMIR to help make his plans ineffective; or if one feels he is "no good" or a "wicked sinner", he may use PMIR to create for himself "punishing" situations); (2) use of PMIR to perpetuate the quality of a series of life experience (e.g. a run of "bad luck") – owing perhaps to a need for consistency in one's life; and (3) systematic "misuse" of PMIR because of motivational conflicts such as guilt or an approach-avoidance conflict (e.g. the shy boy who suddenly gets up the nerve to call a girl for a date after, unknown to him, she has just accepted a date with another boy for that occasion). The "misuses" may constitute real-world analogues to psi-missing.'

Dr Stanford concludes by commenting that much more experimentation is needed to test the model's full implications. 'The studies *most* relevant to it and to understanding psi in life situations,' he says, 'are those which use ESP (and/or PK) tasks in which an individual can use psi unconsciously in an instrumental fashion, and in which he never knows psi is being studied.' Other supportive work for the PMIR model is being done by Dr Martin Johnson of the University of Utrecht, and Helmut Schmidt and others at the Institute of Parapsychology.

The suggestion here, that spontaneous or 'unconscious' ESP and PK tasks should be gauged instrumentally, puts some of the ultimate responsibility on the steady coordination of new and better instruments to accomplish this paradoxical feat. John Cutten of the British SPR[115] puts a final word to the directional focus of parapsychology: 'If a parapsychologist demonstrates strict observance of an impartial scientific approach, and if, in addition, he can wherever possible use scientific instruments to verify his results, he will not be regarded as inexact, even if the results of his experiments are disappointing. . . . It will be only by the use of instruments that at least some of the problems presented will finally be solved. Merely observing the phenomenal occurrence is not likely to help us understand it, and here again instruments must be employed if we are ever to proceed from wonderment to reality.'

1D THE WORLD OF PSI EDUCATION

ESP research is at the stage where general psychology was about a hundred years ago. People are just beginning to get the feeling that ESP ability might obey laws which can be described. Recognition by the establishment in the Universities should be the next stage.

DR J. B. RHINE[121]

MANY parapsychologists feel that this recognition has been extremely slow in arriving, yet looked at in perspective, Dr Rhine himself would surely admit that there has been a definite upsurge of academic interest in the last few years. While naturally wanting to see an even greater and more serious acceptance into the regular curricula of school and college, today's psi disseminators have some very encouraging facts before them.

As of 1975 (according to the Educational department of the ASPR) there were, in America, approximately 118 courses, 75 of them with credit, in the universities, and almost as many extension or independent courses. Apart from these, adult education classes, psi-research groups, seminars and workshops sprang up in schools and centres all over the United States and in a great many other countries throughout the world.

The actual case as it stands is that if there were more trained parapsychologists (not self-appointed authorities or exploiters who cash in on the occult interest to propagate misleading and sometimes highly destructive misinformation), there would be more courses offered; for the demands for ESP knowledge far exceed those equipped to give it, and every class that does offer it has to turn away applicants for a lack of space or facilities.

The lack of actual departments of parapsychology in the universities – there are only two currently, The State University of Utrecht in the Netherlands and the Andhra University in India (under the Rhine-trained Dr K. Ramakrishna Rao), and only one actual university which emphasizes psi subjects, the Institute for Border Areas of Psychology in Freiburg, Germany – may seem to present a continuing case for the sceptics who still hold that parapsychology is outside the academic establishment.

They are right – in part; it still takes courage of conviction for a teacher to be wholly associated with psi subjects; there is still a risk of loss of academic status and therefore advancement. But the front door is not the only way in to acceptance; there are side and back doors, and ESP has slipped through close to eighty of them as of this writing (and more every month) as adjuncts of Psychology, Philosophy, Psychiatry, Social Studies and even Physics ('Paraphysics') Departments.

Just a few of the credit courses offered have such titles as: 'ESP: Theory and Experiment' (Irvine, University of California, Los Angeles (UCLA)); 'Philosophy, Science and ESP' (ISIU, Colorado); 'Introduction to Psychical Phenomena'; experimental course (University of Minnesota).

In 1973, through a fully accredited, interdisciplinary curriculum in parapsychology in association with the psychology department of North-eastern Illinois University, a student could obtain a BA degree in psychology with special emphasis on parapsychology. At Santa Barbara (UCLA), Dr Milan Ryzl (*see* page 27) offered both an introductory and advanced credit course, and Dr Thelma Moss conducts 'Independent Research in Parapsychology for undergraduates and graduates with volunteers as laboratory apprentices in conjunction with the Psychiatry Department at UCLA'. In England, at the University of Surrey in Guildford, the philosophy department in 1973 added a course in parapsychology, as has the Selkirk College in Castlegon, Canada, called 'Science and Beyond; a look at the Paranormal'.

In 1973 a survey of 'The Academic Status of Parapsychology' was carried out by a writer and teacher of parapsychology, D. Scott Rogo[137] for the Parapsychology Foundation, in which the chairmen of five hundred American college psychology departments were sent an itemized questionnaire and asked to answer it for their departments.

The results proved enlightening. Out of the 47 per cent of the department heads who responded – and these did not necessarily do so from predisposition to the subject, since several were in varying degrees hostile – 62·4 per cent answered positively to the

question: 'Do you think parapsychology should be covered in
undergraduate psychology courses?', 11·8 per cent said 'no'; and
21·8 per cent 'briefly'.

A breakdown of department orientation here showed that
clinical psychology departments were substantially more in
favour of parapsychology than experimental psychology departments. Details of the survey also broke down the reasons for this,
and among them were distinct lack of up-to-date knowledge on
developments in the subject, many revealing that the last article
or book read on the subject dated from the early days of experiment or even before, perhaps reflecting absorption in their own
far from rapid entrenchment process.

The answer to whether or not their departments favoured the
adopting of a regular undergraduate course in parapsychology
was preponderately negative for much the same reason, but to
'Would you favour allowing graduate students in your department
to do research in parapsychology to qualify for a graduate
degree?' the answer was 69·1 per cent 'yes'.

D. Scott Rogo's exhaustive analyses concluded that despite the
remaining areas of resistance and question, parapsychology had
made great strides in securing scientific and academic credibility
on our college campuses . . . few colleges were actually antago-
nistic. Many responded with pessimism but with an interest in
learning about advances in the field. Several colleges wished to
see the results of this study to see how sister colleges were
responding to the new academic interest in parapsychology, and a
few institutions were both open and supportive to the idea of
acquainting students with parapsychology.

Some sceptics have latched on to the youthful element in the
rise of psi-interest, linking it loosely with 'the occult explosion'
and reasoning that it is a fad born of escape from reality, allied to
bemusement with drugs, highly suspect and doomed to pass like
all other self-delusion.

Again, they are right – in part; the fad element cannot be
denied, and the ESP-entertainment, the media-exploitation that
creates a parapsychology-occult 'stew', has inflated this factor
into the illusion of a generality.

Dedicated parapsychologists, trained in caution and moderation, have recognized the possibility that this great surge of psi popularity has its hazards, but they have made use of it as an opportunity to fortify their position, to advance their knowledge, to make inroads of sufficient substance that reversal to a previous status was no longer feasible. Young scientists (if not their peers) became interested and dared to show it, and adult education began to swell the ranks of those wanting to know more about this potential for new dimensions to life.

Nowadays, parapsychology is faced with many problems – how to obtain funds to train more parapsychologists to teach it as it should be taught (although more grants are available than at any time in the past), to further the exciting work begun, to supply valid information and reliable literature, to answer the ever-increasing number and range of questions they are asked, and to offset the over-abundance of damaging and spurious misinformation.

Education in parapsychology has also led to techniques for training psi ability, for enhancing ESP in individuals. Training groups led by parapsychologists experiment in a variety of ways to develop telepathic and clairvoyant skill. Dr Milan Ryzl, for instance, has used a hypnotic state to induce ESP; Dr Gertrude Schmeidler discerned a marked increase in ESP card-guessing after students had listened to a lecture on meditation and breathing; Dr Robert Van de Castle and Charles Honorton also used methods of hypnosis and light trances to heighten ESP, and other test-combinations are being tried in groups all over America and several other countries.

Those who would like to make a career of parapsychology are given this knowledgeable advice by Dr Schmeidler, who after warning 'It won't be easy,' adds (in part):[134]

'Since parapsychology is not a recognized college major, you must major in some other field. But this is good, because the skills you learn will most surely be applicable to parapsychology. Almost everything is, from psychology and biology and physics to computer programming or anthropological field studies or mathematical theory. The general advice here is to study what interests you; it will be relevant.'

Dr Schmeidler also suggests that students take advantage of

workshops and summer apprenticeships where they can obtain actual training in research methods alongside able parapsychologists.

'How do you become a parapsychologist?' she concludes. '. . . I'll tell you how *I* did; took a doctorate in psychology (which trained me in research methods); audited a course with Dr Gardner Murphy, and began experimenting. How did Dr Murphy? He took a doctorate in psychology and did a lot of reading on his own. How did Dr Rhine? He took a doctorate in biology and worked with Dr McDougall. How did Dr Osis? He took a doctorate in psychology and worked with Dr Rhine . . . Dr Helmut Schmidt, Director of FRNM is a physicist; Dr Ullman is a psychiatrist . . . there are a lot of routes.'

Probably the most important need for parapsychologists today is to keep in touch with one another's work, to exchange ideas and mutually evaluate the results of individual experimentation. From a few regular conferences here and there throughout the years for this purpose, the list of psi conventions and symposia sounds like an all-season world-travel itinerary; a parapsychologist could spend most of his life moving between them.

In the last three or four years, a follower of psi progress in its several multidisciplinary aspects, might have attended International Congresses in Moscow, Amsterdam, Rome, Prague, San Francisco, London, Montreal, New York, Los Angeles, Vienna, Texas, Honolulu, Kansas, Philadelphia, Berkeley, Tokyo, Washington, Birmingham, North Carolina, Edinburgh, Reykjavik, New Delhi, Paris and many other places. Some of the titles and names of the sponsoring organizations speak of the broadening perspective of mind-potential: 'Academy of Parapsychology and Medicine'; 'Foundation for Parasensory Investigation'; 'American Academy of Psycho-therapists' ('Beyond the Senses'); 'Human Dimensions Institute'; 'Parapsychology and Psychotronics'; 'Studiecentrum voor Experimentele Parapsychologie'; 'Mind Science Foundation'; 'Centro Culturale per la Gioventu'; 'Parapsychology Today'; 'American Psychiatric Association' ('Science and Psi'); 'Western Hemisphere Conference'; 'Parapsychology and Anthropology'; 'Academy of Religion and Psychical Research'. . . .

When these and dozens more are added together, the isolated investigations seem to merge, clearly-marked boundaries between ESP, and man's physical and spiritual nature blur; definitions lead one into the other, indicating less of a puzzle-solving process than a gradual dissemination of light.

2

A tidal wave of mind control and mind expansion techniques

Beneath man's thin veneer of consciousness lies a relatively uncharted realm of mental activity, the nature and function of which
have been neither systematically explored nor adequately con-
ceptualized.

ARNOLD M. LUDWIG (in 1966)

EVEN as psychology and parapsychology found their slow, uphill
way into science, so have many other aspects of mind exploration
pushed in behind them; today, the above comment of Arnold
Ludwig, a psychiatrist with special interest in 'altered states of
consciousness' (ASC), is no longer wholly applicable.

In these intervening years the groundswell of mental exploration and conceptualization has, if anything, threatened to explode
in excess. Apparently the present generation's hunger to escape
rigidities now suspected of being man-imposed, and to realize
potentials residing within mind often tends to bypass the old
scepticism, making him ever more vulnerable to commercial
exploitation.

Some part of the reason for this sudden acceleration of mind-
interest lies, paradoxically, with the mass misuse of the hallucinogenic drugs (the so-called 'mind-expanding' drugs, such as
LSD (d-*lysergic acid diethylamide*), *psilocybin* and *mescaline*)
which had been administered by psychotherapists in experimental
treatment of severely disordered mental patients. Until then, only
the negative implications of states of consciousness, those not
associated with the social norm, were considered. They were
given names and categories as varying forms of neurosis or
insanity, but that they could have positive, advantageous forms
as well, was generally overlooked.

Although the hallucinogenic (or 'psychedelic') drug experiments were discontinued because of their public abuse and possession of these drugs became illegal, the ironical concomitant

was that thousands of users, preponderantly young, had discovered their 'mind-expanding' qualities. Despite the unfortunate results of unsupervised 'trips' and the obvious hazards and inadvisability of indiscriminate psychedelic drug ingestion, there had been incredible visionary and mystical experiences for a great many, revelations of indescribable beauty, colour, dimensions and constructs, sweeping comprehensions of truth, compassion, understanding, love, a sense of oneness with themselves and the universe.

It may not have been entirely intelligible in the recounting, but it tied in with much of what the enlightened, the spiritual leaders, the mystics of the ages had so often attempted to convey. Their interest in religious philosophies of the East was stirred. For these, meditation took on a new significance. A different kind of search was on – for the uplifting and beneficial states of consciousness – hopefully without the use of drugs.

Gradually, but consistently, hundreds upon hundreds of those formerly dependent on the chemically-induced 'high' of hallucinogenics, began to experience what Aldous Huxley[62] described in part as a process 'in which the subject-object relationship is transcended, in which there is a sense of complete solidarity of the subject with other human beings and with the universe in general . . . also a sense of what may be called the ultimate all-rightness of the universe, the fact that in spite of pain, in spite of death, in spite of all the horrors which go on all around us, this universe is somehow all right . . . a sense of intense gratitude for the privilege of being alive in a universe as extraordinary as this, as altogether wonderful . . .'

It seemed that at long last the 'mystical' East had something tangible to offer the 'materialistic' West. As the young (but not always the young) began to apply themselves to strict inner disciplines such as Zen meditation, Yoga meditation and many other venerable systems for 'purifying' the mind and attaining mystical experience, and it was seen by science that they were attaining for themselves what neither medicine nor psychology alone or combined had been able to attain for them, the time appeared propitious to take a scientific measure of what was going on in the body while the mind was so occupied.

Thus did the device of a young German scientist called Hans Berger, for recording minute electrical impulses in the brain, the electroencephalograph (1929),* which later (1952) led Eugene Aserinsky, a physiologist, to note the rapid-eye-movements occurring at regular intervals during sleep, come into more extended and portentous function.

Among the non-pathological studies by means of EEG correlates had been *sleep* (one altered state of consciousness) and *dreaming* (another), and experiments continued in the sleep and dream laboratories. Other states of consciousness emerging for consideration and measurement were: the '*hypnagogic*' state – occurring just before sleep, with special forms of imagery unlike waking, dreams or sleep; the '*hypnopompic*' state – occurring just before waking, at the end of sleeping and dreaming with imagery differing again from the mental activity (or imagery) of wakefulness, sleeping or dreaming at other times; *hypnotic* and *autohypnotic* – occurring in response to suggestion by repetition, either by another person or himself, inducing deep relaxation without sleep and removal of conscious self-control; the *meditative* state – occurring as a result of arrested mental activity, diminished visual imagery and restful alertness (and many other less specific states such as *creative reverie*, *daydreaming* and *ecstasy*). As Gardner Murphy has said:

'There are psychological states for which there are no good names, including feeling states, cognitive states and volitional states, upon which human destiny almost literally may depend . . .'

Facilitating the instrumental assessment of altered states of consciousness (ASC), have been countless cooperative subjects who have allowed themselves to be wired up to the EEG machines under all kinds of conditions for purposes of psychophysiological exploration. Through them have come even more discoveries via brainwave cycles known as 'alpha, beta, theta and delta'† (originally used primarily for diagnosing such disorders as epilepsy and brain tumours).

*He had originally hoped to pinpoint the energy-sources of telepathy, but could not account for long-distance ESP with such small electrical currents.

†The brain is a mini-electrical instrument, producing small electrical currents that fluctuate, with changing states of mind, up and down a normal

Among these have been Zen and yoga monks, who permitted their meditation to be physiologically monitored. In a series of studies of zazen (Zen meditation – a sitting meditation which forms an important part of Zen-Buddhism's religious training) undertaken by Drs Akira Kasamatsu and Tomio Hirai of the University of Tokyo in 1960,[152] forty-eight Zen priests and disciples ranging in age from 24 to 72 were fitted with electrodes and hooked up to machines which would record not only their brainwaves throughout the stages of their meditation, but their pulse rate, respiration and galvanic skin response (GSR – the resistance of skin to small electric current), all this without disturbing their meditation.

To balance the tests, an equal number of non-meditators were asked to imitate the zazen method, which consists of sitting in a cross-legged position with eyes open and gazing downward at a point about a metre in front of them, their hands lightly joined, for about 30 minutes. They, too, were fitted with electrodes for the same instrumental recording.

The general Western view has been that Eastern meditators are in some kind of a trance-state, or hypnotized, and it has long been associated with an escape from, rather than into, reality, a mental 'opt-out' from frustration rather than contact with inner revelation and enlightenment.

The results of these complex and many-faceted experiments

---

spectrum of about 2 to 28 'cycles per second', the basic unit of electrical measurement. This general range is divided by scientists into four zones, each having definite rhythms and characteristics.

The *beta* frequency (13 to 28 cycles) is present when the mind is operating actively in the realm of five senses, and especially when there is tension and anxiety. Nervous people and heavy smokers seem to stay at high beta most of the time.

Alpha (8 to 13 cycles) is a lower frequency of higher awareness. Can be controlled and sustained. Induces feeling of relaxation, calm well-being and inner peace, and alert mind, and side effects of increased efficiency and harmonious human relations. The average individual dips into this wave length intermittently several times a minute, but usually only for a quick second or two. (The dream state stimulates prolonged alpha.)

The *theta* rhythm (4 to 7 cycles) accompanies moods of involved creativity and problem-solving, and also sleep.

Delta waves (2 to 4 cycles) are normally characteristic of deep sleep.

proved interesting. In summary, from a psychological point of view, the experimenters state that Zen meditation is purely a subjective experience completed by a concentration which holds the inner mind calm, pure and serene. And yet Zen meditation procures a special psychological state based on the changes in the electroencephalogram. There, Zen meditation influences not only the psychic life but also the physiology of the brain corresponding to relaxed awakening with steady responsiveness.

Technically, the experimenters reported that 'The appearance of alpha waves were observed, without regard to opened eyes, within 50 seconds after the beginning of Zen meditation. These alpha waves continued to appear, and their amplitudes increased. As Zen meditation progressed, a decrease of the *alpha* frequency was gradually manifested at the later stage. Further, the rhythmical *theta* train with the amplitude modulated *alpha*-background was observed in some records of the priests. These EEG changes could be classified in 4 stages: the appearance of *alpha* waves (Stage 1), an increase of *alpha* amplitude (Stage 2), a decrease of *alpha* frequency (Stage 3), and the appearance of rhythmical *theta* train (Stage 4).' (Until *alpha* waves disappear altogether and strong *theta* appears, amplitude increases continually.)

In other words, the Zen meditators had not only gone immediately into *alpha* waves, those which corresponded on the EEG with a state of serenity, well-being and peaceful alertness, but had maintained them and produced even more as the meditation progressed, ending with *theta*, the waves that correspond with creative reverie. They had produced no *beta* waves, correlates of open-eyed mental activity. They had not fallen asleep; on the contrary, they came out of meditation even more deeply refreshed than if they had had several hours of ordinary sleep. Of course, what they had experienced mentally, itself eluded record (and words), but the fact was established that it had physical correlates that could be measured, and which seemed beneficial to both mind and body. Science could confirm what centuries of mystics had known.

The yogis do not keep their eyes open during meditation and become essentially oblivious to their environment. Experiments reported by B. K. Anand, G. S. Chhina and B. Baldev Singh, of the All-India Institute of Medical Sciences, New Delhi,[152] showed that *alpha* continued through various tests with outer stimuli such as strong light, loud noises, vibration of a tuning fork and immersion of hands in ice-cold water for 45 minutes. Although the yoga adepts blinked, their *alpha* activity was prominent and persistent.

Apart from the generation of *alpha* rhythms, other demonstrated effects of the meditation were reduction of the rate of metabolism, decreased consumption of oxygen (about 20 per cent) and reduced output of carbon dioxide, indicating in combination a slowing of metabolism. (This served to explain the process by which yogis could survive in buried containers, so long a mystery.) Meditation was showing scientists that there was some kind of 'involuntary' mechanism in the body, most likely the autonomic nervous system, which could be 'voluntarily' controlled.

That meditation was thus electrically measurable, created something of an explosion of interest in research scientists. Bewildering, however, were the array of techniques in existence for meditating, ranging from strenuous physical activities to focusing on breathing or a particular object. Also, since most of the disciplines required vigorous training, it was not easy for scientists to be sure which meditator was an adept, which a novice, thus making the choice of suitable subjects difficult. Eventually, however, because one widespread yoga technique was sufficiently standardized and uniform for the selection of sufficient subjects, it was chosen for several large-scale tests.

The technique, now familiar as 'transcendental meditation' had been developed by Maharishi Mahesh Yogi,[40] the closest disciple of Swami Brahmananda Saraswati (1860–1953), a renowned Indian teacher, whose views reflect ancient Vedic tradition. After the death of his teacher, Maharishi remained for two years in silence and solitude, then in 1957 he began to teach, inaugurating what he called the 'Spiritual Regeneration Movement' on a world-wide basis. A small, gentle man with large brilliant dark eyes, flowing dark hair and white robe, with a flower in his hands while he spoke, Maharishi had a ten-year mission to show people what he felt was a natural process for achieving inner and outer harmony of being, individually, and eventually collectively.

He arrived in America at a time when drug addiction was at its height and the young took him to heart to such an excess that he became an over-publicized idol. It was said that Maharishi 'signalled the beginning of the post-acid generation'. But as the yoga and Eastern tradition was still generally in contempt, and because exchange of money was involved with learning, his technique of meditating, and his over-exposure in the press and every other media generated a backlash of hostility, Maharishi's return to India created the impression of failure.

When the Beatles and other well-known young people followed him there, only to leave later seemingly disappointed, the public assumed the day of the Maharishi was over.

The reverse was true. Not only had thousands of people taken

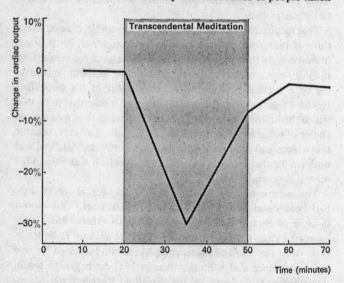

Figure 2 **Change in cardiac output.** During transcendental meditation cardiac output markedly decreases, indicating a reduction in the work load of the heart. (This result is from a deep meditation, one subject.)

(Reference: Robert Keith Wallace, *MIU Press*)

up transcendental meditation with gratifying results in their lives (including the abandonment of hard and soft drugs and even alcohol), but in India, Maharishi was augmenting his 'World-Plan', expanding his objectives – from a few hundred to thousands – and increasing his teaching staff.

The vital impetus towards this objective had emerged inadvertently from the scientific studies of transcendental meditation (TM) undertaken in the early '70s. One of the most famous of these was conducted by Dr Robert Keith Wallace and Herbert Benson at the Harvard Medical School, the results of which were published in *Scientific American* in 1972.[168]

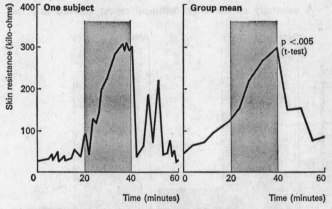

Figure 3 **State of relaxation.** During stress or anxiety skin resistance decreases. During transcendental meditation skin resistance increases significantly, indicating deep relaxation, reduction of anxiety and reduction of emotional disturbances. The chart on the left shows a deep meditation for one individual and the chart on the right is the group mean of fifteen subjects.
(Reference: Robert Keith Wallace, Herbert Benson and Archie F. Wilson, *MIU Press*)

Differing from Zen and yoga meditation, TM required no intense concentration or strict discipline, could be learned in a few short periods of training and involved no specific religious beliefs or philosophy, and consisted simply of two daily sessions of 15–20 minutes of sitting in a comfortable position with eyes closed and repeating a 'mantra' (a sound without special meaning for keeping the wandering mind gently in tow).

A group of thirty-six American subjects, with experience of TM from a few weeks to nine years, were observed at the Thorndike Memorial Laboratory (of the Harvard Medical Unit at the Boston City Hospital) and others at the University of California at Irvine. The subjects, seated in chairs, spent part of each experimental session in meditation, and part out. The subjects were hooked up for measurement of blood pressure, heart rate, rectal temperature, skin resistance and EEG events, and at ten-minute intervals were taken for analysis of oxygen consumption, carbon dioxide elimination, etc.

A summary of the long, technical report showed that the

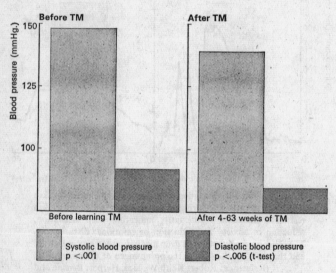

Figure 4 **Decreased blood pressure.** Systolic and arterial blood pressure was recorded 1,119 times in 22 hypertensive patients before and after learning transcendental meditation. The decreases in blood pressure after practising TM were statistically significant and indicate the clinical value of TM meditation in helping hypertensive patients.

(Reference: Herbert Benson and Robert Keith Wallace, *MIU Press*) subjects in what was termed a 'wakeful, hypometabolic' state, had all the same physiological signs of Zen and yogi adepts with fifteen to twenty years of hard training. 'In these circumstances,' the report concluded, 'the hypometabolic state, representing quiescence rather than hyperactivation of the sympathetic nervous system, may indicate a guidepost to better health. It should be well worthwhile to investigate the possibilities for clinical application of this state of wakeful rest and relaxation.'

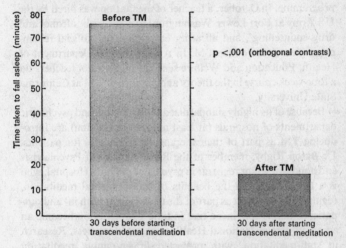

Figure 5 **Relief from insomnia.** Transcendental meditation significantly reduced the time taken for insomniacs to fall asleep. As a therapy against insomnia, TM was found to be simple to administer, immediately effective, stable over time, and without unfavourable side effects.

(Reference: Donald F. Miskiman, *MIU Press*)

Many other studies followed, physiological, psychological and sociological, on the effects of TM, by universities and institutions throughout the world. Findings appeared in scientific and medical journals, supporting the benefits of this twice-daily practice for improving mental and physical coordination, speeding up learning time, reducing nervousness, aggression, depression, irritability, increasing sociability, self-assurance, good humour, outgoingness, efficiency, decreasing tendency to dominate, inhibition, emotional instability. All stress diseases, psychosomatic disorders due to tension, it appeared, were candidates for improvement.

Currently, transcendental meditation[158] has a massive following (of at least one million) in all professions, businesses and walks of life. In May 1973 a resolution passed by the general assembly of the State of Illinois, USA, approved the use of TM in schools and requested that the drug abuse section of the state's Department of Mental Health incorporate TM in its rehabilitation programme. In October, a teacher of meditation was hired by the US Army at Fort Lewis, Washington, to assist with 'alcohol and drug counselling', and all army bases have had official recommendation to introduce TM. In August the US Department of Health, Education and Welfare sent 125 high school teachers on a four-week course in the theory and practice of TM at California State University.

Because of its highly standardized form, doctors and psychiatric departments of hospitals (at least a dozen in London) are introducing TM as part of their therapeutic techniques for patients. Dr Byron Rigby, member of the Royal College of Psychiatrists and honorary senior registrar in psychiatry at Guy's Hospital, who is a firm believer in the benefits of transcendental meditation, regularly prescribes it as part of the treatment of both in- and out-patients, and is convinced that in time TM will soon become an accepted part of National Health treatment for stress. Research in staff-meditation, with projected fifteen-minute meditation breaks every three hours, is under way at one London hospital and at St Bartholomew's, Dr J. A. Bonn, consulting psychiatrist, is planning research into the possible benefits of TM in connection with the treatment of anxiety. An aviation study is currently in progress at the Maudsley Hospital, London, where doctors are conducting rigorous experiments to ascertain possible benefits for airline pilots who are forbidden alcohol, tranquillizers or antidepressants for the relief of tension during stressful flights.

These are only a few of the substantial organizations and professions that are investigating the benefits of TM, and plans for the teaching and spread of the 'Science of Creative Intelligence',[158] which Maharishi believes is reached through transcendental meditation. In 1972 his International University was given the task of implementing the World Plan by establishing 3,600 centres, one for each million population, to teach SCI, to train teachers of SCI and offer courses for primary and secondary grades and undergraduates and graduate degrees.

Figure 6 A visual concept of the process of transcendental meditation, before, during and after TM.

(*MIU Press*)

'Each World Plan Centre will train 1,000 teachers of SCI and maintain their strength through refresher courses year after year. This will provide one teacher of SCI for 1,000 people in every area of the globe for generations to come.'

The message of the World Plan is to 'Improve the quality of life on earth and to solve the age-old problems of mankind in this generation'.

Naturally these plans seem excessive to those who have not meditated, but to those who have, and do so regularly, they seem but a logical outcome of harmonizing of the finite and infinite, by the combining of deep physiological rest with freed creative intelligence, thus breaking away from the unnatural rigidities of daily life that drain energy, and restoring man's innate capacity for growing, and therefore natural state of happiness.

In 1975, in Switzerland, the Maharishi Mahesh Yogi inaugurated his 'Age of Enlightenment', an approach to an even greater potential for TM based on a new statistical proposition that when one per cent of the world's population practices transcendental meditation fifteen minutes twice daily, a global 'phase transition' from chaos and confusion to order and peace will result.

Support for this has emerged from a study by a research team from the Maharishi International University in Fairfield, Iowa, USA into the value of TM in regard to increasing orderliness in society. 'A study on 12 midwestern cities in the United States,

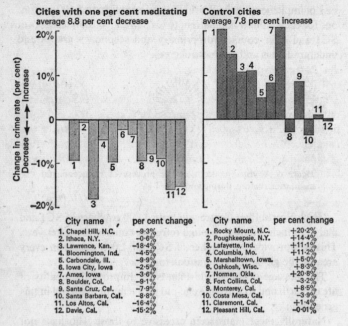

Cities with one per cent meditating
average 8.8 per cent decrease

Control cities
average 7.8 per cent increase

City name	per cent change	City name	per cent change
1. Chapel Hill, N.C.	−9·3%	1. Rocky Mount, N.C.	+20·2%
2. Ithaca, N.Y.	−0·6%	2. Poughkeepsie, N.Y.	+14·4%
3. Lawrence, Kan.	−18·4%	3. Lafayette, Ind.	+11·1%
4. Bloomington, Ind.	−4·5%	4. Columbia, Mo.	+11·2%
5. Carbondale, Ill.	−9·9%	5. Marshalltown, Iowa.	+5·0%
6. Iowa City, Iowa	−2·5%	6. Oshkosh, Wisc.	+8·3%
7. Ames, Iowa	−3·6%	7. Norman, Okla.	+20·8%
8. Boulder, Col.	−9·1%	8. Fort Collins, Col.	−3·2%
9. Santa Cruz, Cal.	−7·9%	9. Monterey, Cal.	+8·5%
10. Santa Barbara, Cal.	−8·8%	10. Costa Mesa, Cal.	−3·9%
11. Los Altos, Cal.	−16·4%	11. Claremont, Cal.	+1·4%
12. Davis, Cal.	−15·2%	12. Pleasant Hill, Cal.	−0·01%

Figure 7 According to transcendental meditation research, crime
is claimed to be decreased when 1 per cent of a city meditates.
These figures were collected 1972–3. The pillar graphs on the
right show the corresponding increase in crime in cities used
as a control.

(*MIU Press*)

having populations over 25,000 people,' reads an official report,
'revealed that when the number of people practising TM reach
1% of the city's population, the crime rate dramatically decreased.
In another 12 cities matched for population and geographic
location, crime rate continued to rise as usual. 1% of the population practising transcendental meditation reversed the trend of
increasing crime by 16·6%.' New research in 18 other cities in the
US shows each city to have a decrease in its crime rate* when the

---

*Figures based on those of the United States Justice Department for city
crime rate.

meditating population reach one per cent. In this study as well, the matched control cities continued to show an increase in crime at the usual 7·8 per cent per year. More inclusive and far reaching studies of 300 cities in Europe, Canada and the US that had reached one per cent of meditators by 1974 are under way.

Scientists attending the inauguration, one a Nobel Laureate in physics, spoke of how this one per cent orderliness principle fitted in with their respective sciences. One explained that in the coherence of the light of a laser produced by the emission of photons (particles of light) from the atoms of the laser, orderliness is induced by the coherent emission of light from a small fraction of the atoms. Magnetic strength in a piece of nickel or iron, explained another, is maintained by an orderly relationship between the atoms, each of which acts as a microscopic magnet. If one per cent of the total number of electrons contribute to the magnetism of each atom, the orderliness of the atoms, and therefore their magnetic strength, can be maintained at room temperature.

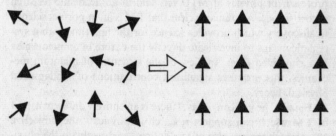

non-magnetic at high temperatures   magnetic at low temperatures

Figure 8 Phase transitions. The third law of thermodynamics is that there is increased order from reduced activity.

(*MIU Press*)

Another explained that the crystallization of a supersaturated solution can be induced by placing a 'seed' crystal in the solution, the atoms of which may represent a fraction of one per cent or less of the whole solution. And one other explained that the gene-important molecule DNA represents a very small fraction of the material of each cell; yet the high degree of ordered information in the DNA molecule maintains the orderly structure of function of the whole cell. All in all, the implications of this 'one in one hundred' effect are vast.

As the TM movement gathers world-wide momentum and infiltrates the general awareness of the public, some of its statistical conclusions and sweeping assertions have been challenged. Dr Herbert Benson, who conducted the pioneer physiological research of TM with Dr Keith Wallace, has now broken away to develop his own technique of relaxation therapy, which incorporates Zen and yoga techniques of meditation, autogenic training, hypnosis and the use of biofeedback devices. The system is called 'relaxation response' and develops the idea that there is an integrated hypothalmic reaction characterized by decreased oxygen consumption, respiration rate, heart rate and blood pressure, and an altered state of consciousness.

There will undoubtedly be other challenges and questions, as the TM Research University is well aware and is itself established to investigate them to the full, and answer. As Lawrence Domash, professor of physics at MIU has said in an academic research report[158] ... '... it remains clear that TM is an important scientific discovery which provides science for the first time with a systematic means to investigate directly the nature of consciousness in a simplified form. In view of the structure of quantum mechanics, this promises significant contributions of fundamental physical theory.'

'Finally,' he goes on to say, 'there is an entirely different aspect of TM which can support research in physics – the subjective effect which the practice of meditation has directly on the physicist's own mind and on his ability to be successfully creative in understanding nature. The greatest physicists, such as Einstein or Feynman, display as their chief characteristic a profound inner intuition, a direct personal feeling of inner contact with the working of nature. This capability has up to now been regarded as an admirable but mysterious gift. If, however, we fully understand Maharishi's description of the mind in *The Science of Creative Intelligence*, we realize that depth of intuition is to be equated with purity of consciousness – and this can be systematically developed through TM. Heisenberg wrote that the mathematical laws of quantum physics deal "no longer with the particles themselves but with our knowledge of the particles" and to this we add Maharishi's aphorism that "knowledge is structure in consciousness".'

In parapsychology, the trend moving towards experiments with ASC, in order to explore possible latent sources of ESP, led to controlled tests with subjects under the influence of psychedelic drugs, without highly significant results. The difficulty, as reported by Robert Masters and Jean Houston (whose research in drugs led to the book *The Varieties of Psychedelic Experience*),[88] Karlis Osis of the ASPR, Dr D. J. West in England, and several others who have done psychedelic ESP research, is that there is a division between the two tasks. Either the drug effect is too absorbing for the subjects to consider ESP factors, or what seems like ESP could be part of the drug effect, since the drug experience is known to be largely influenced by the state of mind and expectancy of the user.

Although the spontaneous experiences of ESP during the drug state are impressively confirmed, laboratory-attempted psychedelic ESP cannot match them, despite the fact that emotionally-charged material has proved effective in other forms of testing. Perhaps as Stanley Krippner of Maimonides suggests, 'Psychedelic drug usage typically gives an individual the subjective impression that he is extremely psychic . . . whether this impression is valid remains to be empirically demonstrated.'

Experiments were also carried out in the ASC realm of meditation. One, carried out over a three-year period (1969–71), was conducted by Karlis Osis and Edwin Bokert of the ASPR[111] with the expert advice of leading parapsychologists. It consisted of ascertaining the subjects' changed states of consciousness by means of pre- and post-session questionnaires, as well as free tape-recorded descriptions. Two ESP tests involved closed circuit television and art-work slides. In the former, the percipients sat in a curtained booth, their hands extended beyond the booth to a table on which was a matrix of twenty-five squares made of 2 inch by 2 inch tiles, while an agent at the other end of the building watching them on a TV screen attempted to influence them to move certain specific tiles. In the latter, agents tried mentally to transmit coloured pictures projected on the wall to percipients (receivers) in another room.

In all these tests, the subjects had first been meditating, and the object was to maintain the meditative state while carrying out the ESP tasks. The meditators had had a period of training and preparation, but essentially each member of the groups meditated according to individual preference, some using Zen and Raja yoga methods, others using self-hypnosis, depth-imagery of various concentration techniques. Each ESP test followed a half-hour meditation period.

From the complexities of self-induced ASC and their relationship to ESP, the experimenters found three areas of potential significance. These were: self-transcendence and openness; mood brought to the session; and the meaning dimension (when a revelation of personal importance to subject arises from meditation).

Of these the meaning dimension was the least functional state, the inner revelation tending to both overwhelm and diminish the importance of any ESP messages; the mood brought to session was confirmed as a chief influence over the effectiveness of the meditation *and* ESP, but self-transcendence and openness (unifying of external and internal world, dissolving boundaries between self and others) was revealed as the most important area for ESP performance and further investigation. In other words, it seems that psychic abilities may be a side-effect of a deep and genuine meditative state. This would bear out the Eastern contemplative traditions in which ESP has an integral but unemphasized place in the advanced consciousness of the true guru; the enlightened would consider that seeking it *per se*, for display or proof, is a mark of ignorance, for in the ultimate state of oneness there is no division of the senses, no division of mind in any of its manifestations.

Another altered state of consciousness explored for ESP has been hypnotically-induced dreams. Up until the days of J. B. Rhine, hypnosis and ESP tended to be an inseparable public image (despite much zealous and authentic work in the nineteenth century), overcast with connotations of exploitive and sinister powers, or the stuff of purely theatrical hocus-pocus. Parapsychology attempted to withdraw and escape the pseudo implications, as did clinical hypnotism. Today, they have become somewhat of an oil-and-vinegar combination, only occasionally promising to blend. Such an occasion was the experiment carried out in the late 1960s by researchers Charles Honorton (presently Research Director of the Division of Parapsychology and Paraphysics, Maimonides Medical Center) and John P. Stump[59] at the Institute of Parapsychology, Durham, North Carolina. Here, six subjects, known to be hypnotically suggestible from previous testing, were hypnotized and while in the hypnotic state told they were to dream about a picture contained in an opaque envelope, randomly selected out of a pool of 115 prints.

One set of experimenter's instructions are given as follows: 'When I count to three, you are going to have a dream. You will have a very interesting dream. It will be a very vivid and realistic dream. You will dream about the target in the envelope. It will be as though you are walking right into the picture in the envelope . . . you will participate in whatever action is depicted, and you will observe the picture from that standpoint. You will see everything very clearly because you will be part of it. You will dream for about five minutes and then awaken by yourself. When you waken, you will remember the dream very clearly and you will be able to describe it in great detail. When you finish reporting your dream, I will again count to three, and when I reach the number three you will be in the same deep, relaxed state that you are now in.'

The target envelope was placed by the subject's chair. When awakened, the subject described the dream impressions, which were recorded, he was then returned to the hypnotic state and given additional suggestions to deepen the hypnotic impression.

Seven experimental sessions were completed, and the results, although mixed, were significant: many subjects judged which picture they had dreamed of without having described it adequately, while others described their dreams adequately without recognizing the target picture in the waking state.

One subject's reported dream-impressions were based on the target 'The Green Violinist' by Chagall, a green-skinned figure playing a fiddle while seemingly dancing in a mist, with a distant background of houses, and a scattering of small, disconnected figures.

'First I got the impression of an odd, mottled, leaf-like texture of pale green and dark green with a deep perspective ... Then the greenish overall perspective drew me and I disappeared into it and was suddenly in another place ... a kind of misty place where there was this old castle-like structure in the background ... and I was running through the mist of this place, so free and infinitely happy ...'

It did seem that the subject had followed instructions to 'enter the picture and become part of it, to participate in it', even though unaware of descriptive details. There were others who described mere details without much participatory feeling; enough promise, all-told, to warrant further experimentation.

Dr Rhine views the state of hypnosis as one of 'highly restricted consciousness to the point where attention is focused in a highly controlled fashion on a small area designated by the hypnotist', while the subject retained normal consciousness; and that the meditative process results from the narrowing of attention to its most concentrated focus by excluding as much sensory stimuli as possible. Encouraged by this correspondence, parapsychologists have further applied his principles to their experiments with ESP in altered states of consciousness, using techniques of 'sensory bombardment' and 'sensory deprivation'.

In sensory bombardment, the subject is immersed in a kind of audio-visual assault, involving lighting, musical and other effects that 'over-load' his senses, the object being to create 'psifavourable' state, in this case possibly by keeping all senses busily employed that might otherwise block ESP function.

Specialists in this form of altering consciousness, Robert Masters and Jean Houston, who conduct the Foundation for Mind Research (founded in 1964 in New York), have developed many audio-visual devices and environments, as well as what they call 'Mind Games'[88] (instructions for which can be read in their book of the same name, discussed later).

In cooperative experiments with Stanley Krippner of Maimonides Dream Laboratory (now the Division of Parapsychology and Psychophysics) 'thematic telepathy' was attempted.[76] Chosen subjects were wired with electrodes and put to bed at Maimonides while at Masters' and Houston's laboratory an agent was placed in an audio-visual environment in which he sat between stereo loud-speakers that blasted out music in keeping with the mood of slides being shown on an 8-foot screen that curved around him, each one dissolving into the next at twenty-second intervals, randomly selected by computer from a pool of thousands, to accentuate the emotional feeling of a selected theme to be transmitted.

Several variations of this experiment produced some unmistakable impressions in the dreamers, with verdicts of 'hits' from the judges. Encouraged, the experimenters tried 'Long-Distance Sensory Bombardment'. One notable experiment in 1971 was with the rock group 'The Grateful Dead' at the Capitol Theatre outside New York, 45 miles from Maimonides.[76]

Here, after being saturated in the music and perhaps an element of psychedelic drug-effect for the alteration of consciousness, an audience of two thousand young people concentrated its attention on a slide that was projected for fifteen minutes, attempting to 'send' it to the subject, Michael Bessent (known at Maimonides for his psychic abilities), while the rock group continued playing.

This procedure was repeated for six nights, and out of these Michael Bessent had four matching impressions, or 'direct hits'. The fact that two thousand people concentrated on the target picture, however, was not considered a vital factor; they had not succeeded any better than a single sender. The experimenters believe that more significant is the attitude of the participants; that they feel the project is possible rather than impossible, being more important than the amount of people involved or the distance.

Other forms of bombardment techniques were employed in an experiment attempting clairvoyant perception in four different states – the ordinary waking condition; while involved in an audio-visual experience; while under stroboscopic stimulation (a film projector and a reel that rotates, providing a flickering effect), and after application of 'electro-sleep' induced by a device called the Electrosone 50 (a device which applies low-voltage electric current by means of electrodes attached to the subject, claimed to cure insomnia, but used in this context for the alteration of consciousness).[74]

These were combined with detailed self-reports to enhance the data. A gradation of the results when analysed showed that this combination had been valuable in discerning states which were potential or favourable for ESP and those which were not, as well as the possibilities in the Electrosone 50 (which effectively altered consciousness) as an added parapsychological 'tool'.

Recent experiments in 'sensory deprivation' have had even more significant results. At Maimonides, subjects' eyes have been covered with devices that resemble halved ping-pong balls and have the effect of completely shutting out all light. Their ears are covered to shut off hearing, and an intense white light is beamed at their covered eyes, causing what seems like an expanse of screen before them onto which images in their minds project like pictures.

In one particularly fruitful test, the sender in another room focused her full attention and feelings on a series of randomized slides all concerning Las Vegas.

When giving her impressions to the experimenter, the subject saw many splintered visions of a place and atmosphere. They began to seem familiar. Suddenly she exclaimed – 'It's Las Vegas!' The agent was informed, and she and the subject were so excited when they conferred that they hugged each other. This hardly needed the careful monitoring or the judge's verdict of a hit.

At present, parapsychologists are looking with growing interest at the possibilities of ESP in association with the 'alpha' state. This involves biofeedback training of subjects, complex approaches to the generation and suppression of alpha waves, together with self-report scales, and post-session interviews. There is much to be learned, but the fact that alpha has beneficial physiological correlates, suggests that it may also provide psi favourable correlates.

Meanwhile, the experiments reach further and further into the diminishing borders between one mind frontier and another – as does biofeedback training.

2A NEW METHODS OF MIND CONTROL THROUGH BIOFEEDBACK TRAINING

The new dimension that biofeedback brings to the evolving mind is the mind's ability to use information to control the material substance of man's being. More directly, biofeedback may have provided the instrument to excise the cataracts of scientific vision that so long has prevented participation of the mind in the survival and evolution of his own consciousness and psyche.

BARBARA BROWN[16]

ALTHOUGH an index of various brainwave activities could now be referred to for research, Dr Joe Kamiya, a psychophysiologist now at the Langley Porter Neuropsychiatric Institute of the California Medical Center in San Francisco, in the late 1950s posed a further question about brainwave activity:[152] Could people be made to discern their own brain rhythms, learn to recognize alpha, for instance, to detect when it was present or absent?

To seek the answers, experiments were run in his Chicago laboratory in which EEG electrodes were attached to the subject's scalp in the usual order to register the alpha brainwave frequency. When a bell rang the subject was to guess, 'A' if he felt alpha was present at that moment, or 'B' if it was not. He was then told at once if he was correct ('feedback').

This strangely interior form of test had surprising results. After an hour or so of haphazard guessing, the subject would begin to guess correctly up to 60 per cent of the time. After three hours, some subjects became up to 80 per cent correct, and a few learned to guess 100 per cent correctly . . .

People could learn to 'read' their own brain!

But – how? Dr Kamiya and his colleagues wondered. When questioned, the subjects found they could not explain articulately what made them know whether they were in or out of alpha, they just 'knew'.

With the next experimental task, however, further enlightenment came. The subjects were now asked to try to produce the state called 'A' on command – when a bell rang twice; when it rang once they were to switch over to the state called 'B'.

The amazing discovery was that the subjects had somehow learned by the preceding training how to put themselves into either level.

This led to the next logical question: Could people be trained to control their brainwaves without this training, by themselves?

When Dr Kamiya became associated with the Langley Porter Institute, he set up an electronic device that turned on a signal tone whenever alpha was present, and turned off again the instant it wasn't. Subjects were asked to try to maintain the alpha waves as long as possible. They were also asked both to suppress alpha and to generate it, deliberately.

All these, subjects were able to do, and after a while their descriptions of what the states felt like began to tally. 'A' generation was achieved by a kind of 'passive blankness', a 'calming-down' of the mind, the release of judgements or questions, a mental 'letting-go'. It was in some way 'very pleasant', and preferable to the 'B' state of suppression. Suppressing it, on the other hand, was easily achieved by visual imagery.

Dr Kamiya ran many different kinds of tests, devised many different kinds of feedback signals and generally extended the range of information on this new potential of mind-body self-regulation. He found that there were 'high' and 'low' alpha states, and that people with experience of meditation, as well as those who were creative and expressive, learned alpha control more easily, but cautiously drew no conclusions as to where 'alpha-training' itself would lead; for him many years of further research lay ahead.

When the media aired these findings, and those of other bio-feedback researchers confirmed them, the public were not so reserved. The possibility of 'do-it-yourself' alpha-training, of 'instant satori' by means of an electronic brainwave feedback device, promised to be the answer to all ills of modern man. Instruments with brand-names like 'Alpha Sensor', 'Alpha Pacer', 'Alpha-phone', were commercially marketed and people could be seen in the US wandering about parks and streets wired to their portable battery-operated devices, obviously concentrating on maintaining the magical 'bleep-bleep' or 'buzz' of alpha rhythm. Despite admonitions that their expectations were excessive and that all the alpha waves in the world could not replace meditation and self-understanding, and the warnings of such authorities in biofeedback research as Dr Barbara Brown, chief of Experimental Physiology at the Veterans Administration Hospital in Sepulveda, California, that 'pop alpha' could damage the promise of serious scientific work, the alpha bandwagon rolled on.

Based on the premise that this new form of self-mastery not only circumvented years of training in Eastern techniques but held the key to many other powers of the psyche, groups sprang up that systemized and packaged courses of alpha-training. They provided courses for the achievement of better health, prosperity, happiness, peace of mind, vitality, improved sleep, greater creativity, control of harmful habits (like smoking), control of weight, control of pain, the ability to solve problems, heal and help others, and the development of ESP.

Although using the term 'alpha level' in their approach, these groups do not actually work with the EEG instruments so much as they teach their students how to achieve the alpha state mentally and physiologically. They do this by a combination of means, among which are techniques for deep relaxation, positive thinking, meditating, physical exercises, programming the subconscious mind by suggestion, and learning to visualize people for the purpose of healing them.

The 48-hour courses consisted of lectures and 'conditionings'. Lectures explained what mind control could do, about relaxed states of consciousness, and answered the student's questions. The conditioning demonstrated their actual techniques for getting into the alpha level, the students set about practising such initial procedure as going to sleep without using sleeping pills, and waking up exactly when they wanted to in the morning without an alarm clock.

While dangers inherent in such a wholesale suggestion, such as possible ignorance of an individual's stage of mental development or some prior imbalance, produced strong scientific scepticism, the spread of the courses in America continued, gradually accruing respectability through numbers, particularly from the business world.

Today there are many variations of alpha-training courses throughout the country, but perhaps the most successful one was founded in the late 1950s by Jose Silva, an electronics technician whose original school was the Mind Control Institute at Laredo, Texas. There are now well over two hundred of his schools, across America, in Mexico, Canada and England.

It has been said often by brainwave researchers that anyone can learn to control their brainwave rhythms, and that 90 per cent of all people produce alpha when the eyes are closed and the body relaxed. It has also been pointed out that the home-devices for monitoring them are seldom accurate enough to pick up the faint signals and voltages of the brain, but are more than likely picking up voltages produced by blinking, or muscle twitches. Nevertheless, it is agreed that the commonly-accepted 'autonomic' nervous system has by now been sufficiently re-evaluated to constitute a breakthrough, that the day of mind control of 'involuntary' states has definitely dawned.

In this area, the work of Dr Elmer Green, head of the Psychophysiology Laboratory in the Research Department at the Menninger Foundation in Topeka, Kansas (and consultant on Autogenic-Feedback Training to the Maryland State Psychiatric Center), has provided substantial scientific support.

Dr Green's research in the 'Voluntary Controls Project'[49] at the Menninger Foundation evolved from two initial sources: keen interest in the numerous reports of British doctors as long as 250 years ago of extraordinary feats by yogis in India, such as stopping their hearts, being buried alive, walking on fire, etc. – and surviving; and the mind-body training methods developed in Germany by Dr Johannes Schultz in the early part of the century (later to be known as 'Autogenic Training'), which attempted to replace reliance on a hypnotist, often engendering the patient's unconscious resistance, with 'meditative exercises' leading to their own physiological control. Both these forms of mind-body regulation, Dr Green suspected, were variations of one another.

In 1965, Dr Green and his wife, Alyce, decided to test Dr

Schultz's methods (which were better known in Europe than in the United States) at Menninger. Their first experiment was with thirty-three housewives, who were asked to practise preliminary autogenic exercises for two weeks. These consisted of attempting temperature control of their hands, of relaxation and phrases of self-suggestion that their hands were growing warmer and warmer.

At the start and end of the test, the subjects were measured physiologically – brainwaves, heart rate, breathing rate, skin potential, skin resistance, blood flow in the fingers, the temperature of hands, front and back – and although only two of them achieved the objective (increasing their hand temperature by 10°F) this success encouraged a much more ambitious programme.

It was a suggestion of Dr Gardner Murphy's that biofeedback be included in the new research. If subjects could 'see' their tension registering on a meter, he thought, it would be far more real to them, and in observing its fluctuations, they could gain practice in trying to make it diminish as well as receive immediate confirmation of success.

In 1967, with this combination, which was called 'Autogenic Feedback Training', Dr Green launched a series of experiments, using increasingly sophisticated EEG and other electronic equipment covering every possible facet.

The first of these was a five-week attempt to train eighteen male subjects to control three physical factors at once – muscle tension in their right forearm, the temperature of a finger on the right hand, and alpha brain rhythm for a ten-second period.

Interesting aspects were revealed. It was shown that when a subject brought his will to bear on any of these controls, the meters would register the opposite result. When, however, he would relax, mentally 'tell the body what to do' then detached his attention from the results, he would almost invariably succeed. Also, if able to focus his attention inward, 'observe without looking', he could achieve alpha waves without closing his eyes – very much like the eyes-open technique of Zen meditation. The object was the same, too, *to train* the subject to be both in the inner and outer world simultaneously, to be in the alpha state yet alert enough to answer questions.

Tests made to see if the ability to remember was increased in the alpha state proved positive, pointing to invaluable benefits in education.

Although the over-all results of the main experiment showed that no subject could in fact control all three physiological variables at once, they did find that some could control one or another and, occasionally, two at the same time.

En route, more also had been discovered about the four brain-wave levels. As we have seen, while most people focusing on the normal daily world were in the beta frequency, if they closed their eyes a mixture of beta and alpha could result. If they became sleepy, theta appeared and alpha and beta tended to fade, and delta appeared only in deep sleep. In a pilot study (in theta training), Dr Green found that in theta subjects experienced imagery similar to the hypnagogic state (just before sleep), and would get 'full-blown' ideas and pictures without effort, often in the way described by creative geniuses.

In the laboratory this state became known as theta 'reverie', and because it suggested much potential data on creativity, a new experimental project was conceived called 'alpha-theta brain-wave feedback, reverie and imagery'. For this musical tones were devised for the feedback signal. Beta waves produced a 'piccolo' pitch, alpha that of a flute, theta an oboe and delta a bassoon.

Instruments and amplifiers allowed two brainwave channels to be studied at the same time, and by attaching electrodes to both sides of the subject's head, he could get feedback information on frequencies from both his cerebral hemispheres – or, his right ear could listen to the right side of his brain and his left ear to the left side.

Basic to success in this training, it was found, were the credibility attitudes of the subjects. As Dr Green puts it, 'seeing is believing' when it comes to the manipulation of 'involuntary' states. If the subject is not convinced that he can control his nervous system, then an attempt to raise the temperature of a hand, for instance, would result instead in the temperature dropping. This adverse result, however, would in itself illustrate to him that his mind could affect his body. A belief would be established.

In turn, the belief would lead to some measure of control, confirmed by the feedback signals, and from this he would now not only believe, but *know*: from then on it would be a matter of developing his control. (Again, the paradoxical comparison with Eastern and metaphysical philosophies which teach the mind to rule the body, the conscious mind to direct the subconscious. That it is accomplished instrumentally, and compares to learning to drive a car, seems proof chiefly for science and the sceptic.)

Involved in biofeedback training is an understanding of the divided functions of the subcortical brain (the 'old' brain structure shared with most animals), which is the domain of involuntary and unconscious processes, and the cerebral cortex (the later brain) which is the domain of conscious and voluntary processes (*see* Figure 9 overleaf).

Recent brainwave research has shown that when the older brain is electrically stimulated (by means of implanted electrodes) it effects changes in the emotions, and conversely, emotional changes make changes in the old brain, which is often called the 'visceral' brain because it contains a section of the limbic system and is highly significant in understanding psychosomatic inter-relationship.

This research has led Dr Green to what he calls the psychophysiological principle: 'Every change in the physiological state is accompanied by an appropriate change in the mental-emotional state, conscious or unconscious, and conversely, every change in the mental-emotional state, conscious or unconscious, is accompanied by an appropriate change in the physiological state.'

In 1970, Dr Green had the opportunity to test this principle in a telling East-West fusion of the 'hardware' and 'software' of self-regulation with an Indian yogi named Swami Rama.

Swami Rama from the Himalayas, trained since he was four years old in yoga disciplines, in the course of his first visit showed he could control several 'uncontrollable' processes with ease (despite the unfamiliar and distracting environment of the laboratory and the unnatural encumbrance of electrodes).

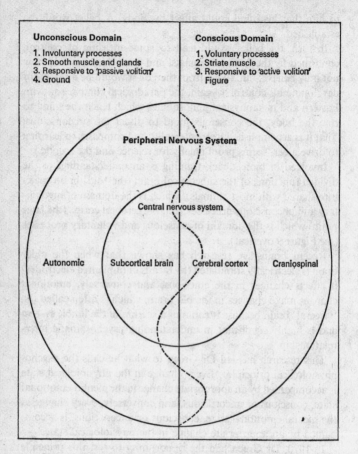

Unconscious Domain

1. Involuntary processes
2. Smooth muscle and glands
3. Responsive to 'passive volition'
4. Ground

Conscious Domain

1. Voluntary processes
2. Striate muscle
3. Responsive to 'active volition'
   Figure

Peripheral Nervous System

Central nervous system

Autonomic   Subcortical brain   Cerebral cortex   Craniospinal

Figure 9 This diagram shows the relationship of the conscious and unconscious parts of the mind to voluntary and involuntary processes. The solid vertical line separates the central and peripheral nervous systems into functional subregions. The dashed line (conceptually visualized to be continuous undulatory movement) separates the conscious and unconscious areas.

(Elmer Green)

In one instance he gradually caused a temperature difference of 10°F between two separate spots on the palm of one hand; one spot turned blood red, the other dead-white. In another instance he both slowed and quickened the rate of his heartbeat.

On another visit, Swami Rama promised to show them that he could stop his heartbeat altogether, by control of his vagus nerve. Dr Green had some misgivings, but Swami said that he would sign papers, if necessary, to state that the responsibility was entirely his own. Nevertheless, Dr Green asked that he limit his offer to stop his heart for three or four minutes, to ten seconds.

An arrangement was made to call him on the intercom from the control room when the time was up. The Swami practised by slowing and speeding his heart, then said he was ready and that they should be prepared for a shock. After about twenty seconds, Dr Green's wife called 'That's all'. The Swami contracted his stomach muscles, then relaxed.

The shock turned out to be the fact that his heart rate, according to the instrument in the control room, had not slowed, but leapt from 70 beats per minute to about 300 for a period of 17–25 seconds. The Swami was not puzzled. He explained that the heart still 'trembled' in him after stopping. Dr Green conferred with Dr Marvin Dunne, a cardiologist, who recognized this as the state called 'atrial flutter', in which the heartbeat goes at its highest rate, blood does not fill the chambers and the valves do not function normally. The proper result should have been unconsciousness.

Later visits of the Swami to the Menninger Foundation tested physiological brainwave correlates. At first it seemed that he was quite unable to generate anything but beta waves – until it was discovered that he was inhibited by the thought of so much polygraph paper being used at the rate of $16 a box! When told the expense was not considered restrictive, he relaxed and was able in five 15-minute sessions of brainwave feedback to generate 70 per cent alpha waves for five minutes, 75 per cent theta waves for five minutes and to perform a yogic feat which consisted of creating the delta waves of deep sleep while hearing all that was going on, and recording afterwards exactly what had been said in the control room by Alyce Green.

The Swami said that this sleep is similar to a dog's sleep in which it is apparently oblivious, but actually aware of outer stimuli and able to respond instantaneously. It was, he said, extremely beneficial, far more than hours of sleep where the body was prone but the mind had not been stilled by a prior meditation.

The Swami returned to India in 1970 to give lectures there on use of the biofeedback machines. There was irony in the fact that he recommended it to young yogi students as a means of speeding up the training period – to the point where machines could no longer 'follow'.

Much had been learned from the Swami, who had also instructed experimental subjects in a form of breathing which helped to retain alpha while in theta reverie, a state in which he believed there was not only the source of creativity but of healing, of the self and others; creative imagery was the key to both.

This possibility had been postulated by many Western meditators and other eminent scientific researchers; Dr Green sees it as a form of mental instruction achieved in deep reverie, a harmonizing of the volitional and non-volitional conscious and unconscious aspects of mind.

The importance of all these tests and experiments, even those of the Swami Rama, was not the precise feats themselves, they were merely significant clues of a vastly exciting potential. As Dr Green has written:

'Perhaps now, because of the resurgence of interest in self-exploration and in self-realization, it will be possible to develop a synthesis of old and new, East and West, pre-science and science, using both yoga and biofeedback training as tools for the study of consciousness. It is also interesting to hypothesize that useful parapsychological talents can perhaps be developed by use of these reverie-generating processes of yoga and biofeedback. Much remains to be researched, and tried in application, but there is little doubt that in the lives of many people a penetration of consciousness into previously unconscious realms (of mind and brain) is making understandable and functional much that was obscure and inoperable.'

For further studies to bear out these words, in 1974 Dr Green took a research team to India. They found yogis who were willing to be monitored by the equipment of their travelling laboratory, and made extensive tests. Results so far analysed show that at least four of the yogis could produce alpha waves for as long as seven and a half hours.

Dr Barbara B. Brown has observed that 'even at the furthest limits of today's expanded consciousness we resort to the models of mysticism of an earlier age to describe our moments of altered states of consciousness'.

In *New Mind, New Body*[16] she explains it scientifically: '... since the moment of insight is signalled by a specific set of brainwave events, it is logical to deduce that the occurrence of such events had to be preceded by other electrical events which signalled their coming. One can conjecture then that there are specific brain electrical activities that exist which predict the times and conditions when perceptual and conceptual systems become "set" for the optimal utilization of new information. (This might be the peculiar appearance or type of several different brainwave components occurring in specific relationships to each other: obviously if brainwaves reflect mental activity, they must do so in some orderly fashion that the appropriate electronic dissection can isolate and identify, much as complex body biochemicals are isolated and identified.) When such antecedent brain electrical events are isolated and characterized, they can be converted into external biofeedback displays and used in training to reinforce them and bring them under voluntary control. Such control would mean expanded and accelerated awareness, acceleration of the process of recognition and information, and perhaps of the rate and extent of thought processes themselves.'

With present intermingling of Eastern practitioners in the West and Western technicians in the East, it seems that the common denominators of mind power are gradually forming a pattern.

2B MIND-SUGGESTION TAKES
NEW DIRECTIONS

THE altered state of consciousness known as hypnosis, or suggestion, has gone through many ups and downs in scientific acceptance still plagued by its occult image. Today, however, it is not only widely used by the medical profession in countless forms of hypnotherapy, fairly well established academically with respected journals in most countries, but it has begun to break ground in new and extended dimensions.

Explored in relation to ESP, it is also used in such mental innovations as the 'Mind Games'[88] of Robert Masters and Jean Houston in which subjects receive suggestion that they will become more creative, more self-enlightened, freer, happier, generally expand their inner horizons, have non-drug experiences of heightened consciousness, or just the plain fun of inner exploration.

There is no trained hypnotist, but any good psychologist will do who can communicate well and gain trust in his competence. The games (all in the book of the same name) are not played only in the Mind Research Laboratory, but anywhere suitable, and all adventurous readers are eligible. The rules must be followed explicitly and in order, and definitions are given for the altered states of consciousness. A great deal of research has gone into the games, and played correctly, they should prove informative 'Guides to Inner Space'.

The introduction to the Mind Games is a preparation for the games to come, a first exercise in altering consciousness by suggestion: the guide might say, for example – 'make yourself very comfortable now, relaxing just as fully as you can, and now listen closely and discover that you can relax still more.

'Relax your body a bit at a time, beginning with the toes, just let them go very limp and relaxed. Then the rest of the foot, and the ankle, feeling the ankle going limp and relaxed, and that relaxation moving up through your body, to the calves, and the knees, and on up to the thighs, and just going very, very limp in your body as I describe the progression of this deep relaxation to you.

'And now on up into the pelvic area, relaxing, relaxing, more and more relaxed. And the abdomen now, and on up to the chest, going loose and limp all over. The fingers, the wrists, the forearms, the elbows, upper arms, and on up to the shoulders now; feel the relaxation, all strain or tension slipping out and away from your whole body. So that the neck feels so loose and limp now, and the jaw, the lips, the cheeks, and the eyes, right on up to the forehead, and over the entire head.

'The whole of your body relaxed now, and relaxing even more and more, so that you are just as limp and relaxed as an old rag doll appears to be . . . and you really are that relaxed, as you listen now to what I have to say to you, and you will want to listen extremely closely, very, very closely please, as you are listening just to me, becoming aware just of what is said to you, and of your responses to what is being said to you.

'And for a little while now, with closed eyes, remaining relaxed, breathing slowly and deeply, focus your awareness on that breathing, as you breathe in now, and then breathing out . . . in and out, in and out, in and out . . .'

After about two minutes, the guide pauses, then continues (note the age-old techniques of hypnosis, the cooperative role-enactment of the hypnotizer and the one hypnotized, a deliberate surrender of conscious volition by one person to receive direct suggestion to the subconscious from another):

'Let your eyes remain closed now, be deeply relaxed, and there is something of importance and value to you that I have to say to you now.

'So concentrate just upon what I will say to you, very fully concentrate on my words, and on what you will experience when the words are spoken. Remember, and accept without doubt that it is true, and recollect now very realistically a dream that you used to have as a child. You may have forgotten it, but now you remember, and you will recall it most vividly now as I remind you of the details of that dream you used to have, of that dream you are going to have again.

'At night, when you slept, as a small child, the same dream

recurring again and again, so that you were not sure that it was a dream, although it was not your usual waking reality, either.

'And beginning always in the same way, as in the dream, you would get out of your bed, walking across the room to the closet, a door you could never find when you looked for it when you were awake, although often you looked for that door. But now the door opens for you in your dream and you pass through the door to stand at the head of a stone staircase.

'It is a very ancient-looking stone staircase, winding down and around, and in the dim light you begin going down the staircase, not at all afraid, but eager to go down, deep and deeper, descending on down through the dream, going always deeper as you go down a step at a time, until finally reaching the bottom of the stairway to stand at the edge of what you recognize to be dark water, lapping, where a small boat is tied.

'And now, lying on the blankets in the bottom of the boat, the boat adrift and floating in the blackness, dark all around, but rocking gently from the motion of the water, back and forth and rising and falling, gently rocked as the boat drifts on and on, as the boat drifts down and down, as you feel only that gentle rocking, listening to the lapping of the water, nearing an opening and into a warm sunlight.

'Still floating, downstream, feeling the warm sunlight, and a soft breeze that passes over you, as you drift down and down, and along the bank the birds are singing, and the fish are jumping in the water, and there is the smell of flowers and of the freshly cut grass in fields that have just been mowed. Feeling a great contentment, serenity, drifting drowsily down and down and down, with that gentle rocking and now just let yourself feel it for a while. Be aware of this whole situation, the movements, the warmth, the sounds, the odours, as you keep on drifting down and down.'

The guide pauses to let players deepen individual experiencing of the images, then continues, with instructions like these:

'Continuing now to float, to rock, gently, drifting deeper and deeper, until your boat approaches the shore and runs smoothly aground at the edge of a meadow, the grass against your legs, the breezes on your body, and conscious of rabbits in the tall grass, of the smell of the flowers all around, of birds singing in the trees, of the movements of your body as you walk, approaching a large tree and seating yourself beneath it, in its shade.

'Sit there now, taking pleasure in all this, enjoying it just as completely as you can, and in a little while I will ask you to play with me that game we have come here to play, that game we made the long journey here to play.

'But now, for a while, just feel your surroundings, be in total harmony with all that exists here in this world out of time, this world without separations, this world where all is one, where you are one with all that is . . .'

The guide will now tell the subjects to 'wake up!' (If the reader wants to experiment alone, there are 'wake-up' drawings at the end of each game that create a kind of optical shock.)

The guide now notes individual reactions. Some subjects will have deeply experienced the suggested dream, others to varying degrees, some perhaps not at all – the percentage would probably approximate to that of persons susceptible to hypnosis generally.

The games from this point on are of increasing intensity; mood music, breathing rhythms, prolonged concentration (such as on the internal vibrations and responses of a plant), the beat of a metronome, touch perception, chanting, all help to deepen the trance state and the creative range of mind-experience. Groups learn to share a trance state, to 'participate' in space, light, the beauty of nature, in bodiless 'travel', psychic communication, the search for ancient secrets (such as the building of the pyramids); there is no limit to these inner explorations except as the subject himself rules.

This form of hypnosis (and the guide is given background reading to do on advanced professional techniques) has the advantage of diminishing people's long-felt resistance in placing themselves at the mercy of another intelligence. The question of whether or not a person under the influence of the hypnotist can be made to commit an act against his own principles has never been entirely settled, despite a consensus by reputable practitioners that it is relative: as Milton V. Kline, director of the Institute for Research in Hypnosis in New York, has said: 'You can't make a criminal with hypnosis, but you can intensify what is already there.'

In techniques such as the Mind Games, even this fear is removed; the subjects are led in a group through inward journeys that provide an expanded consciousness of life and themselves on the positive side, they are not given instructions beyond the sittings, and they can 'wake up' any time they desire. The result is trusting surrender and, for many, enriched lives.

Another form of innovative suggestions has had the same effect of freeing the subject from fears of submission: this is the measuring and monitoring of hypnotic trance by instrumental feedback to establish physiological correlates. The experimental implementation of this approach has been pioneered in England by C. Maxwell Cade, a bio-physicist, psychologist and Fellow of the Royal Society of Medicine.

In 1973, Maxwell Cade together with Dr Ann Woolley-Hart,[20,21] a physician and physiologist, established the Institute for Psychobiological Research in London (with a distinguished committee of doctors of medicine and divinity). Its objects were 'to examine without prejudice and in a strictly scientific spirit the nature of Mind and its interaction with Brain and Body, and to conduct research into States of Awareness, Psychosomatic Illness, Psychophysiological Correlates of Altered States of Consciousness, Bio-energetic Theory, and other psychological problems bearing upon the Nature of Man as a psycho-physical unity'.

At that time, Maxwell Cade and Dr Woolley-Hart had already been working on physiological correlates of hypnosis for about three years and had established a reliable way of measuring depth of hypnosis based upon changes in the electrical conductivity of the skin.

In 1972, they had carried out their first study of deep psycho-physiological relaxation (DPR) with a group of twenty volunteers who, for two hours every Friday evening for ten weeks, gradually learned how to relax themselves to an extraordinary extent simply by watching the needle of an electrical skin resistance meter and mentally following imaginary experiences softly intoned by Maxwell Cade. His idea was to find out whether, in hypnotherapy, it was the suggestion of the hypnotist or the deep relaxation which was the major factor in obtaining cures.

Among the factors which had been taken into account in the design of the experiment were the following: (1) Experiments in sensory deprivation carried out at Princeton University in 1960 have shown that sufferers from colds, sore throats, and poison-ivy rash, all recovered completely – without medication of any kind – after two or three days of sensory deprivation; (2) Experiments of the French physiological psychologist, Michel Jouvet, had shown that, in cats, the part of the brain known as the reticular activating system was responsible both for rapid-eye-movement sleep, sleep, in which dreams occur, and for a depressant action upon the spinal cord which prevents the dreaming animals from living-out their dreams in physical movements; (3) American experiments which allegedly showed (*a*) that skin resistance did not change during hypnosis, and (*b*) that hypnosis was ineffective in the treatment of certain conditions which strongly suggested that, in fact, the experiments had not clearly distinguished between hypnosis and shamming or there was more faith in the hypnotic technique than in the instruments.

Based on these findings, Maxwell Cade and Dr Woolley-Hart decided that it was useless to carry out experiments upon the effects of hypnosis or deep relaxation unless the physiological state of the subjects was *at all* times monitored by suitable instruments.

The instruments consist of a pair of electrodes about 11 cm square attached to the palm of each hand and a voltage meter that measures resistance of the skin (electrical skin resistance: ESR) to the passage of the current. The skin resistance is read at the beginning of the session in the waking state, and during the session readings are compared to determine the percentage differences. As the subject relaxes, the resistance increases, and the greater the trance state the greater the percentage of resistance change. The device measures the number of ohms per sq. cm. Some examples are:

	ohms per sq cm
Panic state	100,000
	(or less)
Normal state	400,000 to 900,000
Sleep	2,000,000
	(and upwards)

Although skin resistance depends on many variables, such as recent intake of food or drink, smoking, drug ingestion, fatigue, depression, anxiety, excitement – and particularly the time of day, since a person's state of arousal (degree of activity in the nervous system) usually climbs throughout the day and then declines progressively towards night – Maxwell Cade says that a single ESR reading gives an immediate idea of what a person's hypnotic susceptibility would be.

Also in order to check these ideas in a convincing manner, it was necessary to experiment with larger numbers of subjects, and the first task was to set up induction courses in meditation, creative reverie and hypnagogic imagery training where variations on the DPR theme could be tried out on whole classes of subjects (who would at least learn how to relax properly and might gain much more besides).

As a result of these experiments, students not only volunteered reports of improvements in self-confidence, 'cures' of insomnia, migraine, psoriasis, asthma, and ability to give up the use of tranquillizers and sleeping pills, but the biofeedback equipment showed that they had all learned to enter deep trance states at will. There was considerable reduction of chronic anxiety, increased creativity, improved memory, a more positive attitude to life, and 75 per cent learned to meditate easily alone, 100 per cent in class.

These and more recent and extended studies confirmed the experimenters' hypothesis that change of electrical skin resistance measured at the palms of the hands is an 'almost linear physiological correlate of neutral hypnosis and autohypnosis'* (although Maxwell Cade believes there is no such thing as hypnosis – only autohypnosis) and that this also holds true for other states of awareness. They have concluded that if the skin resistance remains

*'neutral hypnosis' means when the subject is neither receiving nor executing suggestions.

substantially unchanged, or decreases, then the subject is simply not in trance.

Also confirmed was that biofeedback techniques for the induction of hypnosis, in which the subject feels himself always to be fully responsible for the procedure (and therefore presumably less apprehensive), result in more rapid, more profound hypnosis than traditional methods.

One of the inadvertent findings of the experimenters was that when there was very high skin resistance in the waking state, particularly in young people, it was noticed that the subject's pupils were also únduly contracted. Looking into this curious fact, Maxwell Cade and Dr Woolley-Hart found that all these subjects were drug-takers. A detailed investigation revealed that sharp exercise or challenge did not alter the ESR in these subjects. This discovery pointed to a simple and effective method of screening sample populations for drug-takers. There is one reservation: it has to be a test for non-users rather than users, because absence of response may also indicate extreme fatigue, or the presence of a systemic debilitating disease. Also the measurement must be on the palm of the hand, because measurements of the back of the hand do not show the differences between drug-takers and normal subjects.

In regard to the difference between meditation and hypnosis, the experimenters were interested to note that a group of meditators they studied who 'had a remarkable ability to sit crossed-legged with closed eyes, absolutely motionless for 10 minutes or more', showed no instrumental evidence whatever of electrical skin resistance increase. Obtaining permission to use their techniques, the experimenters were able to teach them deep autohypnosis (40 to 60 per cent electrometric trance) in about 15 minutes. The likelihood is, they conclude, that many so-called meditators are in fact 'cat-napping', which may well account for the proportion of meditators who are disappointed with the physical benefits.

The sum of all these variations on monitored altered states of consciousness seems to be that most ASC are a form of deep physiological relaxation. The significance perhaps is that no matter how attained, or what called, this state appears to be the fount of new possibilities for health. (Maxwell Cade and Dr Woolley-Hart's methods are claimed to have been successful with high blood pressure, epilepsy and gastric ulcers, as well as for improved qualities of mind.)

2C SCIENCE LOOKS AT MIND TRAVEL AND MIND SIGHT

THE impression of leaving one's physical body and travelling about in a kind of etheric counterpart that retains self-consciousness, is an age-old experience of mankind. It has been related to dreaming, psychological symbolism, hallucination, mental imbalance, 'astral' (or psychic) projection, 'travelling clairvoyance' (Eileen Garrett's term) and biological disturbances.

Many autobiographies have been written on these experiences, vivid accounts with extraordinarily similar fundamental details, particularly in regard to the seeming division of the psyche where one 'self' becomes the observer of the other in life-and-death crises of illness.

The subject has, however, posed difficulties for research. Despite painstaking studies by eminent scholars and careful recording of individual accounts, of which there have been thousands, a core of discomfort about out-of-body experiences (known nowadays as OOBEs) had prevented them from being taken seriously. After all, there was no physical evidence that they existed, but only the 'word' of the experiencer; none of the 'substantial' stuff of science.

In 1958, starting with the systematic approach to his own disturbingly vivid and regular OOBEs, Robert Monroe, a successful businessman and electronics engineer from Virginia, caused new scientific speculation on out-of-body experiences. The reason was that in his case there seemed hope of that absolute of science – a respectable experiment: Robert Monroe could induce these experiences deliberately, at will, and offered to do so under laboratory conditions.

Robert Monroe's initial experiences, leading to later journeys out-of-the-body, were alarming enough to make him suspect a brain disorder. As he settled down on the couch for a brief nap on a Sunday afternoon when his family had gone to church, a sudden strong beam of light struck his body, causing it to vibrate violently. He was unable to move, as if 'held in a vice'. After tremendous straining to do so, he was at last able to sit up, and the vibration gradually stopped. Only a few seconds had passed, and at no time had his eyes been closed or his senses dulled to outer noise.

This was puzzling, but he might have dismissed it as some form of hallucination had it not occurred again – nine times – in the following six weeks, always when he lay down for rest or sleep.

He consulted a doctor and had a thorough physical examination. The doctor did not accept his suspicion of a brain tumour and suggested that Robert Monroe had been working too hard, should rest, cut down on smoking, take care of himself generally.

Robert Monroe decided to look objectively at the next experience, if he had one. He did, that very night, and this time instead of attempting to fight out of the 'vice' he lay still to see what would happen. The 'vibration' proceeded right through his body, like painless electric shock, and made a roaring sound in his ears. After about five minutes, it died away.

These experiences were repeated, with variations, for some time. He had not told his family, but now he was frightened for his mental condition. Luckily he had a friend who was a well-known psychologist, and he decided to risk his secret with him. The psychologist not only laughed at the possibility of some incipient derangement, but suggested, rather, an in-depth study of the experiences. He spoke of feats of Eastern yogis who claimed that they could travel out of their bodies whenever they wanted to.

From then on, Robert Monroe assumed the role of both experimenter and subject. His experiences grew increasingly eventful and frightening.

He would lie down, feel the vibration begin, and then without any sense of difference in his consciousness, begin to move through strange variations of reality. In one such experience, the fingers of his hand that dangled from the side of the bed began to scratch at the surface of the rug and found they could penetrate it, then the floor itself – he felt the rough masonry of the ceiling of the room below, a triangular chip of wood, a bent nail, sawdust. He pushed deeper, and his whole arm went through – then he felt water, and deliberately splashed it . . .

Suddenly he seemed to realize the alteration and was awake still in his bed in the moonlight room, but with all the sensations still with him. His arm was still through the floor, and although the vibrations were fading, he felt the possibility that if they died out altogether, he would be left with his arm through the hole and the floor might close in. He jerked his arm out of the floor quickly and drew it up onto the bed. It occurred to him that it was the vibrations that had somehow made the hole. When they stopped, he got up, put on the light to look for the hole.

It didn't exist. His wife was lying quietly asleep in the bed, there was no water on his hand; all was as usual.

Extremely shaken by this experience, he sought more advice, tried to apply his scientific, engineering background to what had seemed to occur. His doctor, impressed with the vividness of the account, even suggested cutting a hole in the floor to see if there was, indeed, the triangular chip of wood and nail he described.

But this was only the beginning of Robert Monroe's sleep 'happenings' – later seeming extremely mild by contrast. For now they ranged further and further from the bed. He passed through walls, met people, visited friends in distant places. He became aware of a world that was similar to the 'normal' one but where *he* did not seem to be seen, and which was somehow lacking in detail.

Of prime significance was the fact that he could induce the transition from his normal body to the 'second' body, learning to breathe in a certain way that caused the vibrations to work up in him like waves, and at a precise moment he 'rolled' out of one body into the other. Whenever he had become frightened and panicked, he had awakened promptly – so confident now that he could always get back into his substantial body, by 'wanting to', he allowed himself to explore and experiment, and he kept impeccable records, developed a kind of technical language to describe and define the experiences. He met with scientific groups and bodies to discuss them, addressed meetings, and found that there were many hundreds of people who had had experiences of similar nature, who had been afraid to talk about them openly, but were now eager to compare notes.

Although he knew there were quite a few psychologists who took these experiences seriously, found them revealing and meaningful, even *humanly* corroborative of extended dimensions of life and other planes of existence, they were no closer to solid 'proof positive' – and the matter came to rest against a wall.

Determined that some form of answer be found, however, Robert Monroe looked for a scientist who would be willing to put him through an experiment with his out-of-body journeys, under laboratory conditions. He found one at last who agreed to donate a certain amount of time to assay both their parapsychological and physiological aspects. His name was Charles T. Tart, Professor of Psychology at the University of California, Davis.

Initial studies were made over a period of months in 1965 and 1966 in the University of Virginia Medical School. Basically simple experiments were designed for the hoped-for OOBEs. Robert Monroe, hooked up to various electronic instruments, was asked to convey his 'second self' into an adjoining room of the laboratory to observe the monitoring technician there, and to 'read' a five-digit number* placed on a six-foot high shelf. Measurements were made of his eye movements, brainwaves and heart rate.

Robert Monroe, on an army bed, with an electrode clipped to his ears, found it difficult to relax and induce the usual conditions for his 'separation'. On several nights he failed to do so, but on the eighth he made two brief forays. He turned over gently, 'rolled-out' of his physical body, but felt as if he had fallen to the floor. When he felt no impact, he knew he had 'separated'. He moved into a darkened area and came upon two men and a woman, strangers to him. They conversed, obliviously. He pinched the woman very gently just below the ribs, hoping to make her aware of him, and thought she reacted. Then some un-

*Recent research on out-of-body perception indicates that letters and numbers are not seen by subjects, only visual images.

easiness decided him to return to his physical body for 'reorientation' and try again.

His eye movements, according to Professor Tart, had shown normal dream pattern, but his blood pressure had shown a sudden drop lasting eight seconds, then just as suddenly returned to normal.

On the second try, after a long, recorded, light-sleep-stage, Robert Monroe succeeded in separating again, and this time followed a wire he saw, which he believed would lead him to the control room; but instead it led to an unfamiliar area, and this somehow unnerved him again, and he went back again into his body. Later, however, his description of the area was found to match an interior courtyard of the building, exactly where he would have gone had he taken the opposite direction to the control room. There were no significant measurements in this effort.

The physiological results of the experiments in general were not particularly meaningful and approximated the dreaming state, but Professor Tart observed that this was 'an over-simplification'. In the remarkable book Robert Monroe had written about his experiences (*Journeys Out of the Body*[100]), he has described the sharp differences between his dreaming and his out-of-body state, and if these experiences were an ordinary dreaming state, Professor Tart commented in the introduction, he estimated that there would be far more rapid-eye-movements, and they would not take place so soon after sleep (the normal time for dreaming is after about eighty to ninety minutes of non-dreaming sleep). He thought it possible that the OOBEs might be a substitute for this non-dreaming stage.

There is also the question of forms of experiment – these had been parapsychological tests (in fact another subject had succeeded in reading the five-digit number, but her experiences were more 'accidental' than induced), and there were countless other possible designs of a more imaginative nature that could be tried.

In one personal test with Robert Monroe, Professor Tart was 'seen' by a friend in New York, when in reality he was in California; this coincided with an experimental arrangement with Robert Monroe (with whom he was spending a night on his way to a conference in Washington). He writes in the Foreword to Robert Monroe's book:

'Some time after dawn that morning (I had slept somewhat fitfully and the light was occasionally waking me), I was dreaming when I began vaguely remembering that Mr Monroe was supposed to try to get me out of my body. I became partially conscious, while remaining in the dream world, and felt a sense of "vibration" all around me in the dream world, a "vibration" that had a certain amount of indefinable menace connected with it. In spite of the fear this aroused, I thought that I should try to have an OOBE, but at that point I lost my thread of consciousness, and only remember waking up a while later, feeling that the experiment was a failure. A week later I received a letter from a colleague in New York . . . he was writing to me about an experience his stepdaughter, Carie, had spontaneously reported . . . that she had seen me in a restaurant in New York on her way to school that morning. This would have been roughly about the time I was having the dream. Neither she nor her father knew I was on the east coast.'

'Coincidental?' he asked himself. 'Again, something I would never present as scientific evidence of anything, but something I can't dismiss as meaningless.'

As a sequel to these events, in 1972 OOBEs became the subject of a new research project at the ASPR. Their central hypothesis was as follows: 'That a human being has an "ecsomatic"* aspect, capable of operating independently of and away from the physical body. This part of the personality may also be conceived of as leaving the body at death and continuing to exist. We want to combine all our information, OOBP (out-of-body perception), apparition cases and deathbed-observations, to see whether this ecsomatic-existence hypothesis is strengthened by our new data and its theoretical integration.'[110]

Incorporated in their experimental designs was equipment for

*Celia Green,[48] director of the Institute of Psycho-physical Research, Oxford, defines an *ecsomatic* experience as one in which the objects of perception are apparently organized in such a way that the observer seems to himself to be observing them from a point of view which is not coincident with his physical body.

recording physiological data, and the enlisted cooperation of
several physicists, engineers and psychologists.

Their first major subject was with an artist named Ingo Swann,
whose spectacular metaphysical paintings, representing what he
termed 'extended awareness', or 'cosmic art' had been exhibited
at the New York World's Fair in 1964. Ingo Swann had always
believed that he moved out of his body, that he had extended
vision and was able to see without his physical eyes.

The ASPR wanted to find out if it was possible for him to
prove his ability at will, and he had agreed to try. Janet Mitchell,
a psychologist associated with the ASPR, conducted the exploratory sessions.[150] Ingo Swann sat in a dim room attached to a polygraph (which records brainwaves (EEG), heart rate, respiration,
etc.). Arranged on a shelf, suspended two feet from the ceiling,
were several objects of distinct design and colour, such as in one
instance, an apple, an umbrella, a black leather scissors-case.
Partitions concealed them from view on either side.

After a time of meditation, Ingo Swann would indicate he was
ready for the test and the monitoring mechanisms would begin
to measure his physiological condition. Then he would sketch
the objects he felt he was seeing, as well as describe them verbally.
Later, his sketches would be matched to the target by an independent judge who had not as yet seen them.

In the sessions that took place, the judge (another psychologist)
correctly matched them all – the chances of this 100 per cent score
was about forty thousand to one.

Sometimes Ingo Swann could not provide precise identification
of some aspect of the target object – it was found that he would
have got a partial obscuration from the angle and light of his
projected vision (and in later experiments the fall of light was
accounted for in the target arrangement). This showed a clear
difference between extrasensory perception and direct out-of-body
perception. The question it raised was whether or not the latter
followed the visual laws of optics.

As for the physiological changes, instruments recorded his
'waking' state and out-of-body state for comparison and found
that there was a loss of electrical activity during his experimental

task and a speed-up of the brainwaves in the visual, occipital region of his brain. His heart rate and other processes of the autonomic nervous system remained normal, indicating that there was no danger to the system in the out-of-body state.

Subsequently, Ingo Swann's abilities have led to further scientific observation. As part of their broad plan to attempt 'to discover relationships between extraordinary human functioning and known physical laws', the Stanford Research Institute [151] have conducted experiments with Ingo Swann, one of which involved a magnetometer protected by superconducting shields, and considered impervious to any form of outside influence. Ingo Swann, it was found, could, at will, cause an increase or decrease in the magnetic field within this magnetometer – a feat beyond belief, achieved through mind alone.

Another incredible experiment with Ingo Swann, carried out by Dr Gertrude Schmeidler in 1973, showed that he was able to alter temperature, at a distance, in graphite thermistors.

More challenging experiments continue to be carried out with Ingo Swann at Stanford Research Institute, and with researchers all over America, the results of some for possible security reasons, not made publically available.

Recently Russell Targ and Harold Puthoff carried out tests of what they call 'Remote Viewing' of natural targets, with Patrick Price, a businessman in the coal industry, who can describe with remarkable accuracy and detail, geographical or man-made sites at a distance of anything from two to two thousand miles.[151]

In each of the experiments with Pat Price, remote locations were chosen on the double-blind basis. A set of twelve very different target locations, each within thirty minutes driving distance of the Institute, had been selected from more than a hundred environments by the Director of Information Sciences at the Institute, who was not connected to the experiments.

Pat Price 'viewed' these distant locations from various places, an outdoor park, a double-walled copper-screen Faraday cage and an office. Another experimenter selected a location from the previously randomized twelve sets of travelling instructions, kept under the control of the Director and otherwise unseen. A team of experimenters consisting of two to four SRI personnel, then proceeded to the target location without any communication with Pat Price or the experimenter who stayed with him to hear his descriptions and ask questions in order to clarify them.

A thirty-minute interlude followed, during which Pat Price 'observed' and spoke his impressions into a tape recorder. When the 'demarcation' team returned, they compared the location they had visited with what Pat Price had 'seen'.

The results were amazingly precise, Pat Price showing ability to describe such details as structural materials, colours, atmospheres, activities of people, as well as buildings, roads, gardens, etc., but because there were some inaccuracies, the experimenters sought the independent analysis of five scientists not associated with the experiment, then a numerical evaluation of accuracy was obtained and the consensus confirmed that the 'functioning of a remote perceptual ability' was indicated.

To extend their investigation, the SRI experimenters chose two other potential 'remote viewers' from a screening experiment of 147 volunteer subjects, an SRI scientist and a professional photographer. These, too, showed accurate results, sometimes viewing targets as distant as Central America where one of the experimenters travelled and conducted the experiment by means of a detailed record of activities, including photographs, and five daily responses by the subjects at set hours.

Since further testing with Ingo Swann had revealed that he also had this form of his out-of-body perception, Russell Targ and Harold Puthoff reported their conclusions as follows:[151]

'We have presented evidence for the existence of a biological information channel whose characteristics appear to fall outside the range of known perceptional modalities. The precise nature of the channel or channels is as yet undefined, but may involve either direct perception of hidden information content, perception of mental images of persons knowledgeable of target information, precognition, or some combination of these or other information channels.

'We have worked with three individuals whose remote perceptual abilities were sufficiently developed that they were able to describe geographical material blocked from ordinary perception.

'From these experiments we conclude that:

'A channel exists whereby information about a remote location can be obtained by means of an as yet unidentified perceptual modality.

'As with all biological systems, the information channel appears to be imperfect, containing noise along with the signal.

'While a quantitative signal-to-noise ratio in the information-theoretical sense cannot as yet be determined, the results of our experiments indicate that the functioning is at the level of useful information transfer.

'It may be that remote perceptual ability is widely distributed in the general population, but because the perception is generally below an individual's level of awareness, it is repressed or not noticed. For example, two of our subjects (H.H. and P.P.) had not considered themselves to have unusual perceptual ability before their participation in these experiments.'

How is this non-spatial, non-physical projection of consciousness accomplished? Perhaps, as hoped, prolonged experimentation will provide the answer.

Research in altered states of consciousness has sometimes taken great courage, as in the case of Robert Monroe, who has fought fear of the unknown, fear of dying, to pursue revelation of possible value to man's self-knowledge. In the case of Dr John Lilly, a psychoanalyst and scientist who has done research in fields of biophysics, neurophysiology, electronics and neuranatomy, there was need for courage to surrender all volitional grip on normal consciousness in pursuit of what he called the 'far out spaces' of consciousness.

Dr Lilly, whose twelve years' work with the relationship of dolphins and humans became well known (*Man and Dolphins* and *The Mind of the Dolphin*),[83] and who had specialized in studies on solitude, isolation and confinement, as well as with some of the important early research in LSD, always believed a researcher should undergo the experience involved in the research himself, not just understand it from reading, study, or the accounts of others. In this regard, he had gone through extensive first-hand exploration with LSD and experienced so much enlightenment about his own life, the contents of his mind and emotions, his character and problems that he felt actually 're-born'.

As well as this, he had had mystic experiences of immense power. Since these are considered the highest form of altered states of consciousness, he took a scientist's interest in them, and among many of his notable experiments were those in 1958 and again in 1964, when he decided to test a neurophysiological hypothesis that the brain stays in a waking state due to outside stimuli (through the end organs of the body), through a device to isolate himself from all external stimulation (as far as physically possible) – a tank filled with water in a soundproof, completely darkened room in which he would remain suspended for a period of several hours.

Together with these conditions was the second factor – he would take carefully prescribed amounts of LSD (approximately 300 micrograins in total). Thus, he combined what was later called 'sensory deprivation', with a total of interior experience of 'inner space'.

The extraordinary results (detailed in his book, *The Center of the Cyclone*[83]) were more than parallels of traditional mystical experience, they were a synthesis of psychoanalytical self-exploration, minute physical observations and mind expanded to realm beyond realm, layer beyond layer of visionary grandeur, philosophical amplifications and universal 'journeying'.

The following excerpts give only a glimpse of the far reaches and complexity of the experiences, but may convey at least a partial impression:

(Having established in initial experiments that he did not need a head-mask and could keep balanced and afloat, that clothing was distraction, and that there was no need to fear that he would not 'get back into his body' – by the same means as Robert Monroe – he fully abandoned himself to the blackened silence, the 93°F water, and the effect of the drug.)

'. . . I was still holding on to the usual cognition spaces of the body . . . the idea of a central point of identity and consciousness. Later this was found to be unnecessary, except during extreme states when I needed a rest. At these times I would return to zero point.

'This zero point is a useful place. It is not complete separation from one's previous ideas, but it is separation from the body. It is space that still represents the darkness and the silence of the tank, but with the body nonexistent . . .

'. . . suddenly I was precipitated into (universal) spaces. I maintained myself as a central point of consciousness, of feeling, of recording. I moved into universes containing beings much larger than myself, so that I was a mote in their sunbeam, a small ant in their universe, a single thought in a huge mind, or a small program in a cosmic computer . . . I was swept, pushed, carried, whirled, and in general beat around by processes which I could not understand, processes of immense energy, of fantastic light, of terrifying power. My very being was threatened as I was pushed through these vast spaces by these vast entities. Waves of the equivalent of light, of sound, of motion, waves of intense emotion, were carried in dimension beyond my understanding. I became a bright luminous point of consciousness, radiating light and warmth, and knowledge. I moved into a space of astonishing brightness, golden light . . . I sat in space without a body but with all of myself there . . . exhilarated with a sense of awe, wonder, reverence. The energy surrounding me was of incalculably high intensity . . . in the great vastness of empty space filled with light . . .

'. . . I am out beyond our galaxy, beyond galaxies as we know them. Time is apparently speeded up by 100 billion times. The whole universe collapses into a point. There is a tremendous explosion and out of the point on one side comes positive matter and positive energies, streaking into the cosmos at fantastic velocities. Out of the opposite side of the point comes antimatter streaking off into the opposite direction. The universe expands to its maximum extent, recollapses, and expands three times . . . the "guides" say "man appears here and disappears there" . . . where does man go when he disappears until he is ready to reappear again, I ask. They say, "That is us".

'. . . I was merely an observer of microscopic size, and yet I was part of some vast network of similar beings all connected, somehow or other responsible for what was going on. I was given an individuality for temporary purposes only. I would be reabsorbed into the network when the time came.'

Describing a trip 'down into' his own body, he writes:

'. . . looking at various systems of organs, cellular assemblages, and structure. I traveled among cells, watched their functioning and realized that within myself was a grand assemblage of living organisms, all of which added up to me. I traveled through my brain, watching the neurons and their activities. I traveled through my heart, watching the pulsations of the muscle cells. I traveled through my blood, watching the business of the white blood corpuscles. I traveled down through my gut tract, getting acquainted with the bacteria and the mucosal cells in the walls. I went into my testes and became acquainted with the formation of the sperm cells. I then quickly moved into smaller and smaller dimensions, down to the quantum levels and watched the play of atoms in their own vast universes, their wide empty spaces, with the fantastic forces involved in each of the distant nuclei with their orbital clouds of force field electrons and the primary particles coming to this system from outer spaces. It was really frightening to see tunneling effects and the other phenomena of the quantal level taking place. I came back from that trip realizing what a lot of empty space I had in myself and what vast energies were locked in the matter of my own body. Having seen nuclei disintegrate before my eyes, releasing fantastic radiation energies on a microscopic scale, I had a new respect for what I was carrying around and what I, in a sense, was at these levels of reasoning and functioning . . .'

After ten years of work in these isolation tanks, together with all his other experiences of inner space, Dr Lilly came to the conclusion that the amplifications and elaborations of one's consciousness come from what he calls self-'meta-programming' of the 'Human Biocomputer' (he has written a book of the same name). And from this, he states his arrived-at principle: '*What one believes to be true, either is true or becomes true in one's mind, within limits to be determined experimentally and experientially. These limits are beliefs to be transcended.*' From this base, Dr Lilly's scientific self-exploration has led on in many directions, through the expanding region of 'mind-body' integration known as Humanistic Psychology, and the esoteric disciplines of Oscar Ichazo's Training Group in Africa, Chile.

3

Expanding horizons for non-medical healing

The afflictions suffered by the body, the soul
sees quite well with shut eyes.
HIPPOCRATES

FOR thousands of years 'witch doctors', shamans and 'medicine-men' of primitive cultures, instinctively acknowledged man's mind-body interrelationship with 'magic' healing that combined psychology and herbs. Centuries of medicine shared this awareness; Hippocrates, the first Greek physician (*c.* 460 B.C.) believed doctors should have 'knowledge of the whole of things', and physicians of the Middle Ages ministered the 'sick soul' of man with potions and theology, agreeing with Martin Luther that 'heavy thoughts bring on physical maladies . . . when the soul is oppressed so is the body'.

The language of mind-body connections is so familiar that it goes unnoticed: dying with grief or a 'broken heart', fainting with terror or passion, going white or becoming frozen with shock, clammy with nerves, ice-cold with panic, stomachs tying-up with knots of alarm, sinking with despair, hearts that race, become light or heavy to describe anxiety, gladness and depression, are only a few showing every emotion to have a physical counterpart.

But in the second half of the nineteenth century, when Lister, Pasteur and others brought emphasis to the germ theory of medicine, and specific micro-organisms were assigned the chief role in most human disease, the mind-body cleavage gradually conditioned both physician and the 'enlightened' patient that ailments had either physical or mental causes, two quite separate departments.

With the advent of psychoanalysis and hypnosis in the early twentieth century, mind was brought back into focus; psychiatry formed its link-up of both mind and body, so that either could be examined for the seat of a patient's trouble without risk of over-looking one or the other, and in the 1930s, with her concept of 'psychosomatic' (from the Greek psyche=soul, soma=body and in 1954 her impressive work, *Emotions and Bodily Changes*[37]) interrelationships, Dr Helen Flanders Dunbar of the Columbia University College of Physicians and Surgeons brought the mind-body interrelationships back into recognition again, with medicine acknowledging that at least 75 per cent of human ills were mentally caused. A full circle has been completed in the interfusion of thinking and feeling and their effects on physical states. An unhappy mind could make you sick, but conversely a happy mind could keep you healthy.

The subject, however, remained mysterious. Limits appeared to what the most skilled form of medicine could do; there were still 'incurable' illnesses, and with the increase of 'stress diseases' in modern life, many symptoms remained immune even to the most sophisticated drugs – which often proved to be stop-gaps, at best bridges, with the deep-seated cause left untouched, perhaps to manifest again and again. The administering of 'placebos' (valueless pills), or treatments which frequently alleviated the patient's symptoms, even acute pain, with a high percentage of efficacy, and the cliché 'bedside manner' and sympathetic ear still removed the symptoms, even when the patients were still diagnosed as physically ill.

Was it possible, then, that the age-old biblical and historical references to 'spiritual' or 'faith' healing had some substance in fact, that somehow psychology and medicine needed to meet in another, more intangible dimension? Medicine knows that it does not of itself perform the actual healing, that it simply creates the favourable conditions for it to take place, and that it is nature which automatically restores, knowing how and doing it by its own inexorable law. Was there this other way, however, to create the 'favourable' conditions, could medicine afford to rely more on a 'divine' power of healing? Were all the unorthodox forms of healing that persisted in curing the 'incurable', in easing pain and suffering in those given up by doctors, the result of coincidence, of natural remissions or the power of suggestion (this last, itself part of the mystery)? After all, only a quarter of the world's population of approximately 4,000 million had recourse to the science of medicine – what about the rest? What about the tenets of Eastern mysticism that named the source of all healing as spirit – were they less esoteric, more practical than Western medicine had understood?

Even the questions were resisted by the majority of physicians, let alone the answers. Was it not irrational to 'progress' from medical ignorance to medical science only to regress? Wasn't it more likely that even greater knowledge of the organism was needed, more sophisticated techniques and drugs? Above all, there was the loss of standing in the professional community through association with the 'fringe' areas of healing, possible exclusion from respectability. The call would have to come from the people in overwhelming demand before the medical and psychological profession could afford open alliance . . .

And this call has begun to be heard. In the last ten to twenty years it has grown louder and clearer, and more and more physicians, psychologists and psychiatrists have stood up to be counted as open-minded to non-medical healing, both in practice and research. Some now report 'miraculous' cures they have witnessed or experienced themselves. For instance, in the case of Dr Richard O'Wellen of Johns Hopkins Hospital in Boston, he saw his own daughter cured of a congenital hip dislocation by the healer Kathryn Kuhlman. He had no explanation for it – except 'God'.

With or without doctors' verification, Kathryn Kuhlman has won untold thousands of followers in America.[80] An ordained minister of the Gospel, she has filled the Andrew Carnegie auditorium to overflowing for sixteen years, 'miraculously' healing countless 'incurable' people 'on the spot' with her fervent prayers and total conviction of the power of God to heal. She has built a great foundation of religious and charitable works and dedicated herself totally to her 'calling', which is not just healing, but 'service to the soul' of man. Nor does she rule out medicine, believing that all healing is 'divine'.

The very proper scepticism of healing miracles, persisting mainly because of charlatans and hysterical claims that fell apart on close examination by the medical profession, has no adequate refutation for Kathryn Kuhlman's long list of total cures that remain lifelong.

Healers like John Scudder,[108] an engineer who is also pastor of a local church (which gives him entrée into hospitals), treats some one thousand people a year by a combination of breathing techniques, 'magnetic passes' of his hands over the patient's body, and a psychological approach to the 'subconscious mind' to alter preconceptions and expectations of sickness. John Scudder claims that he healed himself of cancer through meditation.

Norbu Chen,[108] before he went to Tibet and studied a process of healing that transmits energy to afflicted areas by pressure on certain other parts of the body, was an ex-convict from Kentucky by the name of Charles Alexander. Nowadays wearing exotic black robes and sandals, he has had such phenomenal success with ailments that range from headaches to paralysis, that several doctors not only send their patients to him, but go themselves for his strong, powerful form of treatment. In fact, these powers of Norbu Chen's, which he claims are like acupuncture only 'more advanced', are being studied at the Institute of Noetic Sciences. It seems that after he has chanted 'to raise his vibration level' and meditated a while, he is ready to 'shoot his consciousness' for energy, which he then channels to his patient. Three months of observation at the Institute, has seen cases of hepatitis remissed in four days, face deformity normalized, gall stones and arthritic deposits dissolved. Filed reports and doctors' verifications must wait for publication until the permanence of the cures are ascertained, which may be up to several years.

Apart from these and other outstanding healers in America, there is the proliferation of prayer groups and prayer circles for present or absent healing. The Association of Research and Enlightenment (ARE), with substantial national headquarters in Virginia Beach, Virginia,[2a] was founded in 1947 for the purpose of disseminating information on the 'readings' of Edgar Cayce, the world-famous psychic who could self-induce a trance state at will, during which he was able to diagnose ailments of people he had never seen or heard of, prescribe treatment and discourse generally on philosophical questions asked him, none of which he would remember on awakening.

Altogether, it is estimated that Edgar Cayce entered this trance or sleep-like state at least 16,000 times during his life. Some

9,000 of his recorded monologues were concerned with the mind and the body. Others dealt with religious and moral issues, with human-relations problems, and with generalized advice. Although he died in 1944, the fact that his diagnoses and prescriptions, often extremely unorthodox, were equally often amazingly accurate later led to ceaseless dissection of his ability, as well as analyses of his thousands of remedies by many prominent physicians.

Born in Kentucky in 1877, Edgar Cayce[15] was a simple man relatively unschooled who in waking life could not have known what he was able to express with authority under trance. His only explanation for his talent was that at the age of seven he had had a vision in which he was asked what he wanted to do with his life. He answered that he wanted to help others, especially children. Later in life, he took hypnotic suggestion hoping to cure a loss of voice and found that he could lie down, fall into a sleep-state and answer questions on any subject put to him; he seemed to have contact with some forms of 'infinite wisdom'. He then dedicated the rest of his days to this form of service, at sacrifice to his private life and financial progress.[149]

Today, however, all his hopes have been more than realized. The headquarters houses a collection of some 8,000 volumes devoted to psychical research, and a vast tape library. A R E offers programmes of conferences, seminars and lectures to people from all over the nation, has a medical research clinic for healing experiment, a camp for members' youngsters, family and adult retreat workshops, its own press, and over 1,400 nationwide study groups in which techniques for spiritual healing are taught and developed.

Annual gatherings draw a large attendance of doctors, psychologists, psychiatrists and psychotherapists as well as hundreds of people interested in non-medical healing or seeking help. Leaders of the 'workshops' are mainly medical practitioners and nutritionists, for Edgar Cayce advocated a combination of healing factors, proper diet, rest and exercise, music, colour, a clear conscience: 'All healing is from God,' he maintained. 'Healing is allowing the life force to flow through, and its action is to stimulate and arouse and awaken each cell of the body to its proper activities.'

Also growing in popularity are the healing workshops of the Spiritual Frontiers Fellowship (SFF).[145] Organized in 1956 to foster an open exchange of views between the church and parapsychology and for the spiritual restoration of healing, the SFF has not accomplished this primary aim, so much as to itself become an answer to the current demand for practical research and development in non-medical healing. In this direction, it sponsors lectures by scientists, mystics, doctors, psychiatrists, researchers in any field with a contribution to make to spiritual enlightenment, and has seventy area groups with workshops where techniques of healing are conveyed in detail, with demonstrations of group and individual healing. The methods taught in association with SFF are primarily based on faith in God, sometimes through the healing power of Christ, and consist of preliminary variations of music, spoken prayer and meditation to intensify or 'raise' spiritual consciousness and induce inward and outward 'attunement', then the laying on of hands (with or without contact, sometimes merely a touch) and making statements of faith and expectation of healing.

In their individual healing work SFF leaders have substantial success. The Reverend Alex Holmes, a presbyterian minister, observed that the preponderance of their patients have been given up by medical doctors, yet some 85 per cent of them show improvement, of which one per cent is cured instantly, about 20 per cent improve progressively, the remaining do not respond but fulfil the doctor's verdict. In all instances work is done in conjunction with medical treatment, for medicine is considered an aspect of God, though the power of healing itself is God's.

While many established churches in America are slowly returning to spiritual healing, a few have done so with force and vigour.

At El Santuario de Chimayo in New Mexico,[108] known as 'The Lourdes of America', thousands of people attend healing services; and in St Louis, Missouri, the Baptist Church of the Good Shepherd has a congregation of 2,500 who come for the faith healing of its pastor, David Epley.

In England, more and more churches are holding regular healing services, and the work of The World Healing Crusade, whose headquarters are in Blackpool, has spread to over 100 countries. Based solely on the power of prayer to heal, this ministry is not a church or even a movement. Its leader, Brother Mandus, says: 'We have no ambitions other than to serve and help mankind. We so freely do this in all kinds of churches, and for all kinds of people with many varied faiths – simply because we offer and share the basic truths of all denominations and religions.'

People who want healing, or help of any kind, need only to write their problem in a letter and send it to the headquarters. The sealed letter (never opened) is placed on the altar and the Brothers of the Crusade, acting as intercessors, pray over it. All help is given without charge of any sort, and a magazine, *Crusader*, is sent free to all who ask. Brother Mandus travels the world holding meetings. His healing method is to join with the patient in thanking 'the Father' in the faith that the healing has taken place. Healings are not counted, but many thousands of sick people have benefited.

Many churches, such as the Pentecostal, have always incorporated the laying-on-of-hands in their services, and spiritual healing is an integral part of the indigenous New Thought Movement, whose several divisions include Christian Science[26] and the United Churches of Religious Science. In Christian Science healing there is no resort to medicine, although nursing care is provided where needed (there are Christian Science nursing homes), while the spiritual healing is in process. Disease is considered contrary to God's will, and healing consists of realization of 'Perfect God, Perfect Man', in the thought of the practitioner, who sees the whole and 'real' person behind the apparent; while the person seeking the healing attempts to put off material illusion and 'turn unreservedly to the divine mind'. The cure may be a result of 'absent healing', thereby precluding the element of 'suggestion'.

Religious Science (or Science of Mind),[133] which has some quarter of a million followers in America and other countries, does appreciate and cooperates with doctors because it holds that a person's degree of spiritual conviction of healing may not as yet be adequate to the disorder, and that any form of healing that alleviates suffering is good. Its main principle is that there is but one mind, one infinite creative intelligence in all, through all, as all, and that 'as a man thinketh in his heart, so is he' is a description of the law of thought. Whether a person is aware of it or not, thought is always creating his experience. If his thinking is negative, it must manifest as disorder in the body or affairs; if it is positive, it must manifest as health and harmony. Healing is accomplished in the thought of the person, by realigning it with the one mind, which is perfect and knows no opposites. Called 'scientific prayer' or 'treatment', it amounts to a conscious direction of the subconscious, which this philosophy believes is the creative medium of life which must by its nature mechanically respond, by corresponding.

In 1973 the United Churches of Religious Science established a Research Foundation in honour of its founder Ernest Holmes,[58] for the purpose of working with scientists to try and determine *why* their 'programming' of the subconscious for healing is effective. Among the scientists, doctors and healers on Foundation's advisory committee are Dr Edgar Mitchell, Dr Elmer Green, Dr Carl Simonton and Dr William Tiller.

Another form of non-medical healing has sprung from the successful church of Dr Norman Vincent Peale, whose terminology (and book of the same name) 'the power of positive thinking' has become familiar to most of the Western world. Based on the statistical fact that 21 million Americans suffer one form or another of emotional illness, and that 80 per cent of the nation's emotionally troubled remain untreated due to a lack of trained practitioners, The American Foundation of Religion and Psychiatry was formed (originally in 1937) to train clergymen in the art of counselling. The premise was that most disturbed people first seek the help of the local clergy, and that since there were more than 250,000 of these available, and a conversely acute shortage throughout the US of practising psychiatrists, it was logical to extend the scope of the clergy. Revolutionary at the time, the idea gradually became a reality. Today, the clergyman counsellor is likely to be a trained healer of the 'whole person', rather than simply the state of the soul, perhaps leading his patient back in a roundabout way to a more substantial core of faith. The Foundation offers many other aspects of healing service such as group therapy, marriage counselling, individual counselling, and has a clinic staffed with psychiatrists, psychiatric social workers and psychologists.

Also believing that the fundamental source of all forms of healing is God, is Olga Worrall, who with her husband Ambrose[175] until his death in 1972 conducted a healing ministry in Baltimore, Maryland, for over forty years and became world-famous for quietly remarkable results, many of them spontaneously verified by doctors, and attested by thousands of appreciative letters.

As associate director of the New Life Clinic at Mount Washington United Methodist Church in Baltimore, Olga Worrall finds the demand for non-medical healing greater than ever, and she is continuing cooperative work begun with her husband with scientists who are trying to discover the essential nature of the healing process achieved by healers like herself, whose success over the years in gradual and instant cures of almost every kind of human ailment cannot be relegated to any categories of orthodox scepticism. (These are usually that if a disease was cured, it had had a wrong medical diagnosis, was a 'spontaneous remission' – that is, cured itself – or didn't exist in the first place.)

Olga Worrall, who insists she is an ordinary housewife (she is a Ph.D. and her husband was a successful aeronautics engineer from England), has nevertheless the zeal and approach of a scientist towards an art that has been recorded since about 3000 B.C. 'It is unfortunate,' she says, 'that in five thousand years this knowledge has not been reduced to law and embodied in a system acceptable to science.' For despite the many illnesses she has known to respond to her laying-on-of-hands and prayers, such as tumours of all kinds and sizes (one appeared to melt from a woman's neck as she returned to her seat), diseases of the kidneys, stomach, spleen, liver, colon, brain damage in children, alcoholism, and countless other disorders, she still maintains that a 'proper definition' of this non-medical form of healing must eventually come as a result of scientific research.

Like Edgar Cayce, she has shown clairvoyant ability to diagnose at a distance, and has several times done so with accuracy that has astounded and confounded doctors when it led them to a cure for 'hopeless' malfunction.

'Is it the healer?' she has written. 'Is it the patient? Is it the environment? Is it medication or manipulation? Or is it none of these or all of these? Perhaps something else is at work. One physician called it "the wisdom of the body", another, "the intelligence of the cell". A member of the clergy would call it "God". A scientist may say "it is the operation of law". We can conclude that the most any healer can do is to provide conditions that permit healing to take place.'

Not mentioned by her is the ingredient of compassion and dedication to helping others, for never over the long years of faithful healing assistance for anyone who asked for it, have Ambrose or Olga Worrall asked remuneration or even 'love offerings'.

Channelling this healing power over the course of time, not only to humans, but to dogs, cats, horses, birds and chickens, in 1967, the Worralls agreed to participate in a novel distant prayer experiment with Dr Robert N. Miller, an industrial research scientist who hoped to prove the power of prayer on the growth of plants.[98]

3A SCIENCE LOOKS AT HEALING POWER

DR MILLER had become interested in 'the power of prayer on plants' when reading a book of that name by the Rev Franklin Loehr,[85] which described a group of people praying systematically for plants to thrive, resulting in a growth acceleration up to 20 per cent. But the experiments had not been undertaken scientifically, and therefore lacked veridity.

Using apparatus based on a method originally developed by Dr H. H. Kleuter of the US Department of Agriculture, Dr Miller would be able to measure the growth rate of plants to within a thousandth of an inch per hour. The tip of the plant would be connected to a lever arm which was mounted to a pivot on an electro-mechanical transducer capable of translating the motion of the lever arm to an electrical signal, and in turn going to a strip chart recorder which gave a read-out. When the plant grew at a constant rate a straight line would be generated and the slope of this line would be proportional to the growth rate of the plant.

After some difficulty in finding plants that grew in a way convenient for testing Dr Miller chose rye grass seeds, because rye grass grows from the bottom of its blades upwards, enabling measurement by the apparatus.

Ten rye grass seeds were planted in good soil and growing conditions assisted by fluorescent lighting and daily watering. They soon began to sprout, and when Dr Miller had stabilized the growth rate at six thousandth of an inch per hour for several days, he felt the time had come for the test prayers to begin. Telephoning the Worralls in Baltimore from Atlanta (some 600 miles distant), he asked them to start their prayers for the plants at their usual nine o'clock prayer-time.

The Worralls complied. They visualized the plants growing vigorously and luxuriantly under ideal conditions. The next day, when Dr Miller studied the strip chart, he found that at nine o'clock precisely the trace which had been constant began to deviate from a straight line, and by eight o'clock the next morning the growth rate had increased to 0·0525 inch per hour, an increase of 840 per cent.

Although in the next forty-eight hours the growth-rate decreased somewhat, it never returned to its former rate. Dr Miller checked lighting, temperature, humidity and every conceivable variable, but no explanation other than the Worrall's prayers could be found for this extraordinary burst of growth.

Another experiment, in January 1974 (sponsored by the Ernest Holmes Research Foundation), involving Dr Miller, Olga Worrall and Dr Philip B. Reinhart, head of the Physics Department at Agnes Scott College, Georgia, has exciting promise for the possibility of determining whether the energy of a healer's hands is of some scientifically measurable type.[133]

For the purpose, a cloud chamber was used. This is an atomic detection device developed by nuclear physicists to make the path of high energy particles visible, and the experimental procedure was to place hands around the apparatus to see if they might exert influence on its uniform vapour pattern.

In preliminary experiments, members of the research team in the physics laboratory held their own hands around the chamber, without effect – but when Olga Worrall placed hers at the sides of the chamber and visualized energy flowing from her hands (as she does when healing patients), the researchers saw a wave pattern develop in the vapour parallel to her hands, and seemed to move vertically from her palms.

Presently, to test the validity of the waves, Olga Worrall altered the position of her hands by 90 degrees; the waves also altered course, and moved at a perpendicular angle to their first direction.

In March the same year, another experiment attempted to determine if Olga Worrall could achieve the same effect at a distance. On an arranged evening, when the cloud chamber was confirmed as being in a 'steady-state' condition, the research team telephoned Olga Worrall 600 miles away in Baltimore and asked her to begin. She then repeated both the experiments 'mentally', using her normal absent healing technique. The cloud chamber was again affected in the same way. Photographs were taken of the vapour before, during and after the experiments. It was discovered that the aftermath of energy turbulence in the chamber took about eight minutes to subside.

Olga Worrall herself felt that this followed the usual process of healing energy, that it equated with the healing activation of the cells, but the researchers, while finding support for the theory of some form of measurable energy-emission from her hands, and, in the cloud chamber, an acceptably scientific measuring device, could not make a definitive statement without many repeated and even more rigorously controlled experiments. Such experiments are being continued under the auspices of the Ernest Holmes Research Foundation.

Healing power had been subjected to another kind of experiment two years earlier, when Dr Bernard Grad,[47] of the Allan Memorial Institute of Psychiatry at McGill University, Montreal, conducted a rigorously scientific experiment on the biological effects of the laying-on-of-hands.

For his experiment he used forty-eight female mice all of the same strain and age, all equally treated, fed, housed (in single steel 'stalls'), and kept at the same room-temperature, but for the test divided into three groups. All were anaesthetized and an oval-shaped piece of skin measuring $\frac{1}{2}$ inch in diameter cut from their backs. A tracing of the wound was made on paper, to record its exact size, and the removed skin weighed.

One group of mice was treated by a man called Oskar Estebany, a retired Hungarian Army colonel from Montreal who had considerable success with healing by the laying-on-of-hands. He would place the treatment cage in his hands with the cage resting on his left hand and place his right hand over the cage without touching it, and attempt to heal the wounds of the mice for two periods of fifteen minutes each per day, for five days a week. The other groups of mice did not receive the 'radiation energy' of his hands.

At the end of fourteen days, the wounds of the mice given the laying-on-of-hands treatment were only two thirds as large as the wounds of the mice who were not held. A statistical analysis was made of the wound-measurements taken on the eleventh and fourteenth days, and to be sure the results were accurate, another test was run by Dr Grad; the second results were the same. There was significant indication that during the treatment period some form of healing energy had flowed from the healer's hands to the mice.

In previous experiments with Oskar Estebany (who had treated people with thyroid diseases before he came to Canada), Dr Grad who had done studies in thyroid physiology studied the effects of healing on mice made goitrous by a low-iodine diet, which he accentuated with a drug to produce abnormal enlargement of the thyroid.

The object of the experiments had been to see whether laying-on-of-hands could prevent this enlargement process from manifesting. The very technical details are omitted here, but basically the experiment consisted of the three groupings of mice, two control groups and one receiving the laying-on-of-hands treatment in the same fifteen-minute, twice-daily pattern as the later experiment. One difference was that the control group was given an

electro-thermal heat treatment to duplicate the temperature of
heat in the box under the hands of the healer: this was to ascertain
whether the heat element from the hands was a factor in the
healing effect.

This was a six-weeks experiment, in which it was found that
while the laying-on-of-hands did not totally prevent the goitre
enlargement, it significantly slowed it down; the control group
developed goitre faster in both the extra heat and unheated
conditions.

Dr Grad acknowledges that this iodine-instigated goitre condition in mice does not compare with the often psychosomatically-
caused goitre of humans, but the healing element nonetheless
seemed confirmed.

In another goitre experiment, two groups of mice were treated
alternately, one as the control group, the other treated this time
not with unobstructed laying-on-of-hands, but with cotton-and-
wool pads which had been held between Oskar Estebany's hands
to permeate them with his 'healing energy', then placed in the
cages with the mice for one hour in the morning and afternoon
each day. The results were exactly the same as with the unobstructed laying-on-of-hands.

Even another, the third of Dr Grad's thyroid-healing experiments, was approached from a different aspect. This time the
goitres were allowed to develop for a period of six weeks prior
to healing treatment. Again divided into two groups, one group
was given the extra electro-thermal heat, and the other the regular
laying-on-of-hands. The mice, at the end of the six weeks, had
also been taken off the iodine-deficient diet and given adequate
iodine, so that without the healing treatment the goitres decreased
– but with the treated group the decrease was significantly greater.

Like Dr Miller, his next project was to study plants to see if
healing worked as well as it had on small animals, and perhaps to
find a quicker form of experiment (the previous ones had been
exhaustingly time-consuming). The first experiment was an
attempt to germinate barley seeds on damped blotting paper to
see if one lot germinated faster than another with healing treatment – but it did not. So next, Dr Grad and his colleagues
attempted the same experiment with seeds planted in soil – but

the missing element was a way to make the plants 'sick', in order to prove healing.

They did this by dousing them with salt water, a well-known method of inhibiting plant growth. Putting the seeds in a state of moisture-need, Oskar Estebany would place his hands on the seed pots and also 'heal' the saline solution before it was poured on. Another set of pots was left untreated.

From this experiment it was discovered that the pots did not even need to be held if the saline solution had first been treated by the healer, and only the first or initial water with its 1 per cent of salt needed to be treated. The results showed that all treated plant material came up higher and more abundantly than the untreated. But to rule out chance, the experiment was later repeated, minus any laying-on-of-hands of either group, to see if the variation was simply biological. The result here showed a decided difference that had to be attributed to the healer's treatment of the saline solution.

Carrying these healing experiments to their furthest limits, Dr Grad and Oskar Estebany now worked to see if saline solution in glass-stoppered bottles held in the healer's hands for half-an-hour, then applied to the barley seedlings, would also stimulate their growth more than the controlled, untreated group. It did, significantly.

Dr Grad went on to search out the possible positive or negative effects of people's states of mind on plant growth. Working with subjects in psychotic depression and other neurotic states, and with those of opposite disposition, he persuaded them to hold disguised bottles of saline solution in their hands for half-an-hour at a time. There were control subjects, and sometimes the study subjects were told what the object was they were holding, sometimes not.

This large, ambitious experiment showed that the most acutely depressed person had the most adverse effect on the seed's growth, but apart from that, the human variables, the changes of mood and feeling, made the experiment too complex for concrete assumptions.

Science and healing met again through another experiment involving Oskar Estebany. This time with a study undertaken by

Sister Justa Smith,[143] a Franciscan nun, biochemist, and Chairman of the Natural Sciences Concentration at Rosary College in Buffalo, New York.

After a talk given at Rosary College by Dr Grad, Sister Justa had suggested challengingly that if the healer, Oskar Estebany, could do these things, he must also be able to affect enzyme activity. A grant resulted, and a project towards which Sister Justa retained her reserve of scepticism. A slim, orderly person (she wears ordinary streetclothes) of balanced enthusiasm and purpose, her proposal was to compare the laying-on-of-hands of Oskar Estebany with 'the magnetic field effect' (the area of study in which she had received her doctorate) on the enzyme, trypsin. These enzymes (organic substances produced by living cells, which act as catalysts in chemical changes) were in crystalline form as opposed to those already in the human body (where the healing might be discounted because the disorder could have been imaginary to begin with), and would remain intact for just four hours. Only within this limitation could any healing effect be properly appraised. Each day, therefore, new enzyme trypsin was prepared in a solution of 0·3 normal hydrochloric acid. At first, Oskar Estebany was asked to treat the solvent itself, and then the solution was made up with the enzyme, but there was no effect from his healing treatment. However, when the healer held the vials of water-like solution in his hands for long periods of the allotted time, there was definite increased enzyme activity.

Dr Grad said that healers were never asked to heal a well person, and suggested that a more definitive change might result from healing treatment on damaged enzymes, exposed to a wave length of ultraviolet irradiation at 2,537 angstroms. Samples of undamaged enzymes were prepared for comparison, then Oskar Estebany held the vials of damaged enzymes in his hands for periods of ninety minutes. Every fifteen minutes a technician would enter the room where he was sitting, remove a sample for measurement and re-cork the vial. He would then continue. Another batch of control vials was exposed to a high magnetic field of 13,000 gauss.

The technically complex charts, when analysed for time relativity and other elements, indicated that the healing power of Oskar

Estebany's hands had been equal to the effect of the magnetic field of 13,000 gauss. In other words, their healing effect was qualitatively and quantitatively similar to that of a magnetic field, implying that healing can be induced by a magnetic field. (Research on this very possibility, with animals, was carried out by scientists at the University of Illinois and the Waldermar Medical Research Foundation in Long Island, New York.)

Responding to the question of whether there could be a magnetic field between the healer's hands, Sister Justa and her technicians made a test with an extremely sensitive gaussmeter – there was no registration; whatever the power was, it was not the kind that could, of itself, be measured.

Since many questions remained in Sister Justa's mind, she arranged for the healer to cooperate in a follow-up study a few months later. This time there were several changes in the circumstances of Estebany's working conditions – he could not stay at the college, where he had been very happy and comfortable, but had to be brought there each day by his family. There was violent 'Buffalo' weather, and Sister Justa was so laden with other work that she had to relegate much of the project to helpers. Also, the healer had a personal problem on his mind. The result of these alterations had the effect of decreasing his healing power, and making the outcome negative. However, to Sister Justa this was also significant, for it confirmed what healers themselves had always claimed, that the state of mind of the healer was fundamental to the success of healing.

Other tests on enzymes were conducted by Sister Justa with local people who believed they had healing power. The results were mixed and inconclusive, but in one test, when three healers attempted to release energy in the enzymes, all three effected a *reduction* in the enzymes' activity. Sister Justa ran this test several times, but the results were always the same. Then, examining the requirements of the enzymes more closely, she discovered that if the release of energy had been increased it would have been wasted – so, by slowing it down, a therapeutic conservation had been achieved. This was a case of the healing power exhibiting its own law.

Sister Justa is not very happy with the word 'energy' when

applied outside the measurable scientific spectrum of energies, but feels that there may be another whole spectrum that we don't know about yet.

'My specific contribution to a better understanding of the phenomenon of healing,' she says, 'is based upon several assumptions: first, that therapy by the laying-on-of-hands is an established fact, and second, that disease is a failure of adaptation to environment. Third, whereas medicines attempt to change the environment, paranormal healing assists somehow in the adaptation to the environment by helping to provide the right climate for healing – because we know it is a fact that the body heals itself.'

Healers themselves, what they are like as people, why they are able to channel the healing, and the possibilities inherent in understanding and encouraging their potential abilities, in 1956 became the focus of a long, intensive study by Dr Shafica Karagulla, Member of the Royal College of Surgeons in England, the Royal College of Physicians in Edinburgh, and an orthodox physician with a world-wide eminence in the field of neuro-psychiatry. Persuaded by a friend to read a book about Edgar Cayce's work, she was struck by the incredible evidence of his diagnoses and treatments. His abilities to see fields of force around people (auras), and relate them to their state of mind or health, his profound insights, could not be explained by any known category of her science of the brain and nervous system. Either she could forget about it, leave it a puzzle, or accept the fact that these amazing abilities could exist outside science.

She discovered she could not do the former, and devised a plan: she would spend several months reading everything she could find on unusual gifts such as Cayce's, labelling the talent 'Higher Sense Perception' (higher than the final known sense). Then she would search out as many of these 'sensitives' as possible and establish a research system to test them.

All this tended to be accumulatively elusive. Many proved to be fraudulent, self-deceived, or psychiatric cases. A serious project seemed impractical.

Eventually, however, she found her way to some genuine subjects, her confidence in a project grew, and she decided to take the plunge – she turned down a fine academic post she had been offered, gave up her teaching at the New York Medical School and prepared for what she called 'The Journey of the Open Mind'.

Travelling against the current of orthodoxy was entirely new to Dr Karagulla, but she was too inspired to be daunted; despite occasional rebuff in her world-wide journeying for information, and many fruitless interviews, her huge undertaking gradually gathered momentum. She turned up people in all walks of life, often intellectual leaders or high up in their professions, who had extraordinary abilities of perception. 'Kay', for instance, could 'tune in' on another person, and feel his or her pain, having to shut her eyes to prevent equal suffering. 'Olivia' could tell the emotions that had been connected with an object (psychometry). 'Dr Kim' in London could see 'an energy field' around patients when they came into her office, and there were many others who could see this same 'energy field'. She wondered if perhaps it was the age-old aura depicted by artists around the heads of saints and in holy visions.

And she found an unexpected and serious interest in what she was attempting among her own colleagues. Still trying to be cautious and conservative in her approach, she was nevertheless besieged with requests to speak to professional groups. In the book she wrote later, *Breakthrough to Creativity*,[69] she tells how 'Professors, doctors, lawyers, businessmen and women and government officials' came quietly to talk with her about their own HSP (Higher Sense Perception) experiences. She was astonished to learn how many members of the medical profession had abilities to diagnose illness through an 'energy field' they saw around the patient, or vortexes of energy connected with or influencing the endocrine system, 'a living, moving web of frequency intimately connected with conditions in the physical body'. Some felt a healing 'heat' in their hands.

None of the long list of physicians and hospital technicians who spoke to her had ever wanted their 'peculiar' gifts known, even though they might use them inadvertently in their work. All were fearful of ridicule, or perhaps of themselves. But when it was brought out, they felt relief in sharing with her and others of the same talent. Dr Karagulla found a tremendous similarity in these talents; they formed such a strong design, in fact, that she was certain it was time for science to take 'cognizance of it'.

Her chief problem was to carry out research with such busy people who had practices and exhausting hours to keep. She dreamed of a clinic where they could come for a few hours now and then.

Meanwhile, her case histories mounted, as did her painstaking records. She found sensitives who had almost limitless range of HSP. Mainly, however, with a fellowship from the Pratt Foundation, she narrowed her research to a few of those outstandingly gifted. These people (two of them presidents of corporations and all pressed for time) cooperated with her fully.

'Diane' could see the actual physical organs of the body, as well as any disfunction. In layman's language, her descriptions were nonetheless medically accurate. She also could see a 'vital or energy body, or field' which 'sub-stands' the dense physical body, a light in shifting frequencies, a range of major and minor vortexes within the energy body, looking like 'spiral cones', and a host of other intricate interplays of energy patterns. She was also an accurate diagnostician of the onset of or progress of disease by means of these energy patterns.

In one case, she diagnosed a famous newspaper columnist's 'whole energy field' at a time when all believed this woman was in good health, describing intestinal obstruction in a way that did not even tally with expected medical symptoms for such a disorder. Not long afterwards, however, this woman had to undergo an operation for an obstruction in the colon which showed on the X-rays exactly as 'Diane' had seen it.

'Diane's' abilities were put to systematic test in the outpatients' department of an Endocrine Clinic connected to a prominent New York hospital, where she sat unobtrusively with Dr Karagulla and made observation which Dr Karagulla noted – later requesting the patient's records and making comparisons. The remarkable results are detailed in her book.

Dr Karagulla began to concentrate her studies on correlating the energy fields round both healthy human beings and those suffering bodily disorders, an 'auric diagnosis'. Her methods of research are also in her book, but the consensus of what these sensitives see is three interweaving 'fields' around the body: the emotional field, a foot to 18 inches around the body and the mental field, extending an average of 2 feet or more beyond the periphery of the body, which are a part of the unified field surrounding the human body. From these, the sensitives can discern many interrelating mind-body effects. For instance, in the presence of someone loved, all three fields may brighten; intellectual stimulation brightens the mental field: a sexual emotion clouds the emotional field and dims the mental field; the energy fields of someone acting on the stage seem to glow and expand to include the audience (later, the unified glow breaks up again into individual fields), and other energy field interplays are infinitely varied within the individual and between groups of individuals.

Dr Karagulla's research has shown that sensitives (whom she has never studied in trance state) may be easily depleted of their own energy, often inhibited by environmental conditions or other people; they tend to be allergic or over-responsive to drugs, extremely sensitized to colours and materials (some can 'taste' colours and see them in varying hues and shapes in the energy fields); generally are intelligent, keenly aware of others, yet balanced and usually cautious of showing or using their gifts. They do not seem to have any common denominator in family backgrounds.

Since one of 'Diane's' talents had been to see the energy patterns of jewels and to discern their changes in conjunction with human touch, light and music, Dr Karagulla also made conducted experiments with crystals and magnets, to see how they could be related to the energy fields around humans. She is still pursuing this area.

Meanwhile, she feels many people may have abilities 'far beyond those developed in the twentieth century'. Apart from the inestimable value for diagnosing and preventing illness, in other words, healing before the manifest disorder, she believes that 'A breakthrough in human consciousness gradually producing numbers of people with Higher Sense Perception can reshape our world. Man must become aware of his superconscious and able to tap this creative level with full awareness.'

One of the increasing number of physicians following the pioneer work of Dr Karagulla, and who have themselves the ability to see auras round their patients, is Dr John Pierrakos, a New York physician and psychiatrist. Like Dr Karagulla, he has had the courage to face against the orthodox current and in his well-established New York practice which combines with his conventional procedures, uses innovative diagnosis of his patients' auras. Nor does he stop with personal application of his ability, but conducts extensive research in the energy fields of both man and nature, including the pulsatory movements of the energy field in the atmosphere, the earth and the ocean. Through his work as Director of the Research Division of the Institute for Bioenergetic Analysis in New York (with Dr Robert A. Zimmerman) he conveys his insights and techniques in treating mentally disturbed patients to other psychiatrists and therapists, both in USA and Europe.

In a detailed monograph published in 1971,[119] Dr Pierrakos (whose work was inspired by Wilhelm Reich's 'Orgone' theory and expanded together with Alexander Lowen) describes the aura in this way:

'All living organisms are surrounded by a radiating luminous envelope which pulsates at a specific rate and has specific layering, hue and structure depending on the species and the states of that organism. This envelope is actually a light cast of another body of energy which penetrates the physical body and spreads its luminous radiations outwards in the periphery and is perceived as the energy field, or aura of that organism. . . . The physical body mirrors what is happening in the energy field.

'When a person stands against a homogeneous background, either very light (sky blue) or very dark (midnight blue), and with certain arrangements so that there is a softness and uniformity in the light, one can clearly see, with the aid of coloured filters (cobalt blue) or with the unaided eye, a most thrilling phenomenon. From the periphery of the body arises a cloud-like, blue-grey envelope which extends for 2 to 4 feet where it loses its distinctness and merges with the surrounding atmosphere. This envelope is brilliant and illuminates the body in the same way as the rays of the rising sun light up the fringes of dark mountains. It swells slowly, for 1 or 2 seconds, away from the body until it forms a nearly perfect oval shape with fringed edges, then, abruptly, it disappears completely . ∴. then there is a pause of 1 to 3 seconds until it reappears again to repeat the process. The process is repeated 15 to 25 times a minute in the average resting person.'

Like Dr Karagulla's sensitives, he also describes the energy field as divided (roughly) into three layers. The inner layer, seen only when close to the subject, is transparent dark space bordered in ultra-violet, and appears to reproduce the form of the body in space. The intermediate layer is made up of multiple shapes and forms, is clearly defined in an over-all shimmering blue-grey liquid, particularly brilliant around the head. The effect is that 'of a stream of fire-flies extinguishing their glow at rapid intervals'. The third and outer layer can expand as far as 100 feet from the person, is indefinite, thin, transparent and a delicate sky-blue colour. Its movement is spiral or vertical, seeming to expand in all directions like compressed gas molecules when the volume of the container is increased, becoming diffused and lost at its margins.

This energy field seen in the envelope surrounding the human organism is a modified form of the energy flowing inside the body, and Dr Pierrakos says that by 'studying its characteristics, we can find out its true movement, composition and consistency, and the changes that occur in pathological conditions or in the simple processes of life with its variations.'

So far, this consideration of energy fields (auras) has been through sense-awareness, either natural to certain people, or achieved by HSP training. A more concrete, and therefore more far-reaching confirmation of their existence has emerged from the discoveries of Dr Harold Saxton Burr of the Yale University Medical School.

For forty years, together with Dr F. S. C. Northrup (also of Yale) and other associates, Dr Burr pursued an 'Electro-dynamic Theory of Life', which postulated that there were electro-dynamic fields of life, which he called 'L-fields', around every living thing. With instruments developed to measure these fields, he was able to prove the theory for trees and plant life, but these were not sufficiently sensitive to extend the proof to human beings.

After protracted and painstaking experiment, an instrument was finally devised that could register the tiny electrical voltages in all living systems. This 'voltmeter' (which is nowadays commercially available and found in most physics laboratories), was able to show that all living things on this planet, from seeds to man, are moulded and controlled by this L-field, which is like the blueprint of the living manifestation.

In the book Dr Burr has written of these studies called *Blueprint for Immortality*[19] (of which one half is for the lay reader, and the other for scientists), the L-field, or 'blueprint' is described as that which keeps us recognizable to one another and ourselves, keeps our basic design intact while the material of our bodies is ceaselessly renewed or replaced.

As Dr Burr explains: 'Something like this – though infinitely more complicated – happens in the human body. Its molecules and cells* are constantly being torn apart and rebuilt with fresh material from the food we eat. But, thanks to the controlling L-field, the new molecules and cells are rebuilt as before and arrange themselves in the same pattern as the old ones . . . for example, all the protein in the body is "turned over" every six months and in some organs such as the liver, the protein is renewed more frequently. When we meet a friend we have not seen for six months, there is not one molecule in his face which was there when we last saw him. But, thanks to his controlling L-field, the new molecules have fallen into the old, familiar pattern and we can recognize his face.'

The implication of detecting and recording L-fields goes far beyond healing – showing as it does that the universe is an ordered system, the human organism an ordered component – but for diagnosis of illness and other life processes, it has vast potential.

*According to Dr. Hudson Hoagland, the well-known American biologist, there are 60,000 million cells in the human body and 500,000 million cells of some types die every day and are replaced by new ones – also 'the whole of the protein of which the human body is largely made up is replaced in roughly 160 days'. (*Design for Destiny*, by Edward Russell (1971), with quote of Sir Charles Dodd.)

For example, the measurement of L-fields has already shown that there is a voltage rise during the ovulation period in females which lasts about twenty-four hours. This is helpful for couples who have been unable to have children, pinpointing a favourable time for conception, also for family planning and birth control. In experiments at New York's Bellevue Hospital the voltage measurement was able to diagnose internal malignancies in 95 out of 102 women. These beginnings will undoubtedly lead to many other valuable means of internal diagnosis.

Dr Leonard J. Ravitz, Jr., a psychiatrist on the staff at Yale University, made the original discovery in Dr Burr's laboratory that the voltmeter showed gradient changes during the hypnosis process. His later studies led to revelation that changes in mental states made changes in the voltage patterns of L-fields. Using electro-metric techniques on psychiatric patients in hospitals he showed that symptoms such as schizophrenia, and emotions of fear and stress, could be detected, and that equally the result of therapy could be appraised when the voltage gradients returned to normal. This meant that diagnoses could both anticipate the possible onset of a condition, and confirm its healing.

Possibilities inherent in L-field measurements of the living system stretch as far as the imagination and needs of man, waiting only for more sensitive instruments – for those which have so far been developed can register only an infinitesimal amount of this Life Field that connects us with a universal Field. But since it has been conceived by mind, it will surely be further developed by the same means: some day the voltmeter may take its place in our history as the first scientific probe of the invisible.

3B AN ANCIENT HEALING TECHNIQUE
BRIDGES EAST AND WEST

*The superior doctor prevents illness; the mediocre doctor
imminent illness; the inferior doctor treats actual illness.*
OLD CHINESE PROVERB

WHILE the West put its toe into the increasingly temperate
waters of non-medical healing, followed by a careful foot into
various energy-fields, it was given a sudden, unexpected push in
the back from an ancient method of healing, with no alternative
but to get wet, if not to swim.

The push resulted from a series of events in the early seventies
when several eminent American physicians, taking advantage of
the reopening of China to Westerners, went to observe Chinese
medicine at work and came back to report to the public, the
President and the American Medical Association on the validity
and efficacy of the art of acupuncture.

In turn, this had led to an investigation by President Nixon's
personal physician, Dr Walter Tkach, and a pronouncement by
him in 1972 that something was important here that 'we had
better take a good look at', with a view to using it clinically.

Since the art of acupuncture (Zheu Jiu), dating back at least
5,000 years in Chinese history, is founded on the Taoist principle
of *yin* and *yang* – the female and male aspects of life energy, which
must be kept in balance for health and happiness – this official
boost was in essence a betrayal of orthodoxy.

Soon, however, with all the publicity, the flood of articles and
books on acupuncture and the eye-witness reports (some by Dr
Tkach himself) – of operations carried out with complete anaesthesia achieved simply by the insertion of thin sharp needles into
certain points on the patient's body: with the patient able to
converse and even smile while an abdomen was opened up, and
then get up from the operating table with little or no help and
walk to the vehicles for returning them to their rooms – almost
excessive medical interest resulted. All over the country there

were doctors who wanted to learn how to fit this form of healing into their practice.

They learned that this, unfortunately, was not easy. There was no easily-acquired training: it took time, as much time, in fact, as training for a medical degree, and that while in western Europe there were at least a thousand doctors practising acupuncture, another thousand or so in Russia and a few hundred in South America (Japan has over 25,000 and China over a million acupuncturists), in America there were only a very few to give that training. These had been able to practise only with a letter from a licensed physician that acupuncture was required (otherwise acupuncture is against the law in the US), and now they were suddenly called on to explain and elucidate – for *someone* had to train others, in order to train yet others.

From Chinatown in New York, where acupuncture had been carried on clandestinely for many years, Dr Ching Yuen Ting, only recently established in America, found himself much in demand as a lecturer to medical societies. It had taken Dr Ting, a fourth-generation acupuncturist (whose father had founded the Shanghai Acupuncture School), six years to learn acupuncture, four in school and two as an intern. He had had to learn the five elements of the *Nei Ching* (The Yellow Emperor's Classic of Internal Medicine), metal, water, wood, earth and fire – these symbolized all of nature and man, and all was either yin or yang – the liver, heart, kidneys, spleen and lungs, for instance, were yin organs, and the gall bladder, stomach bladder and small and large intestines were yang.

He also went to school to learn herbal medicine, because in China, acupuncture is only one part of herbalism. It was not very easy to explain this scientifically to American physicians. Nor did Dr Ting know of the more advanced studies of China itself (with which America seemed so preoccupied), with anaesthesia. What *he* did was basic acupuncture treatment.

This treatment consists of an examination, a use of senses in appraisal, particularly of touch to ascertain points of soreness or tenderness, the checking of twelve pulses, which tell him which organs are not in balance, which causing the illness. (He does not use psychology or tell them how the needles work, so no suggestion from him is involved.) The hair-fine needles he uses are up to 5 inches long, but the one he uses varies with the area to be reached and the build of his patient.

The premise of acupuncture is that the body has twelve main meridians (bilateral lines or channels which connect organs deep in the body to surface points), and each of the meridians has a point of stimulation. For example, if the heart point is stimulated, there will be an increase of energy-flow through the pulse of the heart. There is a point of sedation for each of the meridians, and since the organs are paired, if the heart is stimulated, the lung will be sedated. There are perhaps 1,000 acupuncture points on the body, or the possibility of many more. When the fine steel needle (in ancient times they were made of bone, and later porcelain) is inserted at an acupuncture point, and gently twirled or manipulated (they cause no pain), it has the effect of redirecting the energy-flow along the meridians so that the imbalance is corrected. The Chinese call the utilization of this energy-flow 'Qi' (pronounced chee as in cheese), but how and why it works is not understood, only that it does.

As Dr Ting says . . . 'In spite of all those years, there is no explanation for acupuncture. The place I put the needle has no relation to the nerves. If I treat for a toothache, I will put a needle in the patient's hand, between the thumb and the first finger. There is no connection to the jaw. It is very hard for science to prove that acupuncture works. For me, the patients are proof.'

The first over-reactive wave of interest in America, and subsequent scientific resistance, has since settled into steadier momentum of research and cautious application. The National Health Institute in late 1972 announced an intensive study with a committee of experts in neurology, neurophysiology, psychology and neuropharmacology. Their aim was to probe acupuncture's function as an anaesthetic, to determine whether it could make sense in Western traditions of physiology and psychology, and to experiment with normal individuals in contrast to those with certain nervous disorders.

Dr Han Twu Chiang, an anaesthiologist at Massachusetts

General Hospital, planned to study changes in the skin's electrical potential after the needles had been inserted, to try and establish a scientific explanation for how acupuncture works. Several medical institutions, such as the California Medical Center, and the Institute of Rehabilitation and Medicine in New York, have studied acupuncture in the framework of American medicine.

The many clinics and lay practices of acupuncture without proper training do not succeed for long, despite long lists of willing and eager clients. In America, it will still be some time before acupuncture is a routine component of healing therapies. Although there is as yet no precise explanation of how aspirin works, and that despite its known dangers it is one of the most widely prescribed medicines, for acupuncture a verifiable scientific explanation is demanded.

Meanwhile, in Russia, another approach to acupuncture has been developed. Instead of needles this uses an electro-acupuncture detecting instrument invented by the Soviet physicist Victor Adamenko.[112] Called a 'tobioscope', the transistorized instrument contains photo-electric cells which record the skin resistance over 'acupoints' and meridians. When the imbalance is registered, they use various means to restore the balance in energy-flow, sometimes with massage, sometimes electrical stimulation, or salves and ointments. More recently, they have experimented with laser beams. There is complexity in these means because individuals vary, as do races, in their location of acupuncture points. Others, in America, are also experimenting with instrumental measuring of acupuncture points: Kendall R. Johnson, who is President of Paraphysics, Inc. (and associated with Dr Thelma Moss of UCLA), has invented a device called the 'acuometer', for the detection of special points on the skin which seem to tally with those of Chinese acupuncture points. A silver clip is attached to the ear of a subject and a brass probe moves around his body, causing the subject to respond like an electric battery; when a concentration of electrolytes is found by the probe, the instrument gives a signal and a bulb lights up. There is, apparently, a particularly responsive area between the nose and upper lip, and a point like this has, he believes, 'special, electrical, chemical and thermal characteristics'. This approach, too, has its complexities, in that there are disruptive elements such as moisture on the skin, but further experiments are in process.

At a recent annual Congress of the International Society of Acupuncture (headquarters in France) several techniques of acupuncture were disclosed. One was to apply high-frequency sound to the acupuncture point on the body – called 'sono-puncture', and for assistance in diagnosis a computer had been designed to calculate the effects of needle insertions; symptoms could be fed in as information and guidance for treatment automatically produced.

Dr J. R. Worsley,[176] who has practised acupuncture in England for nearly thirty years and is President of the College of Chinese Acupuncture, feels that he needs another lifetime even to understand a fraction of the knowledge filtered down through the ages from Chinese masters of the art. He wonders whether these instrumental approaches can be sensitive enough of the whole process involved, which incorporates an ability on the part of the practitioner to blend his own 'Qi' energy, in mind and body, to balance with his patient's. He feels that each application is individual and personal and that an electrical instrument might be a clumsy intrusion. A sense of the yin and yang of life, of the positive and negative elements of life-energy, the circadian rhythms of 'body-time' which wax and wane, and of man as a microcosm of the universe, all make it a study that concerns the whole person rather than the particular illness involved.

In the past, Dr Worsley's practice has consisted mainly of patients given up by the medical profession, but recently, patients come to him increasingly for symptomatic treatments, or to offset the effects of medication-dependence. He has travelled to the United States to contribute his experience to the training of doctors, eager to devote their efforts and time to a sound understanding of the process.

Dr Felix Mann, a London acupuncturist with a different approach, one that holds no brief for the yin-yang philosophy, believes the process involves 'dermatone', patches of skin that share nerve endings which are linked to internal organs. But the results of treatment are the same – a needle inserted in the foot can relieve migraine, in the arm, asthma, in the leg correct a liver condition; it is still a matter of balancing the energy flow and is accomplished only with long experience of the body's intricate network of inner and outer relationships. Dr Mann, too, has been called on to lecture in America to hundreds of doctors, medical students and other therapists, and he has written several technical books on the subject.[86]

Chinese practitioners consider Western theories together with their own advancing studies of acupuncture. They have ruled out the theory of hypnosis or psychological effects with experiments on animals, particularly rabbits, which show similar stimulation and sedation reactions to the needles as human patients. One of the most important discoveries to emerge from Chinese research has been in the treatment of deaf children.

The treatment was hit upon after one man, in a research team that was hoping to find a method of restoring hearing and speech to a group of deaf-mute children in a school in Peking, experimented with inserting a needle, much deeper than was considered safe, into his own *Yah-min* point (recommended for deafness). When his hands went numb, he stopped and the numbness went away – but then he kept on inserting the needle deeper and deeper – now his hands went numb as if with electric shock, his neck and throat felt strangled and burning. He took the needle out and saw that it had gone to a point where, according to Chinese tradition, he should not have been alive.

Nevertheless encouraged by the possibilities, the researcher inserted the needle to this same depth in the yah-min point of one of the deaf-mute girls for three days running. Suddenly, she could hear, and at the end of the third day, she could also make sounds. The research team then used this procedure on all the 168 girls in the school; of these, 157 were able to hear, and 149 were able to learn to speak. Unfortunately for the West, there is as yet no experience in locating the yah-min point.

Other startling discoveries of Chinese researchers have been with the mentally ill. Using a combination of acupuncture, herbal medicine, drugs and doctor-patient communication, cures at a mental hospital in Hunan province were said to be close to 80 per cent, some long-considered hopeless.

Although the West is just now considering the science of a healing practice based on a philosophy of nature pre-dating the written word, modern medical students in China are taught acupuncture as well as Western methods, with particular emphasis on anaesthesia (it is said that since the cultural revolution, Chinese physicians have performed over 400,000 operations under acupuncture anaesthesia). This situation resulted from Chairman Mao's directive in the 1950s that the 'great treasure-house' of Chinese traditional medicine be revitalized and merged with Western practices.

Today China has developed a health system that fuses its ancient herbal remedies and acupuncture with a massive scheme of preventive medicine, calisthenics, nationwide campaigns against pestilence, and a vast army of 'barefoot' therapists trained to treat individuals in their local communities for every ailment short of serious illnesses. Fear and mystery of the body's functions are dissolved by grass-roots education, which also lessens the mystique of the unavailable physician. Present-day doctors in China, whose remuneration is low, not only have more time to give, and to advance their skills, but do so with humility toward the cause of serving their fellow men. As a consequence, China's health rate has become the highest in the world, indicating that where the whole man is taken into account, not divided into separate compartments, each to be treated as if the other did not exist or relate, the effect may be harmony of mind and body called health.

The unifying energy underlying this health, encoded in Chinese acupuncture and called 'Qi' (Egyptians called it 'ka', the Yogis and Hindus 'prana', the Hawaiians 'mana'), might well be the L-fields of Dr Burr, or that which the Russians call 'bio-plasma'; its scientific identity has not yet been conclusively deciphered. However, some clarification of this could come from a device that appears to capture the energy visibly, on film.

The method, called Kirlian photography, is named after the Soviet researchers Semyon and Valentina Kirlian, who in 1939 re-discovered 'electrography', a form of photography by means of high-frequency currents, and spent over twenty years experimenting with its potential.[112]

The photographic process, achieved without a camera, lens or source of light, resulted from an electric discharge between an object and an electrode. The object, a leaf, coin or fingertip (which is particularly convenient) was positioned between condenser-like plates, and film (any ordinary kind) placed with its emulsion side towards the object, leaving a small gap between. An electrical charge was then pulsed across the plates, and the picture developed in a dark room.

Though some doubts about the validity of the experiments have been expressed (*see* below), the great stir of scientific interest in this technique lay in what appeared on the pictures. For from the objects photographed there emanated radiant patterns of colours, and even more intriguing, these emanations differed in colour intensity and colour-pattern, picture to picture. Experiments in photographing leaves showed not only their intricate internal patterning of lights and colours, but when one leaf was cut from its stem and photographed, the subsequent pictures showed the lights fading away progressively as it withered. Another remarkable picture showed the intact 'energy body' outline of a leaf of which a part had been cut away.

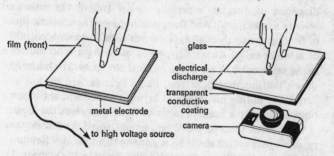

Figure 10 Two types of Kirlian apparatus. (Based on theories of William Tiller and David Boyers.)

(Psychic magazine)

The Kirlians also found, by accident, that photographs of their hands taken when they were in a hurried or nervous state showed dim, blurred emanations, quite the opposite to those taken in calm moods. They experimented with taking a glass of vodka before one photograph and the hand showed a burst o fiery brilliance. It did seem certain that some form of energy was being captured on film.

In the 1960s, the Kirlians gained official recognition for their work. Funds were provided for full-scale research, and well-known scientists, including a group led by Dr V. Inyushin, a biologist at the Kirov State University of Kazakhstan in Alma-Ata, developed the techniques with more powerful instruments, such as a huge electron microscope.

A theory emerged from their innumerable experiments with living plants, animals and humans: they decided that the energy that surrounded all living things, was made up of 'ionized, excited electrons, protons and possibly other particles', and was not just a 'chaotic' system, but a unit, whole in itself, acting as a unit, a counterpart body of energy. They called it 'The Biological Plasma Body'.

It was further posited that photographing this energy (which could be the scientific explanation for the 'aura', or 'etheric' body) would lead to many scientific breakthroughs of knowledge of the universe, as well as having practical applications in early diagnosis of diseases, especially cancer (where the extra cell activity would show). And there was hope for the scientific proof of healing energy through experiments with Kirlian photographs of a healer called Alexei Krivorotov of Georgia, who practised in the same office as his son, a medical physician. The healer had shown that his thumb, at rest, had a light-pattern of dots and flares, but during his imagined laying-on-of-hands, the emanations had shown a beam of radiance flowing towards the subject.

When news reached the West, several noted American parapsychologists visited the USSR (among them Stanley Krippner, Dr Montague Ullman, Dr William Tiller, Dr J. G. Pratt, Dr Herbert Puryear and Dr Thelma Moss), to investigate Kirlian photography. Disappointingly, they were not admitted to laboratories to see it demonstrated, but were able to talk to Dr Inyushin and Victor Adamenko, who had been involved with the Kirlians' work, and were given scientific literature and blueprints of the device.

On return to America, however, electrical engineers had

difficulty understanding the blueprints and no success in making up the device. In 1971, Dr Thelma Moss gave an interested student in her class at UCLA reprints of the Soviet material. To her amazement, he returned at the end of the course with a Kirlian-like picture of a leaf.

The student, whose name was Kendall Johnson, had made up the device in his father's garage. It was crude, but it worked. Since it was not exactly on the Kirlian principle (which employed much higher frequency), even when technically improved, Dr Moss gave it the Western name of 'radiation photography'. She and Kendall Johnson proceeded to make very extensive experiments, taking many thousands of pictures, using hundreds of human subjects.[103]

They found they could not duplicate everything the Kirlian method had produced – the 'cut-leaf' effect eluded them.* But they did produce some remarkable effects of their own, which not only seemed to corroborate the Kirlian discoveries but to supplement them.

Early in their work they found that the emanations could change drastically and sometimes inexplicably, leaving many questions still to be asked, many experiments still to be done – but the significance of certain results were hard to deny.

With leaves, Dr Moss and her colleague found that there was an 'internal structuring of bubbling' invisible to the eye, which may have been what the Kirlians had described as 'the conversion of non-electrical properties of the object into electrical ones'. They found, also, that leaves reacted to heat, cold and changes in weather, and that when a leaf was gashed or pricked, it showed vivid red blotches that looked like bleeding, though the leaves were actually still green. In a whole leaf that had been cut from its stem, the photograph showed the spine seeming to fill with blue 'bubbles', and numerous black patches appeared on the leaf itself.

Every species of leaf had its own unique internal patterning as well as the extended radiation, and the colours of the leaves found typically in radiation photography were pink, blue, lavender,

*Important in the theory that the intact energy pattern could explain sensation of a remaining limb after amputation.

purple and white (though nearly all were actually green) but generally blazing with orange and red when gashed, fading to a uniform pale blue. (Dr Dennis Milner at the University of Birmingham, UK, who had been working with his own form of electrical photography for eight years, revealed that of thousands of leaves photographed in his laboratory, only one had been green – which was just the number Dr Moss had found.) Experiments in healing the bright red 'bleeding effect' of leaf wounds were started by Dr Tiller, who held such a leaf in his hands for a while, after which it was photographed. The result was inconclusive but led to many experiments, using a control (unwounded) leaf for comparison, and more experienced healers. One such healer made 'magnetic passes' over the leaves at various distances, and as a result some leaves showed a whitish luminescence, overflowing the corona, or aura.

After photographing the leaf-healing process with a large number of volunteer healers, it was found that the luminescence of healing was a fairly general result – only a few had the reverse effect of causing a 'brownish effect' in the photographed leaf. As an inadvertent discovery, it was seen that leaves showed an anticipatory effect to being wounded, or to other leaves about to be wounded, showing the black patches that would appear after the wound. This effect showed clearly and consistently through repeated trials. After healing, the leaves also regularly showed an internal rosy hue. (Dr Moss wondered if this could be the 'rose-coloured prana' mentioned by yogis?)

Dr Moss and Kendall Johnson have also photographed finger pads under innumerable conditions. They found that a normal 'healthy' fingertip emanates a deep blue, with a narrow band of lighter blue delineating the finger and a fringed halo, or corona, beyond of darker blue, with some pink and red here and there. (It is the narrow blue band that most shows the changes in the subject's state of mind.) When some distinctly different state of mind is aroused the blues may disappear to be replaced by vivid red blotches, like those seen in wounded leaves, and a pinkish inner area. The researchers also learned that subjects seemed able to change their coronas by deliberately changing their emotion. States of relaxation (such as with hypnosis, meditation and drugs) for the most part produced a more brilliant and wider aura. Excitement, anger, tension, generally produced reddish blotches.

An interesting study was made of the effects of alcohol. A medical student volunteered to drink an ounce of bourbon whisky every fifteen minutes – until he wanted to stop. The first photograph was taken before he started to drink – there was only a small uneven corona, recognizable to the researchers as usual to states of apprehension. Pictures were then made progressively, through the subject's total 17-ounce intake. As the subject became more and more inebriated, so did the photograph show a wider, more brilliant corona.

In the possibility that this effect was related to the vascular system, comparative studies were made of dilation and constriction, but the corona did not appear changed. In other tests for physiological concomitants, the possibilities of sweat or skin resistance as causes for change were studied. Skin resistance was ruled out, and so was sweat – unless, Dr Moss wondered, there might be two kinds of sweat, one for emotions, the other due to athletic exertion – for fingertips encased in a plastic bag to make them hot, the pictures showed a blotchy corona, while after exercise they generally showed a brighter, wider corona than in a normal state.

The most unexpected and decided effects obtained by Dr Moss's experiments came from noting the change in the corona of a male subject when the male photographer (with whom it was necessary to work in an isolation booth) was suddenly replaced by a female photographer. In the photographs taken thereafter, there was a dramatic brightening of the aura. Further experiments were made in which all circumstances remained the same, and in which the photographer would suddenly leave in the middle of the procedure. Invariably, there was a distinct change in the corona. Good friends working together effected wider, brighter coronas than strangers, so did those of opposite sex, while an authoritative, serious experimenter elicited a small, dimmer corona from the subject than one who was easy-going.

The seemingly tangible evidence of energy interchange between people, brought on further research, primarily in healing. It was found that healers showed brighter coronas before the healing process, the patient's dimmer. After the healing-energy had been conveyed, the healer's corona dimmed and the patient's became brilliant. (This was in reverse in the Kirlian process, but Dr Moss believes the explanation for this might lie in the differences of the two processes – the Kirlian method sends the current up through the plate and into the person, while the Western technique sends the current through the person and down into the plate. For the moment, questions must be left here.)

An ambitious study was undertaken with a group of twelve volunteer terminal kidney patients brought to Dr Moss by Dr Marshall Barshay (a kidney specialist). The patients were all on the dialysis machine, and Dr Barshay's proposal was that he should provide Dr Moss with all their medical records and that Dr Moss should work with healers, using radiation photography to appraise the results.

Dr Moss used a group of control healers (those claiming no healing ability) and the experiment ran three months.

There were no miraculous cures, although some patients showed improvements – but some of the photographs were striking. In one a rosy-pink emanation, not present before treatment, appeared after treatment. The healer, who had had the rosy emanation before treatment, did not show it after treatment (laying-on-of-hands). There was no evidence of such exchange with the control healers and patients. But in one instance, the opposite was found, and the healer received energy – the patient was hospitalized shortly afterwards, leading to the possibility of an interchange of energies which can 'sap' as well as restore. (In her book, Dr Karagulla warns that certain people are 'sappers' of others' energy.)

Experimental work with radiation photography and healing energy has also been carried out by an Englishman, Douglas Dean, of the Newark College of Engineering in New Jersey and President of the New Jersey Parapsychological Association. Some of his results were shown in 1972 at the first Western conference of Kirlian Photography, Acupuncture and the Human Aura, in New York (discussed at length in *Galaxies of Life*[73]) and later in Moscow. With the cooperation of a healer named Ethel DeLoach, and using Czechoslovakian-designed equipment of higher voltage, longer pulse, much higher frequency and longer exposure than that of Dr Moss, his aim was to confirm the Russian work.

Ethel DeLoach proved to be an excellent subject. A healer of well-established success who feels she tunes into 'Universal Energy' which instantly responds (equally for all, when it is realized and developed), she has developed a method of passing her hands over the body of a patient following invisible pathways which she senses and re-directs into harmony, much as if she were balancing the energy-flow of acupuncture meridians, with her hands instead of needles.

Pictures taken by Douglas Dean showed similar effect to that of the healer Krivorotov's thumb, in Russia.[35] Photographed at rest, and then when thinking of healing (but not actually in the process), the mid-finger of Ethel DeLoach's left hand showed a marked change; from a moderately bright corona at rest, as she thought of healing, the flares brightened and extended considerably.

This effect was obtained through many repeated trials; also photographs taken during her actual healing procedure showed the strongly-increased emanations.

The implications for high voltage photography and acupuncture were noted by Soviet surgeon, Dr Mikhail Gaikin who, having visited the Kirlians and seen their remarkable pictures, wondered what the reason could be for all the extraordinary effects that looked like fireworks, except for their strangely replicated colours and seemingly ordered patterns. Were these the electrical translations of 'Qi', of the Vital Energy of life in operation? If so, could the several hundred acupuncture points be shown up on film? Could acupuncture and Kirlian photography become complementary techniques, merging the visible and invisible, making claims of the psychics and mystics scientific fact?

Although work of many researchers supports this possibility, there are those not satisfied that factual evidence as yet exists. Recent experiments by Professor Tiller and his graduate assistant, David Boyers, at Stanford Research Institute, sought to explore further the actual processes by which the film is exposed and the colours created.

Their findings supported their theory that the film might be exposed by blue and ultraviolet light resulting from electrical sparks created in the air space between the object and the source of the electricity, and that when they strictly controlled the physical conditions such as voltage, finger moisture, time and spacing, the coronas became consistent and all the mysterious variations attributed to altered states of mind were missing.

The researchers reluctantly assumed that Kirlian photography would have to be re-examined. Since that time, however, Dr Tiller has continued his experimentation and still believes that more sensitive and improved experimental apparatus – which can overcome the difficulty of detecting non-physical energies that exist with purely 'sensor systems' designed only for observation at the physical level – Kirlian or radiation photography will yet become invaluable both as a medical diagnostic aid and guide to altered states of consciousness.

Many other researchers in all parts of the world continue to experiment in this field, which, if validated, would be of major importance to mankind. Funds are the main necessity for its progress, and for the training to combine skills of both East and West.

3C MEDICAL AND NON-MEDICAL HEALING COMBINE IN NEW TECHNIQUES

THE role of mind in disease may have been widely acknowledged in the latter half of this century – but within set limits. There are still diseases which the medical profession, and consequently the public, consider unrelated to mental influence, of completely physical causation. Although the number of these is gradually decreasing as a mind-factor becomes recognizable – as, for instance, in tuberculosis, where emotion has been found of signal importance in both immunization and cure – for the most part cancer is one that stays firmly in the physical category.

In many of the new, less orthodox religions and Eastern philosophies, this view has not been shared; to these, mind is the sole creator, there is no exception and nothing incurable. When mind and emotions are out of balance, the cells of natural immunity lose their efficiency. But just as mind out of balance creates an effect in the body, so the mind may re-create balance and restore the body to health.

Recently, some innovative research and experiment by Dr Carl Simonton,[141] who until 1974 when he went into private practice was Chief of Radiological Therapy at Travis Air Force Base, California, has shown significant evidence of the role of mind in cancer therapy which is gaining support, not only of many potential victims of the disease, but a number of forward-looking physicians of conventional medicine.

His ideas in this direction began to take shape when he was training as a radiation therapist at the University of Oregon and became somewhat despondent about the responses to treatment of cancer patients. There was a mystery in their inconsistency that nagged him – why did those who were expected to recover often get worse, and those expected to get worse often improve? What was the underlying ingredient eluding medical logic? No less sceptical than his colleagues, he nevertheless decided to do some retrospective studies of patients who got well, the ones who defied diagnosis, the 'winners' as opposed to the 'losers', to see if there was some common denominator helping to pull them through.

He had access to and studied many hospital records, spent time talking to older practitioners, and to patients themselves. As the evidence accumulated, it became increasingly clear that there *was* one common factor – the patient's desire to get well, an impelling need to stay alive, a strong will to do so, a strong positive attitude.

Dr Simonton then wondered if there was some way to teach this attitude to patients. Could they possibly take an active part in their own recovery? (He had found that he was not the first to think of this by any means, but there had been no organized research or experiments along these lines within the medical field.)

About that time the work of Joe Kamiya, Elmer Green, Thelma Moss and others with biofeedback, showed a person could consciously control such physiological functions and disorders as pulse rate, blood pressure, gastric acidity, skin resistance and temperature (even epilepsy), and he further wondered if this basic principle could not be applied to other controls within the body, such as of foreign or 'insane' cells.

But first, he must find a way to improve the patient's state of mind. He read up on positive thinking, tried meditation, reviewed what he knew of psychiatry and looked into techniques for galvanizing salesmen to succeed.

From a combination of these, he formed a procedure – then looked for a patient who would be willing to experiment with him. He found a 61-year-old man with far-advanced throat cancer, who agreed to cooperate.

To this man, whose weight was down to 95 pounds, who could not eat, had great difficulty in breathing or swallowing and who was extremely weak, Dr Simonton, after close study of the man's personal history, background and character, proposed the following:

First, meditation: he was to sit in a comfortable position, breathe in and out, and every time he breathed out to say mentally to himself the word 'relax', and to concentrate on relaxing the muscles around his eyes, in his throat and jaw – for no more than two-and-a-half minutes. Then he was to picture a pleasant scene, perhaps one from his past that gave him great pleasure – this, for another minute-and-a-half. After this he was to picture his tumour the way it seemed to him (Dr Simonton had talked to him extensively about it) – and presently to picture the radiation treatment as bullets of energy, seeing them interact with both the normal cells and the tumour cells. He was to visualize how the normal cells would repair themselves and how the cancer cells would die – and his own immunity mechanism – those white blood cells coming in and picking up the dead and dying cancer cells and carrying them out of the body in the normal way, the way the body normally defends and heals itself.

He was to do this three times a day – after he got up in the morning, at noon, and just before going to bed at night. The man did this unfailingly for seven weeks, except for one day when, to his despair, he was interrupted.

Dr Simonton could hardly believe the result; the man, who

had only between 5 and 10 per cent chance to live, could be released and later had no side effects. (Later, using the same technique, the enthusiastic patient also recovered from arthritis.)

Dr Simonton was so encouraged by this initial success, that he continued applying this method when he began practice at Travis Air Base, where he met with cooperation from the medical staff. Here, he set up some scales for measuring the patient's attitude – a five-point scale going from double negative to double positive, from the totally uncooperative patient to the fully cooperative patient. On twelve patients thus assessed the staff voted independently, grading the patients from poor to excellent on composite graphs made of correlating the attitudes with the responses.

Consistently, the negative patients had the poor response – the more positive, the better, and all the excellent responses were either positive or doubly positive. Only two patients out of the first fifty thus scaled did not fall into this predictive category. When the results had extended to 152 patients of all ages, with twenty varieties of cancer between them, and the rates of survival had shown themselves high in terms of 'easy disease' or 'tough disease' (meaning 50 per cent or more chance of recovery for the former, 50 per cent or less for the latter) and still consistent with the grade of the patient's motivation to live, Dr Simonton's approach was further confirmed. The occasional patient who negated it by getting better in spite of poor attitude and lack of cooperation, remained a puzzle – but Dr Simonton had also uncovered many a deep-seated desire to give up, to die in spite of all available help, and that there was usually a justifiable reason for it indicated in the case history.

Dr Simonton, determined not to relinquish his premise, no matter how much resistance or discouragement might lie ahead, continues to conduct his meditation and cancer research and to try and educate people (including the whole family of a patient) to look at cancer without dread and to know that help can be found in their own attitude of mind, that they are not helpless.

He is also investigating and accumulating evidence on why and how the mind can affect the cancer cells. He feels that the effects of mental tension in the body are underrated and that people go for years unaware that they are damaging the normal cells of

their body in this way, just as much as they might do in the case
of less dramatic disorders. He believes they learn to accept stress
as normal, to 'live with it', not recognizing it as connected with
their health problems. The body will always heal itself, given a
chance, and so the deep relaxation of meditation provides this
chance. Visualization might be only a mystical concept were it
not for its tangible effects in biofeedback, so that full relaxation
and concentration of mind arms the body for return to its natural
state.

He also points out, medically, that we all have cancer several
thousand times in our lifetime (if one smokes one has more than
if one doesn't), and our bodies recognize the abnormal cells and
destroy them. In his lectures, given in all parts of the USA, and
recently in England, Dr Simonton shows slides of the cells 'at
war'. He adds that as the will to live goes down, so does the will
to die go up, and vice versa, and the cells react accordingly.

He enlarges that if the doctor said to a patient with severe
cancer 'Why do you think you don't want to live?' it would cut
through a great deal of unnecessary and falsely-conceived attitudes. 'People choose their disease – unconsciously, of course',
he says. It can be traced by a good psychotherapist to some deep-
rooted fear, hurt or feeling of hopelessness some time prior to
the cancer manifestation. He can quote many cases where this is
sharply illustrated.

Dr Helen Flanders Dunbar,[37] the pioneer of psychosomatic
medicine, may have been one of the first to note that personality-
traits play an important part in cancer. Innumerable doctors of
psychosomatic medicine have since concurred, defining it closely
in accordance with accumulated evidence. (Many of these can be
found in *Psychosomatics*[82] by Howard R. and Martha E. Lewis
and *Man's Presumptuous Brain*[140] by Dr A. T. W. Simeons.)

There is a long way to go yet for Dr Simonton to win general
acceptance of his evidence – there is a tendency for those oriented
to the opposite view not to believe even what they see, and this
has ever been so with new ideas – but his support has begun to
snowball and a new frontier for mind and cancer is strongly
indicated.

Also pursuing the hypothesis that mind plays a major role in both the cause and cure of cancer, is a group research project launched by the National Federation of Spiritual Healers in England, headed by the famous healer Harry Edwards, their president.

The NFSH, with headquarters in Loughton, Essex, was formed in 1954 for the purpose of raising the standard of healing and healers through training courses and screening, and to provide a sanctuary and healing service, without cost, for anyone who requested it. It has some 9,000 members, 5,000 of whom are healers, has affiliate associations in most parts of the world, and the approval of the Minister of Health to administer healing as requested by patients or their relatives in over 1,500 national hospitals.

In 1972, the NFSH launched an inquiry into 'The Cause, Prevention and Cure of Cancer', setting a target of £20,000 to finance the initial stages of brochures, widespread dissemination of questionnaires to cancer sufferers and others of related interest, the computerization of their results, and to put forward NFSH views on the subject to the medical profession and general public. Their impetus was derived in part from the statement of Lord Zuckerman (a Scientific Adviser to H.M. Government) in his report in 1972 on the outlook of cancer, that despite much fine headway against several forms of the disease, that with others, despite combined efforts of world-wide cancer research in this century, medical science has come to a 'dead-end' and that the great need today is for a 'new galvanising idea'.

The NFSH believe they have such an idea; it is 'that within the organ concerned, each cell possesses an intelligence which can be influenced by a person's outlook and behaviour. For instance, the cells of the sex organs will be indirectly influenced by stimulation which is received through the senses of touch, vision, hearing, smell and taste and by mental impressions and the emotions of others.

'All that is required is for one cell to become abnormal to commence the tumour. What research has been seeking, unfortunately without avail, is the process which induces that change.

The conversion of a well-behaved, disciplined cell into a renegade, irresponsible cancer cell is the crux of the matter.

'Our theory contends that when a person develops depressive frustration in a primary life's objective, this frustration is communicated to the organ concerned and to the cells, which in turn become frustrated, dejected and despondent, desperate to rebel against the accepted rules of conduct and so deranging its physical function, throwing off the pituitary discipline, and becoming demented. Insanity, also a condition of intellect, is ... propagated in the new cells being produced as quickly as possible without any restraint.

'Medical research will continue to seek ways and means to eradicate cancer cells but a new opening comes with the study of human behaviour patterns aimed at the prevention of the mind stresses which tend to make people cancer-prone. From NFSH research we hope to establish the character of frustration which promotes a tumour in a particular organ, and then most important of all to provide a descriptive analysis for its recognition and counsel to show how to counteract it.

'Everyone admires the tremendous efforts medical scientists have made to discover the cause of cancer, and in their wonderful skill in treating it, but in looking solely to a physical cause, medical science has not been able to explain spontaneous remissions (according to Dr G. Bennette, Honorary General Secretary and Information Officer of the British Cancer Council, there have been "1000 odd of these cases collected since the beginning of the century") any more than its electronic instruments have been able to isolate the cause of cancer.'

Although a majority of the medical profession still refute the mind-role in the origin of cancer there are a growing number who do not rule it out. Of these, Dr Ivan Smith of the Ontario Cancer Foundation has stated, 'One would do well to look for some relationship between retardation of a cancerous growth and the personality of the patient'. Dr Joost Meerloo, a Columbia University (New York) psychiatrist has said, 'Stress, mental shock or maladjustment may be a sensitive factor in cancer', and Dr John Lovatt Doust of the Toronto Psychiatric Hospital says: 'The mind and body cannot be separated. Breakdown is not accidental, it is tied up with a person's inheritance which may well influence the way the site of a cancer is chosen.'

A significant comment on mind and cancer was made by a Greek psychiatrist, Dr N. C. Rassidakis of the University of Athens, who stated in 1972 that: 'The percentage of *mental* patients who die from malignancy is less than one third of the general population who die from malignancy'. His statistical findings were similar in England, Wales and Scotland. Suggesting that the mind-element of cancer is re-directed or escaped by 'madness'. Another view, which may further detach cancer from a physical cause is that of Sir Heneage Ogilvie, the English cancer specialist who remarked: 'A happy man never gets cancer'.

One of the ways this new approach to cancer gathers force is the pooling of ideas between researchers; as the world shrinks, making international travel within their reach, they often find they have been working separately along similar lines. When Dr Carl Simonton visited London to be a speaker in 'The May Lectures' of 1974 (a symposium of advanced ideas in healing, parapsychology, medicine and human potential techniques), it was an opportunity for Harry Edwards, Gilbert Anderson (NFSH administrator) and others of the NFSH cancer research committee to talk with him about his work and to tell him of theirs.

Dr Simonton visited the National Federation of Spiritual Healers' headquarters and learned how Harry Edwards worked with patients, (he has brought about healing in thousands, and annually demonstrates his form of healing before capacity audiences at the Albert or Royal Festival Halls) without medical techniques and, in turn, Dr Simonton outlined his.

The result of this was an influence on each, of the other's techniques. At the NFSH a new healing procedure for cancer is now being carried out by Gilbert Anderson, one of England's leading non-medical healers. It consists of applying Dr Simonton's approach of initial study of the personal history of the patient, psychotherapy, to remove the fear of the word 'cancer' and of the disease itself, and re-creating the *will to live*, explanation to the patient of the nature of the particular manifestation of the disease, daily meditation, training in deep relaxation through group therapy, this accomplished with self-monitored auto-suggestion and instrument feedback (taught and supervised by Dr Ann Woolley-Hart,* now lending medical support to the project) – visualization of the inside of the body and, finally, the laying-on-of-hands. This procedure will be repeated until there is improvement.

Thus has the mind-approach to cancer forgone one, heretofore primary, element – the medical treatment, radiation therapy; it is an all-out non-medical commitment, requiring complete faith in both patient and healer. So far, some early results are extremely promising.

In May 1974, at the Federation headquarters in Loughton, Essex, Dr Woolley-Hart and Gilbert Anderson chose a group of seven patients with terminal cancer and put their theory of a non-medical cure to a severe test. All seven patients had been given up by doctors and given a maximum three months to live. Of the seven, two died before the therapy was organized, but five remained, one with cancer of the bone marrow, whose bones were breaking because they were so thin, one with lung cancer (one lung removed and shadow evident on the other), one with acute leukemia and resultant sores that wouldn't heal, one with abdominal and bowel cancer, in great pain and distress and one with cancer in both breasts spreading to lymph glands.

The patients were extremely depressed when they started, and in the beginning it was not easy to get them to respond to the procedures or to raise their morale. But once they had got accustomed to the meditating, relaxing and visualizing, had some success with the biofeedback instruments and became used to the group therapy, their gloom lifted and their attitude went through a profound change. Gilbert Anderson describes them as an amazingly 'happy and jolly group'.

That was the beginning. Soon they were getting encouraging reports from their medical checkups. Week by week, each patient improved. They passed their terminal point, doubled it, continued to improve. At this writing, sixteen months have passed. Two of

---

*See *The Role of the Mind in Disease* and *The Will to Live* (Dr Ann Woolley-Hart and Gilbert Anderson, in conjunction with NFSH Independent Cancer Research), available through NFSH.

the patients have been told by their doctors that they appear to be entirely free of cancer and the other three are considered to have 95 per cent normal health.

Spurred by this success, Gilbert Anderson and Dr Woolley-Hart will soon start another group of their own. Seven or eight new groups have already formed in different parts of the UK. If they yield a similar sort of result over the next year, then Gilbert Anderson and Dr Woolley-Hart will extend the procedure on to a more national basis.

Meanwhile, one cancer specialist has agreed to run a control group from patients in his hospital and two other consultants have agreed to work with a healer in their vicinities, one of them with medically untreated patients in order to discern the full effect of the non-medical approach without medical interaction.

Although it is early for anything but cautious comment on the significance of his and Dr Woolley-Hart's initial success with their methods, in his thirty years as a healer, treating as many as 150 patients a day, Gilbert Anderson has seen so many recoveries from almost every physical illness that he has little real doubt that cancer will prove equally curable by non-medical means, 'no matter what you want to call them'. Over the years, he has had at least a 30 per cent success with sclerosis (hardening of tissues or arteries), finds spinal troubles 'yield' with great consistency and can usually help almost anyone with disc trouble – in a few minutes if it's tension, over a period of time if it's a nerve condition. When cells are dead, he says, 'they are dead – but the body is creating new cells almost every moment of our lives, so that the thing to concentrate on is the creation of healthy new cells, rather than repairing damaged ones'.

In September 1975, the NFSH became the World Federation of Healers with the object of extending their fellowship of healing world wide and of obtaining a new international headquarters, Healing College and Research and Healing Centre, which will provide administrative services, lecture hall, club, residential accommodation and equipment for expanding healing research.

Not so extreme, but to many equally incompatible with mental causation, is diabetes. However, while preponderantly attributable to an inherited tendency, diabetes may not show itself until stress affects the balance of blood sugar in the system, thereby subtly linking itself to the mind.

In Jaipur, India, a government-sponsored clinic[89] and research centre has been approaching diabetes from a yogic point of view, and in the course of twelve years, producing some significant data. Founded by Swami Anandanand, a mystic with yogic but no medical training, the clinic, a splendid white building in a handsome setting, is medically supervised by two physicians.

In the twenty-bed clinic, yoga loses its connotations of mysticism and becomes the age-old science of India, just as methodological as any Western therapy. Strangely enough, it is the Indians themselves who are the sternest investigators of yoga in practical terms of healing. For not until the sudden onslaught of interest from the West, had they taken a closer look at what their own traditional philosophies had to offer medicine. Prior to that, they had only been trying to follow Western techniques.

The 283 patients who came to the clinic at Jaipur for the original experimental research were all Indian, ranging in age from 13 to 64, and suffering degrees of diabetes from moderate to extremely serious, and of durations from one to ten years, though none was bedridden. They were asked to stay for three months unless there were complications.

The treatment began with a strictly regulated diet totalling 2,900 calories and incorporating 400 grams of carbohydrate, 98 grams of fat, 100 grams of protein. Exhaustive personal histories were recorded, the patients clinically examined and their type of diabetes, prior treatment and prescribed medication checked in detail (it was noted that 90 had hereditary factors). Next came the yoga therapy.

This consisted of four main steps with subdivisions and were programmed for two periods a day, one from 5 to 7 a.m., the other from 5 to 6.45 p.m. Some of their methods seem bizarre to those accustomed to modern medicine, but they have a long-accumulated non-medical wisdom, for yoga combines purification of the mind with purification of the body.

First, in the treatments, is *Shat karama*, for cleansing the interior of the body. This consists of *kunjel kriya* – a method of stomach-cleansing that aids digestion and liver functions – warm water is drunk quickly and regurgitated by tickling the throat; *vasta r-dhoti* – another type of stomach-cleansing, which brings up bile and toxic material, involves slowly swallowing about an 8-yard long, 3-inch wide strip of muslin, rotating it with the abdomen muscles, then lifting out the cloth; *shankh-prachalan* – a combination of repeatedly cleansing the digestive tract with several glasses of warm salt water and inducing purging by special postures; *sukshyan vyayam* – special body and breathing exercises that are salutary to various organs, the nervous and hormonal system and circulation; *isthula vyayam* – more exercises that tone muscles, joints and circulation, and help to lower blood sugar levels; *asana* – yoga postures that calm the mind, relax the body and achieve a balanced coordination of mental and physical aspects of the whole person.

When the patients showed normal blood sugar levels, they were given trial meals that tested their tolerance to certain foods.

Dr Narain Varandani, the senior medical adviser of the centre, who was greatly encouraged by the over-all results of the pilot project, summarized his findings at a 1971 conference of medical doctors in India:[89]

'Of 283 subjects studied in the present series, 51% responded to yoga therapy in the absence of any other medication. Those diabetics who failed to improve with yoga therapy alone may do well with a combination of antidiabetic drugs along with yoga therapy, thereby reducing the drug requirement and delaying the complications.

'The discovery of insulin and oral antidiabetic agents has been a major breakthrough in the treatment of diabetes and with the use of these drugs even the severest form can be controlled and complications cared for . . . but alas, we have not yet discovered any drug that can permanently cure the disease or avert its dreadful complications. A few major problems with insulin therapy are – inconvenience of life-long daily injection, development of tolerance and resistance to insulin, local lipodystrophy (defective metabolism of fat) and hazards of missed doses and overdosage.

'How important it is then to learn to minimize the use of these drugs by observing moderation in life, avoidance of mental distress, proper dietary habits and regular practice of physical exercise and yoga and to reserve these potent medications only for urgent needs.

'I don't advocate the complete replacement of diabetic drug treatment; but certainly yoga can be helpful in the modern management of diabetes by reducing drug dependency and effecting a better mental and hormonal balance. Many pre-diabetics, early diabetics and adult onset diabetics, may be spared a lifetime of drug dependency if appropriate therapy is instituted in the initial stages.'

Dr Varandani thought that the elements which probably helped seventy-three patients normalize their condition, and another seventy-six to show definite improvement (sixty-four did not complete the course and another seventy did not respond), were: removal from the site and circumstance of stress; a regular daily routine and alleviation of responsibilities; a spiritual atmosphere and group prayers to increase peace of mind and self-confidence; meditation for tranquillity of mind; exercise for well-being, and the understanding counselling of Swami Anandanand.

The reason for this may have been that the typical personality of the diabetic found in this study was 'highly intelligent, given to accuracies in life, very sensitive and of a brooding nature – and the case history of each patient had shown some form of maladjustment to his environment'.

This fusion of mental and physical symptoms, while not yet confirming one root-cause for the disease itself, adds another valuable facet to the growing body of research bringing all methods of healing together.

As William James[64]* said at the beginning of the century '. . . May the Yoga practices not be, after all, methods of getting at our deeper functional levels?'

*Professor of Harvard Medical School, medical doctor, philosopher, psychologist, parapsychologist, author and lecturer (1842–1910).

3D SCIENCE INVESTIGATES A FAR-FLUNG
SHORE OF NON-MEDICAL HEALING

THE most extreme form of non-medical healing challenging science today may be 'psychic surgery', a mystifying procedure performed by certain non-medical healers indigenous to Brazil and the Philippines. It may not be explainable by presently-known medicine or science, may not exist at all, but the evidence accumulating that it might is increasingly disconcerting.

One procedure, in which the body of an unanaesthetized patient appears to be 'cut into' by the hands or finger of the healer, the flesh parted and the diseased substance removed, causes no pain, seldom, if ever, leads to infection, despite the lack of precautionary measures, and, as the hands are withdrawn, achieves instant healing of the wound without a scar.

Verdicts of fraud abound, but they seem belied by the thousands of ailing people who have travelled to the Philippines and undergone the 'miraculous' operations, with a high proportion of success. Physicists and doctors, in groups or as individuals, who go to take a hard, close look at the so-called surgery, more often than not find themselves on the horns of a dilemma – for what might have appeared as sleight-of-hand trickery on a film or photograph, at close range reveals none that is discernible – yet they cannot believe what they see, let alone understand it. Thus, few final conclusions have been reached.

Interest in psychic surgery was probably fanned in the West by a team of physicians, including Dr Andrija Puharich,[122] who went to Brazil, in the 1960s, and conducted a field study of the medical skills of Jose Pedro de Freitas, known as 'Arigo' (meaning 'good guy'), claimed to have extraordinary paranormal abilities, and which Dr Puharich described at the first meeting of the newly-formed Academy of Parapsychology and Medicine in 1971.

Dr Puharich told of Arigo's uncanny correctness in diagnosing a patient's illness by just looking at him, often despite the patient's lie or cover-up, of being able to prescribe with the

precision of an exceptionally-skilled physician, using the proper
medical terms rather than informal ones (for major or minor
disorders) and a knowledge of pharmacology impossible to re-
concile with his lack of education and near-illiteracy.

Pictures and films were shown of Arigo at work on fairly
minor problems – major surgery could not be watched. In one
instance, using a sharp knife, he plunged it into the cornea of an
unanaesthetized patient's eye, cut the cornea without hurting her,
and the cornea healed instantly – the whole process had taken
about 20 seconds. In another, borrowing a dull-edged pocket-
knife from someone standing by, he performed surgery on a
patient's boil – and very soon afterwards removed a sebaceous
cyst from the same patient. Both operations healed at once.
(Dr Puharich noted that the wounds healed so quickly that it
was sometimes necessary to pack them with vaseline to keep them
open for draining.)

Allowing the researchers to see even these minor operations
had been an exception to the policy of privacy for Brazilian
healers, and the validity and efficacy of major operations performed by Arigo was based on reliable testimony. There seemed
no major surgery he had not performed, and his local fame was
for curing the incurable. In one case he had cured advanced
cancer of the stomach, and for this there were medical records and
X-rays to prove it; he had plunged his hands through the unanaesthetized man's abdominal wall without using a knife and
extracted a quantity of bloody tissue. The doctor's report had
confirmed that the cancer had been eliminated.

Explaining his amazing powers with the humility of a simple,
earthy man with no ambitions for fame or glory, he told the
group of Western physicians that he was guided in all he did by
the voice of a 'Dr Fritz', who spoke in a small voice in his ear,
giving him precise information and instructions. If Dr Fritz had
left him, he said, he would not know how to diagnose, prescribe
or heal.[43]

Arigo, who died in 1971 at the age of 49, often turned patients
away. If he felt a medical doctor could take care of the complaint,
or that the patient was faking, he would say, 'Don't waste my
time'. And there were times he said, 'God bless you – your time

has come, and I cannot treat you. Good-bye.' He never charged for his healing services, and maintained himself by outside work.

In Brazil there are many thousands of spiritist groups (30,000 in Sao Paolo alone) involved in non-medical healing, and several million in the country at large, whose healing work is believed to be through spirit communication. Since many spiritists also exist in the US, UK and many other countries of the world, scientific attention may one day be focused on the vastness of these numbers which, because they are partially founded on necessity, receive little publicity.

Healers in the Philippines were the next focus of research interest, and here healing methods and healing training could not only be witnessed, but operations undergone by foreigners.[163] This evoked a mixture of new hope for the desperate, as well as suspicion of exploitation, excessive credulity and hard-nosed inquiry. Plane-loads of the sick came from all parts of the world. Watching the healers operate became a tourist attraction, and teams of investigators arrived with cameras and other equipment calculated to reveal the nature of this logic-defying phenomenon.

Throughout the whole influx and flurry, the Philippine healers carried on as they had always done, calmly, steadily, with absolute confidence in what they did, confounding the sceptics by their profoundly religious approach to their work, their undeniably dedicated service to the poor of their own country, whom they had always treated without personal gain and often at cost to their private lives in the belief that they were merely channels of spiritual powers, whether straight from God or 'spirit guides'. Although there were exceptions to the rule, those who used the sudden abundance of available money for trickery, it was difficult to believe that the majority were not sincere.

Philippine healers, most of whom are members of the Union Espiritista de Cristiana Filipinas, spend long years training, acquiring the techniques originated by the healer Eleuterio Terte, taught as a 'gift of the spirit', in which spiritual energy must be invoked, disciplined and developed; the more evolved a healer is spiritually, the more advanced his skills. When he approaches a patient, he has learned to enter a trance-like state, focusing his mind-energy on what he is to accomplish and 'attuning' to the energy of the patient, on which he also draws. When he becomes proficient after performing hundreds of operations, he enters this trance-like state almost instantly, and can talk to others without breaking it.

Healers are widely scattered throughout the Philippines, with many located in remote villages.[93] They work long, hard hours and often go on healing missions. Their healing rooms vary widely in size and shape, but are extremely simple, without cooling systems against the heat, unequipped against infection, and have only minimal lighting. Some healers work happily surrounded by relatives and friends, others require prayers and hymns to help focus their concentration. They are used to treating people unfamiliar with Western techniques, people believing strongly in witchcraft and the devil, in possession and many afflictions caused by evil spirits. The indigenous healer, in deference to these beliefs, sometimes 'materializes' objects such as a corncob, shrimp, or dead mouse, from within their bodies, knowing this will provide his patients with the kind of proof they need to believe they are free and healed. (Whether or not objects are genuinely materialized is another subject of inquiry.) Since 60 per cent of the inhabitants of the Philippines do not have access to regular medical care, and will not have in the foreseeable future, the healers must fill the healing gap according to local expectation.

The Rev. Tony Agpaoa,* whose fame as one of the Philippine healers has spread over the globe, has said that he could open the body of a patient without a drop of blood, but that his people would find it harder to believe in *bloodless* psychic surgery than they do seeing the gore, tissue and organs. These are what Westerners have been led to expect, and these, therefore, must be provided (even as the Western doctor provides placebos?). Though relatively uneducated he was the first healer to specialize in the treatment of Europeans and Americans. Trained in the disciplines of Union Espiritista Cristiana, he operated six days a week for over twenty years, denying access to neither friends nor doubters. A typical operation procedure by Tony Agpaoa begins

*From the first hand report of Marcus McCausland, who visited the Philippines with a group of doctors and scientists to investigate psychic surgery for Health for the New Age.[93]

with getting to know something of his patient. Being unfamiliar with Westerners, he finds them harder to deal with. They are less receptive because of their intellectualization of what is about to take place, and he can treat double the number of Filipino patients in a day.

Tony Agpaoa, who has treated every variation of disorder the body can manifest from a cyst to multiple sclerosis, then meets the patient in a room of mutual choice, bringing with him a young assistant, who carries a briefcase containing a floral plastic sheet, some cotton wool, a towel, a few bowls and forceps. The plastic sheet is placed on the bed, the towel on top, the cotton wool soaked in water, and the area of operation washed. He may make a few preparatory 'magnetic' passes over the prospective patient's head and a cursory inspection of his body which could include foot massage, which apparently tells him of sensitive areas.

Other of the well-known healers may make somewhat more elaborate preparations for operations: Mercado, for instance, gives the waiting patient a 'spiritual injection', done by jabbing with his hand in the direction of their arm, leg or chest. The patient flinches, as if at a pinprick, and often blood spurts from the 'puncture'. (In order to check this a surgeon from Bombay concealed four sheets of thick polythene foil under his shirt before the so-called injection. He reported that he felt a sharp prick. Later inspection with a physicist from the Max Planck Institute in Germany, showed a hole in each sheet of foil exactly as if penetrated by a needle, yet close observation by both researchers, before, during and after the procedure, convinced them no such needle was used. There was also a little blood. They concluded that it was some genuine psychokinetic phenomenon.)

Blance, another healer, asks a bystander to extend an index finger which he grasps and moves in a cutting motion above the area on the recumbent patient's body where he intends to operate. Instantly, an incision appears on the patient's skin. Researchers from Germany had closely investigated the possibility of a concealed razor blade or an incision already made, but no evidence supported this, and at one time the healer made three such incisions within 15 seconds without altering the position of his hands.

Virgilio, using a technique familiar to acupuncturists, touches the meridian points of the patient's fingers and toes for diagnosis of energy imbalances, then he either treats by stroking and massage or by an operation.

Tony Agpaoa, after a short prayer, is ready to operate. He may spread a small amount of cream on the area where he intends to work, then he surrounds the area with wet cotton-wool, and places the fingers of both his hands on the area and starts a rhythmic kneading movement of his hands as if both pulling from within yet keeping open the patient's flesh which seems ready to close the instant he lifts his hands. Blood suddenly appears (checked by many groups of scientists and physicians, and proved to be human blood – although there have been *imitators* using animal blood, thereby increasing the case for scepticism), and between the healer's hands can now be seen what appears to be bodily tissue.

His assistant helps to cut this diseased tissue away with forceps or scissors (also proved to be human tissue on histological analysis). After some further work of this sort, the healer lifts away his hands and the assistant wipes the blood from the skin. There is no scar, no trace of a wound. The entire procedure takes perhaps 2 to 5 minutes. The patient gets up and walks away. Another one enters.

Needless to say, every form of trickery is suspected and searched out. Tony Agpaoa does not bar any kind of inspection and has worked with cameras focused on his every move. His room has been searched before and after. He shows what he is doing to those who ask, and will pause to allow a researcher to see more closely.

In one case, a young woman (a probation officer from Washington) came armed with camera and tripod to record her mother's abdominal operation. In the room was a spectator who was to be the next patient, so that Tony Agpaoa had the combined scrutiny of two intensely interested onlookers. The daughter had arrived early to inspect the room, found nothing suspicious, but was still wary.

Before coming to them, Tony Agpaoa had done brain and heart surgery, now he went right to work on the lower abdomen of this patient. He began with the kneading movement and suddenly his fingers were inside her stomach. The daughter heard her mother give a slight gasp of surprise, but not pain. Her mother talked as the calm, gentle healer showed the onlookers the opening and the tissue he intended to remove. With forceps he then lifted out what he explained 'did not belong there' – dark red tissue, 'adhesions', which were causing the patient's trouble. He appeared to plunge his hands about in considerable blood, some of which spurted out, but just as quickly as he had begun he was pushing the interior material back in place, withdrawing his hands. The assistant wiped the woman's stomach and the healer massaged it a few moments with eucalyptus oil.

After a few moments rest, the healer proceeded to operate again, on the inside of the woman's thigh, removed unhealthy tissue, and closed the opening – a thin line remained on the skin's surface, which disappeared with massage.

The woman returned to her wheelchair, talking animatedly. The combined operations had taken only a few minutes. The spectators were stunned. The daughter said afterwards that it all looked so natural, that she could only believe what she had seen. The other onlooker who got onto the 'operating table' had a tumour removed from behind one eye. He felt only a slight vibration of the healer's hands, but drew a gasp from the women who had stayed to watch (he himself could see only the ceiling) when, apparently, his head was open – its contents revealed. He, too, after massage and lubricating treatment, was up and about in a few minutes, though with one eye bandaged. He was shown the tumour.

Some patients watch their own operations with the aid of a mirror. They may be sickened, but they feel no pain and post-operation reactions are usually from shock that passes off quickly. The effects of the operation are not always felt as immediate improvement. If they have been successful this shows up soon after. There are few instant cures, and few single treatments. Patients coming to the Philippines may undergo a whole series before the healer is confident the disorders (which may be related) are taken care of.

The healers believe a force greater than they are works through them. Tony Agpaoa spoke for many of them with his theory that it is on the 'astral' body the surgery is achieved, the counterpart body which is roughly the same as the material body. Areas are 'materialized' and the disease tissue removed – some time later the process is duplicated in the material body.

A more scientifically acceptable hypothesis may be that of Dr F. Karger of the Max Planck Institute, who feels that if the possibility of trickery is to be eliminated, 'the Philippine healers must have the ability to apply macroscopically visible psychokinesis under controlled conditions. This is of great importance to physics since it affords hopes of determining the principles and type of the interaction responsible for psychokinesis. This phenomenon, occurring only with living systems, is not only of interest to biology, medicine and psychology, but also has a bearing primarily on the foundations of our physics, our knowledge of basic natural laws.'

There are, of course, many other theories being formed. As Dr E. S. Maxey, a biophysicist and Fellow of the American College of Surgeons, commented after closely witnessing Philippine psychic surgery: 'This is the former Doctor Maxey speaking – if all I see is true, I'll have to throw aside 20 years of work and start all over again!'

Meanwhile, a vision experienced by Tony Agpaoa has become a reality through the help of Drs Edwin and Sigrun Seutemann of Germany.

Dr Sigrun Seutemann has flown over 1,000 patients to the Philippines for treatment (most of them considered incurable by conventional doctors), has watched over 7,000 operations and been 'operated' on herself for a cardiac condition which made breathing painful, and which disappeared after treatment by Tony Agpaoa. Her enthusiasm for the healer matched his vision, which was to have a large, well-equipped clinic where patients from other countries could come for treatment. (Dr Seutemann does not believe in the physical existence of the operations. She feels the actual blood and tissue manifested, as far as can be explained, is paranormal. She believes that patients are convinced by the healer's treatment, and this creates in them a state of mind conducive to the body's natural healing process.)

Funds were raised, and today a beautiful old monastery in magnificent grounds on a hilltop in Baguio City, about 100 miles from Manila, has been converted into a seventy-bed clinic with fine laboratory facilities, and a free clinic for poor people of the town. Here, it is hoped, other healers will join Tony Agpaoa's work and the young healers who come to the Philippines to study healing techniques, from simple laying-on-of-hands to psychic surgery (many have been coming for some time from Australia, Switzerland and Germany) will be helped in their development. There are also facilities for scientists from overseas to carry out worthwhile projects connected with healing.

It must be said that much controversy still exists as to the authenticity of 'psychic surgery' on a physical basis, and there have been many attempts to discredit the healers themselves, which has not been minimized by the Island's obvious element of exploitive charlatans. But the fact that healing is accomplished in this way, and has been for many years, and that most of it is done with good intention and without pay cannot be denied. If it should prove no more than another form of non-medical healing, this is noteworthy in itself – and – if a psychokinetic effect is involved,* or 'materialization', on an 'astral' or energy-body, places it all in the realm of the paranormal, the research will have been more than justified. Only time and further scientific scrutiny will tell.

*See *Romeo Error*[170] by Lyall Watson, for thoughts on this.

4

The moving together of metaphysics and physics, of science and religion

Anyone who studies physics long enough, is inevitably led to metaphysics.
ALBERT EINSTEIN

WHILE most of the world's great scientists have agreed with this observation, and have shared Einstein's mystical and spiritual concept of an underlying intelligence of the 'highest wisdom and the most radiant beauty, whose gross forms alone are intelligible to our poor faculties', it has remained more of an inward illumination than a verifiable scientific fact that mind and matter are one.

When material science comes up against the question of mind or spirit, it generally backs off – not because it flatly rejects the idea of a unified version of the world, but because the realm of psychic energy cannot at present be fitted into its general laws of the electro-magnetic spectrum. Here and there throughout the world, scientists attempt to find a chink in these laws, or another form of energy that can accommodate the materially unexplainable.

Today, some of them are making headway by means of instrumentation and pioneer work that appears to be providing nebulous yet verifiable evidence of the mind-thought-consciousness factor of life.

This evidence is at the cellular level known as 'primary perception' and was brought to light inadvertently by a man called Cleve Backster, a polygraph (lie-detector) specialist and expert in this field, in his laboratory in New York City in 1966.[4] Although some doubts have been thrown on his researches, his groundwork is so important that it warrants considerable attention.

Cleve Backster had served as a polygraph consultant for almost every government agency, and ran his own school for advanced training of law-enforcement officers in polygraph techniques. One day, taking a break from his research project, he decided to water a philodendron plant his secretary had bought, and then wondered idly if his polygraph equipment would measure the rate at which the water rose in the plant from the root area into the leaves.

He connected a pair of the polygraph electrodes to the leaf of the plant, one each side, held by a rubber band. Since his speciality was the galvanic skin response, he thought he might get a reading on the rise of moisture in the plant, but nothing significant was recorded by the moving ink-pen.

Suddenly, however, an unusual tracing appeared, similar to the contour pattern of a human emotional reaction briefly aroused. Cleve Backster was astonished and intrigued. He could think of no explanation, but felt impelled to find one.

As a means of experiment the 'threat-to-well-being' principle occurred to him – he knew from his own work that threat was a reliable trigger of sharp emotion. He plucked a leaf from the plant and plunged it into a cup of hot coffee. There was no response; the tracing remained steady.

Perhaps, he thought, the threat had not been direct enough. About ten minutes later, he decided to make an attack on the actual cell tissue of the leaf between the electrodes by burning it. At the instant of his decision, before he had even moved to get the match, there was a dramatic upward-sweeping of the recording pen that almost bore it off the chart.

Was it possible that the mere thought of burning the leaf had triggered it to this violent response? The implications were so exciting that he had to control himself from running out into Times Square at 7.30 in the morning to tell people what had happened. He waited for his associate, a man on whom he could count for scientific reserve, and together they conducted more experiments. When, later, they actually burned a leaf, the reaction was not violent, and when they pretended they were going to burn it, there was no reaction at all. It did seem logical, at that point to suspect that some kind of primary perception was taking place, a communication between mind and plant-cell. After all, a great deal of valuable work had been done in the past by Sir Jagadis C. Bose (an Indian physicist and founder of the Bose Institute of plant research in Calcutta) on the psychophysiology of plant life (and all organisms), proving its extreme sensitivity to sound, touch, temperature, light and the electro-magnetic field, so why not to thought energy? (Bose was knighted in 1917 for his plant work and the magnifying instruments he invented.)

Several months of testing and careful recording of every experiment followed. Effort was made to overcome possibilities of coincidence or unconscious influence on the results. Although many plants were tested, Cleve Backster had had no initial predisposition towards them, no undue sentiment; still it was something of a shock to see what happened to the polygraph chart during one series of experiments in which live brine shrimps were killed by immersion in boiling water.

Three philodendron plants, each in separate rooms, had been wired to polygraphs. The shrimp were programmed to be dropped randomly into the water by automatic equipment with no human being present, or even on the premises. When the registrations were studied, there were spasmodic bursts of violent tracings. The indication seemed to be that when a cell died, it broadcast a signal to other living cells. Some confusion in the charts led to the discovery that some of the brine shrimp were unhealthy, and that when this was so, the plant did not react, as if the element of survival had dimmed. When only healthy, active shrimp were used, the plant's polygraph tracings were consistently violent at the point of death.

After his initial experiments, Cleve Backster called in many scientists, physicists, chemists, neurologists, psychologists, psychiatrists, and asked them modestly if they could help to explain the strange polygraph tracings, and if they fitted into any of their disciplines. Was the answer something quite simple, not at all earth-shaking? He had already been criticized and he was prepared for ridicule. His main object was not to waste any more time.

The scientists went through their 'check-lists', up and down the scientific spectrum, and finally had to concede that they simply did not know – the phenomenon did not fit anywhere into the scattered body of scientific knowledge.

Cleve Backster was confounded. He had always counted on the dictums of science, and now he couldn't help wondering 'if they didn't know *this* – then they might not know *that*' – and, that perhaps this discovery of his had something to do with *that*. In other words, perhaps he was on to something so meaningful that his whole philosophy of consciousness needed reassessment. He had never been religious in the orthodox sense, but this was a hint of confirmation of a spiritual foundation of life that needed thought.

From then on he lost his awe of science. While thousands of scientists wrote to him asking for further information and attempted studies of their own based on his experimental system, he continued wholeheartedly with his research.

Another accidental discovery led to a new area of exploration. First, the plant had reacted to hot water thrown down the sink, and another time the reaction of the plants to some yoghurt he was eating was so marked that he realized they must be responding to bacteria, in the drain and in the live yoghurt. Bacteria were also flora, at a less developed, less complex stage on the evolutionary scale. In experiments at the level of bacteria, he found his experiments were repeatable. He switched his instrumentation over to the electroencephalograph (EEG), and other more sophisticated instruments of measurement, which enabled him to test a much broader range of cell-life.

From experiments with all kinds of plant life, including vegetables, fresh fruit, various mould cultures and yeasts, he and his associate moved on to forms of animal cell-life (such as blood samples – his own – scrapings from the roof of a human mouth, amoebae and spermatozoa): all showed the same emotive reactions to other forms of cell-life and to human thought at its level of *intention*, as if nature provided a warning system to muster defence or 'cry for help'.

Here, another inadvertent discovery was made by Cleve Backster. While breaking open an egg to give to his Doberman Pinscher dog (to make his coat glossy), he noticed that a plant hooked to a near-by polygraph showed sudden, sharp tracing changes. Curious, he decided to make some careful galvanic skin response tests with hooked-up eggs. The result was confounding. An ordinary unfertilized egg was found to have a heartbeat that matched the usual cycle of a 4 to 4½ day-old chick embryo, at the point when the circulatory system of a fertilized egg might first be observed. Stranger still, when he dissected the egg later, there was no sign whatsoever of any embryo development.

Further tests of this kind only confirmed what seemed to be a kind of pre-form, a yet-to-be manifested form at an invisible level that equated with the principle of an 'etheric' body, or the 'blueprint of life', as Dr Burr called the L-field. Certainly, he thought that these implications deserved serious exploration.

Following this revelation with eggs, came another of potential significance. One day, feeling extremely hungry (having worked through his meal times), and not wanting to take the time to go out, he decided to eat the only food available in the laboratory – eggs, three out of two dozen stored for experiment. His conscience bothered him, but hunger won: he did, however, note the polygraph activity of an African Violet – for, at the instant he decided to break open the first egg, the plant (these are among the most sensitive) reacted with the equivalent of human shock that ends in unconsciousness – it 'fainted'.

Later, he discovered that other eggs, hooked up for tests within shielded, lead-lined containers, had shown bursts of activity that coincided with each egg broken open and cooked. Deciding that this form of response would lend itself to repeatable experiment, Cleve Backster and his colleague devised a fully-automated system whereby ten eggs on a rotating plate would be tripped off down a chute at six- to eight-minute intervals into a deep pan and the EEG switched on. No person needed to be present, thus removing any possible interference from human consciousness.

The discovery here was, once more, totally unexpected: when the first egg was tripped off and hit the boiling water, the other nine eggs (all hooked up) 'fainted'. Although Cleve Backster laughs when he tells this, it was, nevertheless, startling evidence.

Among many experiments in plant-and-people cell communication, Cleve Backster has found a good deal of corroboration that plants recognize their enemies despite attempts to confuse them. In one such test, six of his students were asked to think of destroying one particular plant out of three in the room. (This plant was not hooked up, but the other two were.) One of the students was to be the actual destroyer, while the other six were to work up all the appropriate 'intent' to destroy. The students then approached the plant one at a time.

The ruse failed – the two plants remained impervious to all the students except one, the one who was actually to destroy the target plant. As this student approached, the polygraph contours burst into wild activity.

Cleve Backster has travelled far and wide to test other plants in other places and found their forms of response on the polygraph the same. He has also found that plants become 'attuned' to their caretakers and will remain undisturbed by distractions and threats that do not affect the caretaker. An 'attuned' plant will pick up the consciousness of its owner at any distance, just as if nothing separated them. This might account for the absent healing, or 'prayer-effect' as shown in the research project of Dr Miller and the Worralls.

Often asked why plants are not in a constant state of agitation from all the cell-life destruction and threat in process, Cleve Backster postulates that there is a form of selectivity involved. After all, every form of life selects from it that which applies to its survival and well-being and screens out, or is totally non-reactive to the rest (a cat will hear only the mouse behind the wall of a noise-filled room, and won't be dissuaded from its vigil even by food or physical threat).

Recently, Cleve Backster has been narrowing his research. With the help of the medical profession he has been concentrating on cell-culture work. Taking the cell-tissue 'in vitro' away from the donor (initially animal life), he separates it into incubators that are spread apart, for the purpose of seeing how one cell reacts to the needs or well-being of another. Pilot work has shown encouraging evidence that the well-being of one 'disadvantaged' cell can be enhanced by another when the need is there. If this inter-cell-communication can be done in the laboratory with 50 feet between them, Cleve Backster reasons it surely will take place within one body. He hopes to show conclusively that cells have the capability of inter-communication and mutual response.

In his cancer research, experiments have been done to 'trick' the cells into using their own immunology. Asked why the cells needed to be tricked, Cleve Backster answered that this might be the most significant question of all, perhaps in the spiritual realm. But as far as a scientific reply is concerned, he passes it on to other scientists, wishing to act primarily as a catalyst.

At present, scientists do not understand how the antibody can move right to the target; how, selectively, the white blood cell can penetrate the capillary wall, swim through the tissue and fluid of the body right to the area of an infection, cope with the infection, survive the battle, and then go back into the blood stream. The question has passed from one discipline to another, and it is finally conceded that there must be a third dimension of communication, a gap bridged by some form of 'chemical messenger' none of them can yet discern. Cleve Backster feels that if he can at least show science that this dimension does exist, it will allow them to re-approach, in a broader sense, many problems in the medical research field.

The other area of Cleve Backster's specialization is plant *memory*. This experimentation will be automated and consist of six small cups attached to wires which operate in an electrically-driven pulley system to rotate the cups at a horizontal level. Each cup contains seedlings of a different variety from each other and from the test plant, and as each cup (randomly selected) passes the plant, a light shines on it to induce the plant to 'remember' that particular seedling. The plant is hooked up to the polygraph by a light-conducting electrode, and the purpose of the test is to condition the plant, by the 'reward' of light, to 'remember' that particular seedling, without the light itself.

Thus, from a humble plant to human consciousness, Cleve Backster's road of discovery is well posted with signs leading to life's ultimate questions and perhaps some of its answers.

Despite the fact that some of his cell-culture studies have been questioned by other researchers on the grounds that they failed to achieve his results with duplicated experiments, Cleve Backster is pursuing his exploratory work at the Backster Research Foundation. He hopes that in time he may find forms of experiment that convince beyond the margin of error or doubt.

More recently, Cleve Backster's work inspired another scientist, Dr Marcel Vogel,[167] to pursue some ideas of his own on cellular consciousness. Dr Vogel's background could not have been more appropriate: a senior chemist in material science at IBM in San Jose, he was an acknowledged authority on liquid crystals, magnetics and rare earth phosphorous, and while his work in the 'think-tank' of the advanced systems-development laboratory in Los Gatos, California, categorized him as a 'hard-headed' scientist, he was drawn to the subtle implications of the mind-element in 'deaf, dumb and blind' plant life.

Keeping this interest separate from his professional work, Dr Vogel established a laboratory in his own home, with home-made equipment, read a great deal on the subject, particularly the works of Charles Darwin which spoke of the necessity for the 'domestication' of plants – after being removed from a wild environment, a period of adjustment while they adapted themselves to the human environment, or they 'rebelled and died' – and also of the power of movement in plants, that the mind of the plant was in the root stem, and that the root tip turned toward magnetic fields surrounding it to find the substance required for the life form that is in the soil. These observations led him to Darwin's view that the root was the primitive form of the mind of man.

He found stimulus for this in reading of Luther Burbank, the 'father of plant hybridization' who had used thought to influence the genetic code of the plant, conceiving the form of the plant with his own mind. Very remote ideas for science – yet possibly less so nowadays; perhaps this energetic exchange between man and plant was merely a recovery of knowledge, rather than a discovery?

Dr Vogel's method of recording the plant's response was to avoid the direct pressure of electrodes on the leaf by first applying agar-agar paste (mixed with 1 per cent sodium chloride and some preservative moistened with water, to prevent excessive mould growth) which provided an intermediary grip for the electrodes. The wires were fed into a wheatstone bridge, put into a solid-state amplifier which fed a strip chart recorder.

Like Cleve Backster, he found that plants were an extremely sensitive photo-electric instrument; for instance, a car starting up outside, a hundred feet away, made the plant actively respond; much of his initial plant experimentation confirmed Cleve

Backster's work. Now he wanted to expand his research to thought-influence. His problem was to devise an experiment that would show a transfer of his thought to the plant. He started off with concentration on a desire for the plant to continue to grow and remain healthy, and repeated this concentrated emotion at intervals watching the baseline of the recorder for reaction. The result was a stable, solid baseline, impervious to any other forces around it.

Dr Vogel has demonstrated this reaction to other scientists and on several television shows, and despite the intense lighting and strange activity of a television studio the plant would remain stable for a period up to half an hour. This has shown Dr Vogel that the control is within himself; in other words, the experimenter has entered into the consciousness of the plant. If the experimenter focuses on the emotions of another person, this automatically registers on the strip chart recorder, so the experimenter must, if he is to succeed in this achievement, keep quiet and control his conscious mind. He has written a scientific report on his experiences in establishing this evidence of 'baseline and control'.

Following this, he investigated the use of a microscope to bring out the patterns of form that nature has in the microscopic world. Twelve years previously he had discovered (and was afraid in those days to talk about it), that nature predicted its forms by an 'energetic transformation'; before being consolidated into what was called form, there was an energetic change that could be seen under polarized light – first 'a field', a sudden transformation, and then the solid occupied this space. It was like a precise analogue image of what was to be (as Cleve Backster had found with the unfertilized egg).

(In the language of liquid crystals, this is the intermediate state between solid and liquid. The edge of a cell wall itself is a liquid crystal composed of water molecules and phospho-lipids ranged in orderly arrays, and as an electrical charge varies the conductivity and the mobility of the cell wall, it lets go and moves on. The energies released from this vacuum accumulate as aura forms.)

At this point, Dr Vogel made the surprising discovery that

when he focused his mind on this moment of transformation, he could build images, 'thought photographs'. (The sophisticated IBM equipment he uses is worth about $70,000, so he doesn't recommend it for amateurs!) In slides made of these experiments, it is possible to see the deliberate formations of some simple, basic feeling or image held in his mind. First, there is the bluish 'pre-form' in space which is not solid, and then the blue becomes a yellow solid state of the 'thought-form'.

Among the many thousands of these images, or thought-forms, achieved by Dr Vogel over a four-year period with utmost patience and persistence as he sits in a darkened room and concentrates while the pre-form transforms into a solid state, are shapes of a bird, a gargoyle, a witch, a 'beautiful woman', an embryo, a 'trinity'.

Although in these experiments he gave 'free rein' to his imagination, there were many more complex formations as he worked to sort out the difference between reality and imagination and became more adept at mentally influencing and manipulating the pre-form in transit.

The trend of Dr Vogel's work has had a profound effect on him – from a man with a cursory interest in religion, he has become not religious in the orthodox sense, but spiritual, with a belief like Einstein's in a basic unifying intelligence that merges inseparably matter and mind, and it is almost certain that the first manifestations of this have been recorded in action on simple graphical charts.

In Russia, the exploration of the bio-energetic nature of man and the universe continues as a realm of physical science, devoid of mystical overtones, with emphasis on electrical and magnetic correlations or paranormal phenomena, more specifically classed as 'psychoenergetics' for parapsychology and 'bio-energetics' for PK.

The energy field associated with all living beings and given various names in the Western world, is spoken of as the 'biological plasma body' and is considered by Russian scientists in this area to be a 'fifth state of matter' consisting of 'free charged particles' that form organized pattern-arrangements in an unvaried 'web' of energy. Psychic phenomena are not considered outside this web, but part of it, and the job of research is to determine the nature of the whole and the part.

While Western experiment may be less innovative with instruments than the Soviets', its experiments are more rigorously controlled. Since 1971, realization has grown that each has something to learn from the other. Pooling of information has been established by means of large national and international conferences, the first of the latter in Moscow in 1972. In Prague in 1973, for instance, a conference sponsored by the newly-formed International Association for Psychotronic Research of Czechoslovakia ('psychotronics' being the Czechoslovakian term for 'the study of interactions between humans and organic and inorganic objects and their effects')[63] was attended by 250 scientists from twenty-one different countries, including several from the Soviet Academy of Sciences, and total attendance was close to four hundred. The coordinating secretary, Zdenek Rejdak, emphasized the objective of an 'holistic', interdisciplinary approach to the energy fields and the immense range of papers presented reflected this aim.

A Soviet scientist, Alexander Dubrov, reported an extensive investigation, conducted by researchers of the University of Novosibirsk, into a possible channel of communication between cells which could explain the mechanism of psychotronic phenomena. The hypothesis is that during cell division, energy is released that may, in the form of 'quasi-gravitational waves' be focused through the crystalline structure of the cell for telepathic communication. In over five thousand experiments on the nature of cell-radiation under varying conditions, they found that normal healthy cells emitted a uniform 'coded' communication. When there was disease in the cells, the 'code'-pattern became broken up and irregular, and the irregular patterns could also be related to specific disorders. Research was in process to investigate possibilities of both diagnosing and treating diseases by manipulation of the radiation 'codes'.

'Psychotronic generators' were explained and demonstrated by their designer, Robert Pavlita of Czechoslovakia. The devices, he claimed, could magnetize almost any material with purely psychic energy. Since both magnetism itself and psychic energy retain mystery, description of this achievement remained unclear, but it is conceded by some eminent scientists to be a potentially important development in this field. Benson Herbert believes it might involve a mixture of normal and paranormal energies.

The psychotronic generators come in a variety of shapes and sizes and can be used in as many ways to 'energize' objects. Robert Pavlita has spent over thirty years developing these generators which can purify water in a jar by drawing the pollutants to the bottom with psychically 'energized' iron chips; in another the psychic energy can cause a small metal disc to rotate, and in yet another it causes an electrically-rotated motor carrying a copper strip on top of a spike inside a sealed metal box to stop dead still by the concentrated focus of this energy by the inventor (later, he could start the motor up again and rotate it in the opposite direction).

Western representatives at the conference (much of whose work has already been covered in this book), reported experiments in the fields of radiation photography as developed from the pioneer Kirlian process, in acupuncture-point detection, and contributed some general theories consistent with the atmosphere of an 'holistic', multidisciplinary approach to psychoenergetics.

Many more large, multidisciplinary conferences of this order were held in 1974 and 1975 and are planned for 1976 and the years ahead, each one contributing to the advance of paranormal knowledge. It seems that a new aspect of science has firmly emerged and is unlikely to turn back.

4A PARASCIENCE AND THE STUDY OF CONSCIOUSNESS: A BRIDGE OF THEORIES AND PHILOSOPHIES

For scientists who wish to explore the world as consciousness an important tool may be consciousness itself, particularly its wider reaches. Scientists who are capable of personally experiencing such states could gain insight which would not otherwise be possible.

W. G. ROLL

AMONG physicists who are braving the uncharted country of consciousness, is Dr William Tiller, Chairman of the Department of Materials Science at Stanford Research Institute. Known for his work in crystallization, surfaces, and the general materials field, Dr Tiller's interest in parapsychology and the mind seems a contradiction.

Actually, the two interests have co-existed in his personal thinking for some time, converging in recent years when he and his wife joined the Religious Science Church in Palo Alto, California, where he gave a series of talks, which led to his collected essays *Evolution not Revolution* (1970). Later, a period of reading and theorizing on psychical matters while on sabbatical leave at Oxford University, was followed by a research project in Russia as part of a seven-man team investigating Soviet work in psychoenergetics. There, he gathered a great deal of useful information on detection devices and his interest was quickened by the immense potential inherent in the subject generally.

From this combined experience came a strong urge to convey what he had learned and encourage Western scientists to step up their research in the field. To do this, he resigned his scientific post to give lectures and talks. A year later, having aroused many qualified people to carry on psychoenergetic research and communication he returned to his work, and as an extracurricular activity, turned to research of his own.

What he sought in this work had by now shaped in his mind as a concept involving three requisites: first the transformation of man (meaning increased awareness and perceptual understanding by man of both his individual and collective level of being); the nature of the universe (so that man can be better understood); understanding energies of a non-physical nature (how they function in man), and development of reliable devices for detecting and monitoring these non-physical energies.

The model that Dr Tiller uses for his thinking has seven unique dimensions: a positive space-time frame, physically perceived; the 'companion' or 'etheric' conjugate frame (or 'negative space-time dimension' at present not reliably perceived by science); and these two dimensions go together to form the four-dimensional space-time continuum; a transitional, or 'astral' frame in which the emotional energy of the body is manifest).

This last frame, Dr Tiller believes,[156] is the bridge between the temporal and eternal. In the eternal, there are four basic levels in his model. Three have to do with mind – the lowest is instinctive mind, then intellectual mind, and then spiritual mind. Beyond that is the dimension of 'spirit'. The latter four dimensions he thinks of as frames of existence of the 'true man'. Here man is indestructible and eternal and this is where his true growth takes place. To aid his growth, man has the vehicle of a body allowing sensory experience, and reference to the earth frame. The vehicle is temporary and the entity, man, spends much of his time learning to 'work the levers and knobs of the vehicle'. The familiar terms for this condition of body and soul, Dr Tiller looks at in terms of energies and energy correlations.

The seven levels, which Dr Tiller illustrates in Figure 11 can be imagined as a seven-dimensional unity, thinking of each level as a circle of different colour drawn on tracing paper, then the papers placed together so that on looking through all seven colours they are seen as one.

According to Dr Tiller, the seven levels interpenetrate as well as interact with each other. Through the polarity principle they form atoms and molecules and configurations, these influenced increasingly through the agency of mind: mind can bring about changes in the organization of structure in these various levels.

Dr Tiller calls this mind-level that works through the other levels to produce a physical effect (or vice versa), the 'ratchet' effect. It is, he says, based on the yogic philosophy of the seven

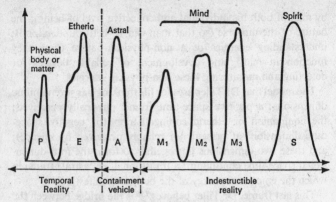

Figure 11 Schematic spectral distribution curve illustrating, along one coordinate, relative radiation characteristics of the seven levels of substance (consciousness).

principles operating in man (in English terms: 7. Spirit; 6. Spiritual Mind; 5. Intellect; 4. Instinctive Mind; 3. *Prana*, or vital force; 2. Astral Body; 1. Physical Body). Each level has its own laws, going from the most apparent, at the physical level, to the subtlest, at the level of spirit. He further postulates that they exist in different kinds of space-time frames in the universe, which gives each unique characteristics of radiation (absorption and emission), or energy fields.

Also related to Dr Tiller's seven levels or dimensions, are the chakras, meaning 'wheels', of Hatha Yoga (the aspect of yoga dealing with the science of bodily health), the six 'subtle' energy centres situated along the spinal column of the etheric body at the location of the spleen, the base of the spine, the navel, the heart, the throat, the forehead, and the top of the head (*see* Figure 12), and connected by 'Nadis', or nerve channels which run down each side of the spinal column. These, together with the endocrine glands, basically at the same locations of the physical body, can be tuned to form a circuit that draws cosmic energy into the etheric, which becomes transduced into a different form for the functioning of the physical body and radiates through the etheric as spiritual qualities. He also relates the acupuncture points to an etheric form of circuitry.

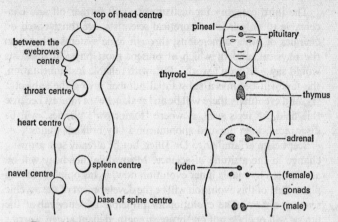

Figure 12 Left: Location of the 7 major chakras at the etheric level of substance.
Right: Location of the 7 major endocrine glands at the physical level of substance.

(William Tiller)

Dr Tiller sums up this blend of energy principles by observing that the primary source of energy in the cosmos is not necessarily electro-magnetic. It could be, of course, but it is more likely to be another source 'with perhaps many different kinds of energy that we presently know not of'. Some day, he says, we will. 'This energy flows in space in great currents, and it passes through our bodies unabsorbed and unnoticed unless we tune the chakras to couple with this power source and transduce some of its energy into the etheric system'.

As for the instruments that will fuse science and consciousness into a unified field, recognizable and available to one and all, Dr Tiller sees good possibilities in the further development of radiation photography, the polygraph and other 'read-out' machines that establish correlates of non-physical and physical energies. Just as important, though, he feels, are 'human instruments'. More work such as Dr Karagulla's with people who perceive other energy bands must be carried out. Substantial numbers of these perceptions must be cross-checked for common denominators and related to man's common experience.

The third category for instruments, still further off and conceivable to only a few theoretical scientists, are those based on energies of other dimensions, through logic systems other than the physical, and of which at present most physical scientists would say – 'it won't work'. But, with reliable instrumentation, the few will become a substantial number giving the subject a try, and eventually there will be an 'avalanche' of interest because this field, he feels sure, is where 'tomorrow's physics' will be discovered, then pursued spontaneously by brilliant minds.

Scepticism is familiar to Dr Tiller, but he already sees growing change in the attitude of science. Meanwhile, headway will be accelerated by man's inner evolution now, in his opinion, taking place. Part of this evolution will be the development of the psychic sensory system. The evolutionary principle of 'survival of the fittest' will operate not on 'brute strength, defiant anger, warrior training or cunning mind', but rather on characteristics of 'inner harmony, balanced behaviour, ability to love, and disciplined mind'.

Dr Tiller observes that 'unique information on man's internal states and perceptions have been lying fallow in the East for a long time . . . the East did not apply these ideas to daily life since they thought of life as an illusion, and often used these procedures to escape the day-to-day world'. If the West starts 'mining and processing these ideas' it will develop a new technology and new viewpoint of the universe. The ideas will change shape, be amplified and become more sophisticated. Man needs to make a major change now if his world is to survive, and this will be one step on the path to collective enlightenment.

As a final comment, W. G. Roll's suggestion that 'scientists who are capable of personally experiencing such states (consciousness) could gain insight which would not otherwise be possible', is put into practice by Dr Tiller. Each day, no matter how busy he is, he meditates for periods of up to an hour. Although he prefers the morning for meditation, he also attunes himself meditatively at other times of the day when he feels the need. His form of meditation is a mixture of approaches that suits him individually. His main object is to still his mind and keep himself 'open to the whole universe'. If he is working out a particular problem, he just localizes his consciousness 'softly, gently in that area – then my mind expands in that area . . .'

Of course, as a scientist who meditates, Dr Tiller is far from alone; there are no qualitative boundaries to meditation's current infiltration – but it does seem to bear out the comment of Dr A. Imich of New York that 'The scientist is the yogi of the West'. Perhaps additionally, the yogi is the scientist of the East.

In practical alignment with Dr Tiller's theories, are the findings of a three-year study by Dr Hiroshi Motoyama of Tokyo, Japan, to see whether the chakras, nadis and acupuncture meridians had, in fact, physiological correlates. His research employed one hundred yogis, whose typical acupuncture circuitry was recorded and measured by a combination of monitoring instruments (EEG, polygraph, etc.) and psychical tests.

· Dr Motoyama's[54] first progress report, which was encouraging, has resulted in the construction of sophisticated electronic equipment. One instrument, fully automated, is already being used in hospitals, research institutions and acupuncture clinics in Japan. His machines are soon to be demonstrated in the West, and one is under experiment with Dr Bernard Watson of the Medical Electronics Department of St Bartholomew's Hospital, London.

Another theory on the nature of consciousness, related to quantum mechanics,* is being developed by Evan Harris Walker, a physicist (Concepts Analysis) with the US Ballistic Research Laboratories at the Army Aberdeen Proving Ground in Maryland.[169] Without attempting to present the highly technical aspects, an abstract of the foundation of his theory taken from written papers, states that 'behind processes of the world that are physically measurable there exist processes that determine the development of events in the physical world'. He believes that although physicists deal with the objective view of the world, it should be ultimately possible to translate any objective format to the subjective, or vice versa, if the explanation is complete. Most physicists disregard the nature of consciousness, feeling that all the physical equations should be worked out and established first;

*Very briefly: quantum theory is a theory of the wave-like nature of matter in which the position of a particle is uncertain when the momentum is fixed.

therefore, this subject has suffered indefinite postponement, unjustifiably he believes, in the light of arguments on the brain already sufficiently settled.

Skipping past the philosophical delineation of consciousness, which has no present means of being directly measured as an object, Dr Walker puts forward his first postulate as a working hypothesis: 'Consciousness is a nonphysical but real entity', until some machine makes this particular postulate unnecessary.

His second postulate is that 'there exists at least one physical quantity that connects the consciousness to the physically real world'. For this, it must be assumed that it is a 'single carrier phenomenon on which pain, pleasure, etc., all ride. Physical reality is connected to the consciousness by means of a single physically fundamental quality.' Consciousness, which for 2,500 years has been associated with the brain, must be associated with a physical process that is correspondingly extended. The nonphysical and the physical are coupled by means of a neurophysiological quantum process to the brain and to physical events.

In his theory, the ideas of life, thinking (data processing of the brain), and consciousness are seen to be distinct. He states that 'the consciousness of the individual who looks at the meter in an experiment for brain correlates of consciousness is, in a sense, the one who determines the outcome'. In scientific language, he speaks of consciousness as involving a communication between 'remote synapses' (a dictionary definition of 'synapse' is – 'point of contact between two cells'), and that all these synapses are somehow in contact.

Dr Walker postulates that personal identity lies beyond the physical body. Ultimately, consciousness is sometimes present and sometimes absent, according to the communication between the synapses, or nerve-cells, and 'hidden variables' which are not accessible to physical determination by any finite set of measurements but which include the variables that describe the conscious state.

Summarizing a presentation of his theory to the 15th annual meeting of the Parapsychological Association in 1972, Dr Walker indicated that his concepts could be developed to provide a foundation theory for psi phenomena. And with regard to religion,

Dr Walker has written that 'the idea of an agency having the properties necessary to interrelate conscious observers is suggestive of concepts such as that of 'Cosmic Consciousness' (a term used by Richard M. Bucke[18] to describe a flash of brilliant illumination that transforms the consciousness, experienced by all the great 'enlightened' ones such as Gautama, Jesus, St Paul, Mohammed and poets such as Blake, Whitman, as well as numbers of unknown but sensitive individuals).

The foregoing is incomplete, vague – except for those scientists who can read in the missing mathematical equations – and therefore does Dr Walker an injustice; but it is presented to show the furthest reaches of physical science to explain consciousness in its own terms.

For Dr E. W. Bastin, of Cambridge University, whose work as a physicist is to consider 'new concepts of the space-time continuum', consciousness cannot be defined as an entity apart from any other, nor can it be defined. There is no separability of life's processes.[6]

Alan Mayne,[90] a mathematical scientist of the University of London, feels that it is possible 'to develop a unified synthesis that combines the best features of the scientific, parascientific, experiential, religious and philosophical approaches, and that this "transcendental" pattern of knowledge will have great beauty'. He believes, further, that this synthesis is urgently needed to lead mankind out of its present predicament, that it will strengthen human ethical foundations in the process, and that sufficient progress has already been made to make practical applications of this new, synthesizing science.

Dr Eugene P. Wigner, Nobel Prize-winning physicist, also believes there is a place for consciousness in modern physics. In excerpts of his work appearing in *Consciousness and Reality*[104] (edited by Charles Musès and Arthur Young), he says:

'All that quantum mechanics purports to provide are probability connections between subsequent impressions (or "apperceptions") of the consciousness, and even though the dividing line between the observer, whose consciousness is being affected, and the observed physical object can be shifted toward the one or the other to a considerable degree, it cannot be eliminated. It may be premature to believe that the present philosophy of quantum mechanics will remain a permanent feature of future physical theories; it will remain remarkable, in whatever way our future concepts may develop, that the very study of the external world led to the conclusion that the contents of the consciousness is an ultimate reality. . . .'

A fellow of the American Association for the Advancement of Science and former head of cancer research at the Biochemical Institute of the University of Texas, Dr Alfred Taylor[104] has observed that while material scientists had necessarily to be extremely careful to keep data free of subjective influences, to be 'realistic', it is obvious that it went too far in assuming that 'ordered sequences can evolve out of materials, solely by random play of forces . . . scientific research itself is based on the assumption of an intelligently ordered world – otherwise research would be impossible . . . Materialism – the notion that life is merely the collocation of inanimate individual units – cannot account for the incredible organization it assumes, and indeed finds.

'. . . since all forms have their origin in one source, we are forced to the conclusion that *organization* is the determining factor, whether energy appears as hydrogen or lead, as a daisy or a man. Something must distinguish one from the other, and that something is organization, meaning, consciousness . . . the *meaning* of the form transcends matter-changes. The same being continues, but not the same materials.

'Physics,' observes Dr Taylor, 'is necessarily becoming more metaphysical as its research progresses. Chemistry is based on elaborate theoretical organizations of chemical elements and associated energies. And the life sciences are primarily involved with the quality of organization. The materialistic hypothesis certainly does not add to the objectivity of scientific research, but rather brings to it a quality more weird than a tale from the Arabian Nights.

'We look at a rose and are under the illusion that the idea of it in our minds is what we receive through the sense of physical sight. But, of course, this is not so. A rose is a meaning, a value that can be appreciated only by an intelligent observer. Our eyes bring to us only different qualities of brightness, of colour. No sense organ can possibly react to meaning or significance, since these qualities are not in physical space or time.

'Scientific knowledge,' Dr Taylor says, 'has revealed a universe of meaning, plan, ideation, intelligence. The more that scientists are able to translate the book of nature, the more astounding is the wisdom revealed. We can be confident that the previous emphasis on materialism will soon be discarded.'

Head of the Physics Department at Birkbeck College, Professor John Hasted, an experimental physicist, has a theory into which mind and the paranormal may fit. He ascribes to 'The Many Worlds Interpretation of Quantum Mechanics' developed in the fifties and sixties by a number of American theoreticians, (Wheeler, Everett, De Witt, Graham, etc.) which, he believes, gets around the difficulty of forming a real mathematical theory of a random event (e.g. when a radioactive source emits a pulse of radiation, it is impossible to predict when that pulse is going to come because the clicks for the geiger counter are truly random and the 'hidden variable' which might explain it remains elusive).[53]

This theory, in essence, is that every time such a quantum event occurs, the universe forks, splits into two universes. Those cohabit the same space, but they cannot communicate with each other in any physical way. Because their way-functions, though normal, are orthogonal (right-angled) to each other, there's no communication possible. However, these quantum events occur millions of times every second in all parts of the world, so if each one makes a new universe, 'there must be an awful lot of universes: fortunately they can't communicate with each other, so we only know our one universe in which an event has occurred at a particular time, which we say is random – in the other universes it's also random, but the relationship between the different universes is not.

'It might be possible to extend this idea', Professor Hasted adds, 'by saying that in the mind one could subtend more than the one universe . . . and if you're willing to admit that, you can interpret most paranormal phenomena, because you simply say they have occurred in another universe, and the subject instantaneously apprehends them. . . . I think it's the central part of paranormal investigation that solid objects can pass through solid barriers i.e. disappear and reappear on the other side (this has happened with Uri Geller and in some poltergeist phenomena). Suppose there has been a quantum event which has split the universes; by means of a very unlikely tunnelling through an energy barrier, an object has been displaced in one of the universes. The subject has the ability to "see" this very rare event, and telepathically he makes us all see it as well. Locally, we are now in a different universe from the one in which we started.'

Although Professor Hasted knows his theory is 'way-out' for current physics, and that there is much work ahead to investigate it, there do exist some potential 'regimes' to explore: while differing from Evan Harris Walker's ideas in this many-universe approach, Professor Hasted feels there is common ground in their view of 'non-local wave functions' (states of knowledge) communicating with each other through those 'hidden variables'.

Professor David Bohm, an eminent theoretical physicist at Birkbeck College, University of London, whose chief endeavour for many years has been in developing new notions of space, time and matter, sees the same inseparability. In his boldly conceived and gradually developing 'Implicate Enfolded Order'[11], in which the movement consists of unfolding an order which is folded up, and therefore not a movement in space or time at all, he proposes that the ways mind works are similar to the ways matter works, that the universe works in a way that is not all that different from the way consciousness works, that all matter has a kind of consciousness, that 'consciousness is a reflection of reality'.

. . . 'Quantum mechanics,' he says, 'implies that there are discontinuous transitions from one state to another, without passing through the states in between. Now that would imply that the nature of time, space and matter cannot be separated . . . the past does not become the present, something new is eternally unfolding – this unfolding is the way in which the past, present and future may be folded all together, that which is implicate, in all its content, becomes "explicate", or unfolded.'

Professor Bohm illustrates this idea by describing an instrument called a 'hologram', in which, he explains, we can form an image in which everything is 'implicit', that is to say folded into each part, and can become unfolded by using light in a suitable way so that you can see a three-dimensional image coming out. The image is frozen in each part of the picture. It is characteristic of this 'holomovement' (or 'indivisible flux') that the whole is in each part, that there is no division of the world. This again is similar to consciousness in the sense that the whole of consciousness is implicit in each element of consciousness. So one might say that the consciousness and the whole of reality are not as different as we had supposed.

In developing this new general world view, or metaphysics, Professor Bohm explains that 'we cannot stop with the attempt to understand matter alone through the implicate order. For we ourselves, along with electrons, protons, rocks, planets, galaxies, etc. are only relatively stable forms in the holomovement. It is necessary to include not only our bodies, with their brains and nervous systems, but also our thoughts, feelings, urges, will and desire, which are inseparable from the functions of these brains and nervous systems. If the ultimate ground of all matter is in the implicate order, as contained in the holomovement, it thus seems inevitable that what has generally been called "mind" must also have the same ultimate ground.'

A theoretical physicist, Professor Fred Alan Wolf, of San Diego University, in 'The Question of Parascience, a Physicist's View' from *Space, Time and Beyond*,[174] presents a view that differs from the classical and in some ways the quantum. 'Classical thinking' he says, 'results from the universal consciousness recognizing itself by dividing into an "I" and a "not-I". The behaviour of the not-I becomes an observable of the I. But suppose we choose to "stop the world" (meaning, the act of perception), like magic, all paths between the event where we started to perceive and an original event, come into existence, or awareness.

'By stopping the world, the I changes its perception of the not-I. A physicist calls this fundamental process of separation of I from not-I, the act of measurement. It is in this process that the not-I universe comes into existence and in this process that it is changed ...

'The state of knowledge itself can be constructed from this view,' Professor Wolf continues, '... we can determine the future and past wave functions once the *now* wave function is known. In essence all we have are fundamental acts of I–not-I separations ... the I in seeing the not-I of itself is defining time itself ... each act of the I–not-I separation is irreversible, each act is a quantum jump into the pool of "is-ness", making a splash and giving rise to waves of information. The infinity of splashes makes an ocean of random waves ...

'We have posed an answer as to how it is that the fundamented act of life, the act of consciousness, by becoming aware of itself, in separation of I and not-I, changes itself. With each fundamented act, with myriads of twinkling star-like acts of awareness, the whole pattern forms an infinite lattice of connection between I–not-I twinkles. Laws of order and motions then appear as the action strands in the cosmic spider web.'

While this abstraction of what seems itself like an abstraction may be difficult to follow, Professor Wolf has this to say of any attempt to put the abstract, scientific or mystical, into words: 'My viewpoint is that one must endeavour, one must struggle, to explain what one is experiencing – therein lies the key to enlightenment, the key to understanding; to keep trying to get ideas and experience into word-form until finally one can get it into a form which is beyond word-form, which is more abstract, more mathematical, which is eventually what we call physics ...

'And if one doesn't make that struggle, if one is not aware of that struggle, then one is never going to find out what mind is.'

Charles Musès, Director of Research at the Centre de Recherches en Mathematiques et Morphologie in Switzerland, and co-editor with Arthur Young of the *Journal for the Study of Consciousness*, has a theory of 'Hypernumbers'[104] to bridge materialism and consciousness. The theory is too complicated to present anything but approximately here, but Dr. Musès postulates that a new kind of number could be used by advanced mathematicians to map and explore the so-far immeasurable and imponderable consciousness.

This one new kind of number 'would more than double the entire mathematical power of all the previous centuries, and would become intimately related to the new physical discoveries in electronics, atomic theory and twentieth-century chemistry'.

In his investigations, Dr Musès has already observed seven kinds of number (although the kinds might be infinite) possessing 'unique and powerful properties', by which great advances into the relationship of consciousness to matter and energy could lead the way to realities that might otherwise have 'lain hidden and unsuspected in the profound obscurity of man's unconscious mind, and in a side of nature he did not see'; in other words, from 'hypernumbers' to 'hypermind'.

In a postscript to the book, Charles Musès reaches out further still, toward 'a love-restored science'. As more sub-atomic particles are revealed to dismay and baffle the physicist, 'what is happening is that infinity is wearying those minds that had futilely hoped to exclude it'. He urgently advocates 'the restoration of love as a prime value in reason as well as in feeling . . . (only then) will the horrors of war, political oppression, ecological pollution, and psychological blindness and unbalance be overcome . . . The love-balanced and love-deepened mind would also see that the bewildering variety of sub-atomic particles means that the basis of the so-called physical world is not simply physical but biological: and that all these countless forms are living creatures in a proto-biological reality governed by powerful tropisms* that appear to us as the "laws" of the physical world. Without these tiny beings acting *en masse* in their accustomed ways, we would be as helpless and unviable as if the hordes of humble diatoms in the seas stopped providing their contribution of seventy per cent of the earth's atmospheric oxygen . . . such is the living vista that a love-restored science will see.'

To illustrate the forward push of scientific interest in mind and consciousness, a unique theme for our civilization was introduced at the twenty-third international conference of the Parapsychology Foundation in Geneva, Switzerland, in August 1974 – *Quantum Physics and Parapsychology*. Here, ten physicists from five different countries gathered to compare their thoughts and theories as to how these two sciences could be related. It was a highly technical meeting, and several intriguing new hypotheses were introduced, but the main importance of the event was that it took place, cor-

---

*Response of plants or sedentary animals in growing towards or away from a stimulus.

roborating that the mind of science has been opened up and is unlikely to close again.

As parascience edges closer and closer to metascience, Robert Ornstein[109] and colleagues at the Langley-Porter Neuropsychiatric Institute in California are casting new light on the apparent objective-subjective dichotomy of consciousness, this time by means of the brain.

Even as a student of psychology, Dr Ornstein was more interested in the nature of consciousness itself than in the methodology of the subject. When biofeedback looked a promising area, he explored its possibilities and was fascinated particularly by the fact that people who practised meditation gained more control over their physiological functions than those who did not. Drawn next into the study of Eastern philosophies, he felt that Western culture seriously undervalued the intuitive aspect of the mind, the way problems could be solved with an 'interior' science.

The two interests combined in a decision to conduct some experiments with a former colleague, Roger Sperry, whose 'split-brain' work with disturbed and epileptic patients had contributed insight into the different functioning of the two separate types of cerebral cortex, the left and right 'hemispheres' of the brain (connected by a dense nerve-bundle called 'corpus callosum').

This innovative research resulted in some highly significant revelations. Based on biofeedback principles, tests were designed to determine whether the two brain hemispheres of normal, healthy people could be monitored in relation to alpha rhythm (since alpha indicated the brain in an 'idling' state).

The left hemisphere was usually associated with rational functioning, and the right with intuitive functioning, so a student subject was given tasks appropriate to each; e.g. composing a letter and matching blocks to a design, while fitted with scalp electrodes.

The exactness of the correlation caused much excitement among the experimenters. Unable to believe it, they carried out ten more experiments with six different subjects. The results held: it was quite clear which task was being performed, by the alteration of alpha activity on the machine.

Since then, a great deal more information has been gathered. It now appears that people who have seemed to have only one kind of ability may only be using half of their brain's capacity while the other half remains undeveloped.

A division of functions can now be more precisely located: the left hemisphere is associated with such activities as calculating, reading, writing, speaking – the right with artistic creativity, music appreciation, visualization, contemplation, abstract thought. In Western culture, Dr Ornstein points out, the left hemisphere dominates. Western education develops the left hemisphere with 'reading, writing and arithmetic', relegating minimal importance to the development of right-hemisphere creativity, abstraction and intuition.

On the other hand, Eastern culture is right hemisphere dominated and centred. Here, education and values are organized about intuition, contemplation and spatial awareness. Both cultures, he believes, are out of balance, but now with an understanding of these two modes of thought that illustrates the two cultures are not just representing opposing philosophic principles but two biological principles, the two can be made complementary.

The brain, a $3\frac{1}{2}$-pound instrument, which from the top looks like the kernel of a walnut, contains millions of individual cells which can, in any one day, make one hundred times as many interconnections as the entire telephone systems of the world. The nearest man-made instrument is the computer which, in its most sophisticated complexity, generates a comparatively infinitesimal degree of left-hemisphere intelligence, and no right-hemisphere activity whatever – no biology, no language, no ability to generate life. The human brain cannot only predict, interpret, build expectations, regulate in response to outside connections in a two-way process, but has a choice of possible neural connections that if written out would come to 1 followed by $9\frac{1}{2}$ kilometres of noughts.

No man yet exists who can use all the potential of his brain, and there are no discernible limits to its capacity. The genius of Einstein was not in his great scholarship – he even failed mathematics at school – but in his intuitive, right-hemisphere ability to see an abstract whole. His brain's less able, but adequate, left hemisphere was then able to translate his intuition into the logic of science. In fact, the genius of many men has been based on 'the flash' of inspiration supported by sequential reasoning which Einstein himself described as the 'combinatorial play' by which he evolved his Theory of Relativity.

It is through this interfusion of the meditative and intellectual processes, Dr Ornstein suggests, that man will become *fully* conscious. Meanwhile, Dr Ornstein is researching the possibility of training people through biofeedback techniques to 'switch' to one or another of their brain hemispheres at will.

4B SCIENCE REACHES INTO RELIGION AND MYSTICAL EXPERIENCE

RELIGION has no name or place in science, even though William James, himself a scientist, said in *The Varieties of Religious Experience*[64] that he did not think psychology would be complete until it included an account of spiritual man. Albert Einstein went further when, in *Ideas and Opinions*, he said: 'Science without religion is lame, religion without science is blind'.

Certainly no scientist has ever conducted a systematic exploration of the nature of religious experience with the intention of relating it to an integral, biological process in man – no one, that is, until 1970 when Professor Sir Alister Hardy,[51] Professor Emeritus of Zoology at Oxford University, started his Religious Experience Research Unit at Manchester College, Oxford.

Sir Alister does not believe that science itself can 'touch the real essence' of religious experience, any more than it can 'embrace the nature' of art. He does, however, hold the view that the scientist can make a systematic, methodological study of written records of man's religious experience and that this could provide enlightening and valuable information. This is the objective of the research unit.

Its first project has been to collect 5,000 samples of religious experience, sent in to them by people willing to write them down. By 1974 there were some 3,500 on files, 1,000 of them analysed.

Initially Sir Alister had written to religious publications asking them to publish requests for experiences, which were to be sent in with the assurance they would be kept strictly confidential. The mere 250 replies were a disappointment. Subsequently, however, he was interviewed by several leading newspapers and wrote some articles for them about his research. This led to a more plentiful supply.

When the experiences are collated, they are carefully studied by Sir Alister and the three qualified academic members of his staff, including Dr Edward Robinson, a philosopher, who has made previous studies of childhood religious experiences. It has not been easy to classify the experiences by familiar systems because they tend to be composite. Now that there are sufficient on record, however, Sir Alister plans to write back to all the contributors asking specific questions that have formed from the aggregate so as to further clarify their components.

Sir Alister and his colleagues have by now become aware of the various kinds of religious experiences people undergo, but not how many people have them in relation to population and location. The unit hopes to employ an opinion poll to sample 1,000 people and to extract some twelve short questions evolved from the unit's analyses that could be asked generally, e.g. 'Have you ever had any of these religious experiences?'

So far, the Religious Experience Research Unit have distinguished fourteen major elements in the experiences on record. Naturally, these are divided and sub-divided, and it is now possible to make much improved comparisons of their main characteristics. Since Sir Alister envisions a long-term programme, he is aware that this preliminary work is more or less 'the natural history' area that is necessary before attempting to apply the systematic methods of science. He needs to amass more records, and appeals to those who feel they have had any religious experience to write it down and send it to the Research Unit. This is a project that needs the help of people, the cooperation of the general public.

In a statement of RERU's aims, Sir Alister says in part:

'Some people may have felt that there is nothing particularly remarkable about their own experiences and that we would not be interested in them. The reverse is true. We do indeed want accounts of these seemingly more ordinary but deeply-felt experiences. Again, some may have been misled by the very term "religious experience", thinking that it must only refer to the more dramatic isolated experiences; I want to make it quite clear that we are just as interested in accounts of that continuing sense of spiritual awareness which many people feel makes a difference to their lives . . .

'I further realize that there are people who feel that their religious experience is altogether too sacred and personal a matter to be exposed to any examination, even though their names will never be made known in relation to it.'

As support, Sir Alister quotes Professor C. C. J. Webb (philosopher and theologian), who also said 'there is a serious danger of overlooking the existence of a genuine religious experience which, although taking forms perhaps less strange and striking (than those of some mystics) is not therefore less real and significant'.

'With these explanations', Sir Alister continues, 'I hope that many more may be able to help us in our work. All those who feel that they have been conscious of, and perhaps influenced by, some Power, whether they call it God or not, which may either appear to be beyond their individual selves or partly, or even entirely, within their being, are asked to write a simple account of these feelings and their effects.

'All such records should include particulars of age, sex, nationality, whether married or single, religious upbringing, present faith, if any, age at time of any particular experience and any other factors thought to be relevant; they should be sent with the name and address of the sender.'

Here are a few extracts from the first thousand recorded experiences:

(1) 'I find it difficult to describe my experience, only to say that it seems to be outside of me and enormous and yet at the same time I am part of it, everything is. It is purely personal and helps me to live and to love others. It is difficult to describe, but in some way because of this feeling I feel united to all people, to all living things. Of recent years the feeling has

become so strong that I am now training to become a social worker because I find that I must help people: in some way I feel their unhappiness as my own.'

(2) 'It seemed to me that, in some way, I was extending into my surroundings and was becoming one with them. At the same time I felt a sense of lightness, exhilaration and power as if I was beginning to understand the true meaning of the whole Universe.'

(3) 'When I was on holiday, aged about 17, I glanced down and watched an ant striving to drag a bit of twig through a patch of sun on a brick wall in the graveyard of a Greek church, while chanting came from within the white building. The feeling aroused in me was quite unanticipated, welling up from some great depth, and essentially timeless. The concentration of simplicity and innocence was intensely of some vital presence. I've had similar experiences on buses, suddenly watching people and being aware how *right* everything essentially is.'

(4) 'I think from my childhood I have always had the feeling that the true reality is not to be found in the world as the average person sees it. There seems to be a constant force at work from the inside trying to push its way to the surface of consciousness. The mind is continually trying to create a symbol sufficiently comprehensive to contain it, but this always ends in failure. There are moments of pure joy with a heightened awareness of one's surroundings, as if a great truth had been passed across.'

(5) 'One day as I was walking along Marylebone Road I was suddenly seized with an extraordinary sense of great joy and exaltation, as though a marvellous beam of spiritual power had shot through me linking me in rapture with the world, the Universe, Life with a capital L, and the beings around me. All delight and power, all things living, all time fused in a brief second.'

(6) 'As far back as I can remember I have never had a sense of separation from the spiritual force I now choose to call God . . . From the age of about 6 to 12 in places of quiet and desolation this feeling of "oneness" often passed to a state of

"listening". I mean by "listening" that I was suddenly alerted to something that was going to happen. What followed was a feeling of tremendous exaltation in which time stood still.'

Apart from religious experiences, the RERU is investigating extrasensory perception, which Sir Alister feels is important and relevant. After all, what is prayer, what is this inner communication with forces-invisible, if it is not extrasensory? 'If the scientific world can be convinced that thought patterns can be transferred from one mind to another by non-physical means, it lends plausibility to the possibility of individuals making contact with something outside themselves, something transcendental.'

Sir Alister is not attempting to postulate what this is, but reiterates the value of qualitative descriptions of a body of facts, followed by the quantitative study of the same facts by experimental method.

The final outcome of this combination, he hopes, may be 'such a mass of evidence that the majority of the intellectual world must come to realize that religious experience is indeed a vital part of man's make up and so bring about a change in our present climate of materialistic culture'.

Scientific in purpose and approach, this research has not yet braved the final borderlands where religion and science can be said to meld in a 'supra-consciousness' of man, an 'omniscience' incorporating mysticism. As Dr D. M. A. Leggett, Vice-Chancellor of Surrey University in Guildford, has said: 'With comparatively few exceptions they (scientists) ask for proof. Our situation today resembles climbers setting out to scale a hitherto unscaled peak. It is useless to ask for proof that the peak can be scaled before setting out. The only proof possible consists in actually scaling it.'

On the other hand, Lawrence LeShan,[81] a psychologist and pioneer in the study of psychic healing in America and the scientific training of healers, has compiled a list of statements made by modern theoretical physicists and acclaimed mystics of various eras and cultures, in which the similarities of description of the nature of reality are all but indistinguishable. Published in *The Journal of Transpersonal Psychology* (1969) (and later in his book *The Medium, the Mystic and the Physicist*, 1974), Dr LeShan had composed them as an experiment. Their significance, he later felt, was not so much that the quotations had been impossible for one or the other of the groups to identify with accuracy, but that it had been 'a difficult task'.

As one of this century's most learned students on the subject of mysticism, Evelyn Underhill[162] describes mystics as a type of personality which 'refuses' to be satisfied with that which other men call experience, and are inclined to 'deny the world in order that it may find reality. These persons are met in the east and west, in the ancient, medieval and modern worlds. . . . Whatever the place or period in which they have arisen, their aims, doctrines and methods have been substantially the same. Their experience, therefore, *forms a body of evidence*, curiously self-consistent and often mutually explanatory which must be taken into account before we can add up the sum of the energies and potentialities of the human spirit, or reasonably speculate on its relations to the unknown world which lies outside the boundaries of sense.'

Dr LeShan points out that while the 'goal of the mystic is to be more at home in the universe, to comprehend and be part of reality, and to attain serenity', by contrast the 'goal of the physicist is to understand and control physical reality'. The incompatibility of the two viewpoints seems to have rested at an impasse as two bodies of evidence, one empirical up to the vanishing point of hypernumbers, and the other solely validated by human experience. Yet in the following quotations, only a few out of sixty-two in Dr LeShan's paper, the divergence appears less conclusive. Can the reader, perhaps, discern which statement belongs to mystics and which to physicists? (The answers are at the end of the chapter on page 228.)

(1) 'So far as broader characteristics are concerned, we see in nature what we look for or are equipped to look for. Of course, I do not mean that we can arrange the details of the scene; but by the light and shade of our values we can bring out things that shall have the broad characteristics we esteem. In this sense the value placed on permanence creates the world of apparent substance; in this sense, perhaps, the God within creates the God in nature.'

(2) 'Nature gets credit which should in truth be reserved to ourselves; the rose for its scent, the nightingale for his song and the sun for its radiance. The poets are entirely mistaken. They should address their lyrics to themselves and should turn them into odes of self-congratulations on the excellency of the human mind. Nature is a dull affair, soundless, scentless, colourless, merely the hurrying of material, endlessly, meaninglessly.'

(3) 'It is immediately apparent, however, that this sense-world, this seemingly real external universe, though it may be useful and valid in other respects, cannot be *the* external world, but only the self's projected picture of it. It is a work of art, not a scientific fact; and whilst it may possess the profound significance proper to great works of art, it is dangerous if treated as a subject for analysis. Very slight investigation shows that it is a picture whose relation to reality is at best symbolic and approximate, and which would have no meaning for selves whose senses, or channels of communication, happen to be arranged upon a different plan. The evidence of the senses then, cannot be accepted as evidence of the nature of ultimate reality. Useful servants, they are dangerous guides.'

(4) 'Every attempt to solve the laws of causation, time and space would be futile because the very attempt would have to be made by taking for granted the existence of these three.'

(5) 'Matter expressed itself eventually as a formulation of some unknown Force. Life, too, that yet unfathomed mystery, begins to reveal itself as an obscure energy of sensitivity imprisoned in its material formulation; and when the dividing ignorance is cured, that gives us the sense of a gulf between life and matter, it is difficult to suppose that mind, life and matter will be found to be anything else than one energy, triply formulated.'

(6) 'Religion and natural science are fighting a joint battle in a second, never-ending crusade against scepticism and dogmatism, and against superstition. The rallying cry for this crusade has always been and always will be "On to God!"'

(7) '(Modern Science) (Deeper Understanding) has demonstrated that in the real world surrounding us, it is not the geometric

forms, but the dynamic laws concerning movement (coming into being and passing away) which are permanent.'

(8) 'We are deceived if we allow ourselves to believe that there is ever a pause in the flow of becoming, a resting place where positive existence is attained for even the briefest duration of time. It is only by shutting our eyes to the succession of events that we come to speak of things rather than processes.'

Although these quotations tend to be philosophy rather than the substance of physics, or mysticism, Dr LeShan's exercise does seem to point up, in a new way, that the veil between them might be thinner than supposed.

4C THE EXPLOSION OF RESEARCH FOR A SCIENCE OF MIND, SPIRIT AND CONSCIOUSNESS

IN the West, the most recent emphasis of mind today – like an eye that is suddenly impelled to see itself seeing – is the turning of millions of young people to religious teachings and philosophies, preponderantly ancient and Asian.

More like a quiet revolution, this phenomenon is not entirely explained as disillusionment with religion that provides nothing relatable or acceptable to their twentieth-century lives, or with a technological society that leaves them essentially unfulfilled and adrift.

It can be partially accounted for by the drug-induced confirmation of expanded realms of consciousness, similar to those described by mystics, by followers of 'pre-scientific' religions. Certainly this might have instigated the re-focusing and re-evaluating of Eastern practices and doctrines of the spirit. And to this could be added the discovery that they often replaced the drug experience with far more insightful and salubrious forms of expansion.

But more than all these, a kind of appropriateness is suggested, a turning-point, a moving on of human self-discovery with evolutionary overtones. Gopi Krishna,[78] author and founder of

The Research Institute for Kundalini, in an article for *Psychic* magazine, observed: 'From the zenith of material prosperity – at which mankind now stands due to the achievements of science – the ascent towards spirituality will begin. Modern knowledge, now almost at the frontier of its survey of the physical world, has but a short distance to cover to gain knowledge of the entrance to the spiritual realm. This is the biological mechanism of evolution in every human body.' And Jacob Needleman, in the preface of his book *The New Religions*,[107] observes that 'it is not because they (the young) have stopped searching for transcendental answers to the fundamental questions of human life, but because that search has now intensified beyond measure'.

He also points out that although students across the country (and in Europe) are 'demanding courses in Buddhism, Hinduism and mysticism, often forming their own "free universities" to study these subjects' that 'psychiatrists, psychologists and clergymen of all faiths are joining the younger generation in this pursuit – not only in order to understand the inclinations of the young and the interests of their patients but of the members of their congregations. They are turning to them, to these areas, to see for themselves if the East has a knowledge to offer our threatened society and our tormented religions.'

Moreover, he continues, 'the individual initiative of countless young men and women practising Eastern forms of meditation or group activity on their own . . . with or without drugs . . . is not the heart of the phenomenon. What gives the whole movement its real significance and life is the arrival (in the West) of certain unusual men from the East who have brought with them practical teachings and forms of organization, each of which in its own way is not only new to the West, but new to the world.

'It is these teachings and the influences they radiate which may well compel the consciousness of the West to take stock of itself in a way that has not happened since the dawn of the Scientific Revolution.'

The 'unusual men' referred to, are the gurus, the 'spiritual' teachers and masters who have come to the West to share their 'enlightenment' with those hungry for their ideas, for growth. Some, Tibetan Buddhists, entered the outside world for the first time in escape from the destruction of Tibet, and travelled West in response to the apparent interest. Some stayed in France, England and other parts of Europe, others went to New York and California. From various parts of India, masters of other aspects of Buddhism, of Sufism, Subud or Yoga, have brought their teaching to all the countries where there were eager students.

In Eastern religions, the guru is usually the means through which individual illumination is attained. The guru doesn't preach (there is no organized church, and the word 'religion' is a Western interpolation of philosophy) or deliver a body of dogma. He (or she) through subtle answers to a student's questions, leads him gently, persistently, to a personal inner awakening. Spiritual disciplines are provided step by step, *en route*. These are varying techniques, according to the particular approach and may include meditation, physical, breathing or psychological exercises.

Reaching enlightenment is far from easy. It has a definite progression from stage to stage that cannot be hurried by impatience, eagerness, or the most ardent desire. In India, millions have meditated around the clock for weeks and months, fasted, tortured themselves, to the point of permanent crippling and death, spent twenty-four hours a day under the influence of hallucinatory drugs, danced, chanted mantras and mastered the most drastic state of suspended animation – all without achieving the yearned-for 'union' with the Divine.

If this is true of India (and other places of similar tradition), it may be true of the Westerner, hopeful of a quick spiritual change. Enlightenment, the guru teaches, comes to those who are prepared by the right kind of understanding and not before. Within bounds of reason, however, nothing seems lost in the attempt. The consensus of participants in the 'spiritual explosion' in the West is that of incredible benefits; more compassion; greater ability to love; understanding of self and others; joy in living; new appreciation of nature; heightened awareness of beauty, colour, sound, taste, touch; increased alertness and energy; higher ideals and ethics; better health; more confidence; less fear of death; strong desire to help others.

In other words, whether true or full enlightenment, the deep awakening achieved by only a few hundreds of men and women over the course of time that utterly transforms them into the concept of 'sainthood', may be the lot of any more in the West than it has been in the East, at least a heightened state of consciousness could become widespread.

As for the possibility of *naïveté* leading to exploitation or psychological damage, Claudio Naranjo, in his book *The One Quest*,[105] says: 'Unquestionably the longing of the new generation has brought onto the scene (or the market) a number of self-styled teachers, American and Asian, who either profit momentarily or derive personal satisfaction from playing the "Master" game, and cultish groups increase their self-esteem by soliciting converts.

'Yet these are peripheral and pathological manifestations of a valid need, and the activity of earnest persons and groups should not be judged on the basis of these fringe elements as most of the great Eastern traditions presently have authoritative channels in the West.'

Many books are now available, translated into English (some for the first time) that explain the fine gradations of the main teachings of the East – Hinduism, Buddhism, Sufism. 'Sadhanas' (a 'liberating' spiritual discipline), Groups and Spiritual Centres have sprung into existence all over the world, their approaches too varied for complete listing. Some excellent attempts to do so are: *Year One Catalog*[41] ('A Spiritual Directory for the New Age') edited by Ira Friedlander, *A Catalog of Ways People Grow* by Severin Peterson,[118] *Aquarian Guide* edited by Francoise Strachan[148] and although not a directory or guide as such, *Religions of the East* by Anne Bancroft (London: Heinemann, 1974) gives a comprehensive survey of the Eastern philosophies.

The answers to Dr LeShan's test are as follows:
1. A. Eddington (Physicist (P))
2. A. N. Whitehead (P)
3. E. Underhill (Mystic (M))
4. Sri Vivekananda (M)
5. Sri Aurobindo (M)
6. Max Planck (P)
7. W. Heisenberg (P)
8. A. K. Coomaraswamy (M)

5

The burgeoning inquiry into extended ranges and reaches of the mind

Mankind now stands at several historical branching points. We are on the threshold of a preliminary reconnaissance of the cosmos. For the first time in his history, Man is capable of sending his instruments and himself from his home planet to explore the universe around him.

CARL SAGAN

AT the far end of the spectrum of mind power, reaching away from the very planet itself and extending outward to the universe, perhaps to infinity, are the recent beginnings of definite research into contacting other minds and forms of being than our own, perhaps other ways of thinking and feeling, of combining matter, intelligence and consciousness. All this could be very relevant to our growing understanding of our own minds and in particular of their potential powers of expansion. In 1971 scientists came to firm grips with 'exobiology', the study of extraterrestrial life.

A symposium unique in objective was held at the Byurakan Astrophysical Observatory in Armenia, sponsored jointly by the American and Soviet Academies of Science.[13] Attended by prominent physicists, biologists, astronomers, cryptologists, cyberneticists, linguists, sociologists, historians and archaeologists, the aim was to discuss problems of detecting and establishing contact with extraterrestrial civilizations.

The fact of great note in this event was that the scientists (who included two Nobel Laureates) now saw promise of finding other forms of life on other planets and communicating with them. They believed that Earth was at last technologically prepared for the serious attempt, and in the position to do so.

It was a momentous statement, affirming the visions of science-fiction; extraterrestrial exploration was an idea whose time had come.

Discussion at the symposium centred about topics such as life's origin, other planetary systems, the origin and evolution of intelligence, problems of detecting signals from intelligent life, and the possible consequence of contact with extraterrestrial beings.

Despite the overwhelming number of seemingly insurmountable difficulties of time and space, and a minority of sceptics who felt the possibilities of contact were nil, the majority of scientists expressed a long-view optimism. For a start, a meteorite that had fallen in Australia in 1969 contained hydrocarbons, undoubtedly of extraterrestrial origin, that might also have been of biogenic origin (though doubt is now thrown on this), 'building blocks' or the primitive material from which life was initially synthesized. From interstellar space, radioastronomers had discovered molecules of water, ammonia, methane, hydrogen cyanide, methyl alcohol and formaldehyde (another building block) all chemical substances underlying complex organic compounds. Since no known law of nature is violated within the radius of 8,000 million light-years (the present observable range of the universe), the laws of these life components would operate everywhere.

Although it is unlikely that the primordial constituents of life would have evolved into any form similar to man, this evidence, the consensus of scientists felt, indicated enough likelihood of extraterrestrial life of other kinds to justify concerted multi-disciplinary research.

The first world symposium to take their pronouncement up for further consideration was organized in 1972 by Professor Richard Berendzen of the astronomy department at Boston University, and entitled 'Life Beyond Earth and the Mind of Man'. Again eminent scientists of all fields attended, as well as theologians and philosophers of science.

Here, it was confirmed that extraterrestrial exploration was a feasible endeavour; moreover, that the discovery of and communication with life on other planets would be the most profound achievement in the history of mankind. It would also provide untold technological and sociological benefits that could help to solve the problems of Earth civilization, though this required an uncharacteristically long-range view and might not be apparent to present-day man. There remained the procedure, the means.

Radio monitoring of the sky has seemed the most logical way to search for other civilizations for interstellar communication, although so far radio engineering has not permitted observation of large sections of the sky at once, and there is no particular reason why signals should be coincidentally aimed towards earth's radio antennae.

The solution could be in specially designed radio telescopes. Instead of searching out each of millions of stars for signals, a whole galaxy containing hundreds of billions of stars can be simultaneously monitored. One such instrument, the 1,000-foot diameter radio telescope at the National Astronomy and Ionosphere Center in Arecibo, New Mexico, could communicate with another like it at any point in the Milky Way galaxy over distances of thousands of light-years.

Other radio telescopes of even greater capability are being tried out at the Gorky Radio-physical Institute in the Soviet Union, and at the National Radio Astronomy Observatory in the US. Even larger radio telescopes that could eavesdrop to inconceivable distances in light-years are not beyond present engineering, only the billions of dollars, roubles or pounds it would cost to build them.[172]

While countless signals from extraterrestrial life might be beaming earthwards as yet undetected, until March 1972 mankind made no attempt to reverse the procedure. With the launching of the *Pioneer 10* spacecraft from Cape Kennedy, the United States sent its first effort of interstellar exploration rocketing out towards the environment of Jupiter.

On board the *Pioneer 10* went a message meant for any form of life that might intercept its lengthy journey (e.g., although it is not directed at any star, it would take 80,000 years or 4·3 light-years to reach the nearest one). Etched on a 6- by 9-inch gold-anodized aluminium plate attached to the antenna support struts of *Pioneer 10* are a male and female figure (the man's hand raised in a gesture of goodwill) and a map of the planets of this solar system. The message describes in scientific representations the location of the planets, the sun, when the spacecraft was launched, its height (which conveys the relative height of the human figures) and *Pioneer 10*'s trajectory from earth, thus hopefully identifying this one star and one year among a galaxy of billions.

Although the plaque might be read even by life-forms without eyes, through 'radio wavelength vision', to extraterrestrials the human figures may be the most baffling part of the message from Earth civilization.

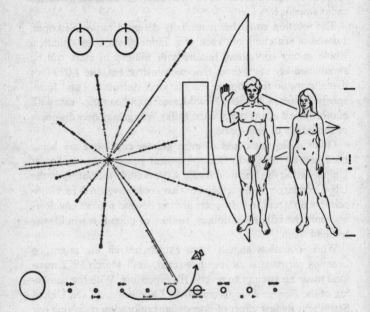

Figure 13 Plaque aboard the interstellar spacecraft *Pioneer 10*. It is hoped that it will tell extraterrestrial civilizations where the spacecraft has come from and what we look like. The spacecraft's trajectory and the relative sizes of the solar planets can be seen at the foot.

(Carl Sagan)

By December 1973, several small unmanned spacecraft were heading out into interstellar space; *Mariner 10* towards Mercury (bypassing Venus), *Pioneer 11* towards Saturn (also bearing a plaque), and four Russian spacecraft towards Mars. But on earth, too, exobiology was accelerating – in the laboratory, where the origin of life here could throw light on life elsewhere. Since the universe as understood by Earth-scientists seems extremely hospitable to life, if the origin has been a simple process, then the chances of it being so everywhere are in equal measure. Also, with *Project Viking* in 1976, instruments will be landed on the surface of Mars to explore the possibility of life-forms there.

Both American and Soviet scientists have expressed the belief that contact could be made at any moment, and probably will be – but the possibility of a two-way exchange between an extra-terrestrial civilization and Earth presents a formidable challenge. A message from a civilization more advanced would doubtless, in scientific terms, require centuries to translate, and though radio signals take only a few days to be transmitted, they take three hundred years to travel a distance of three hundred light-years. A dialogue cannot be anticipated, but valuable monologues of information sent both ways can be realistically expected.

Exobiologists are often asked why Earth should think only of advanced civilizations – why not ones more backward? Carl Sagan, founder of exobiology and Professor of Astronomy at Cornell University, in his book *The Cosmic Connection*,[132] gives this answer: 'There may be millions of civilizations less advanced than we, but we have no way to make contact with them: they lack the technology to receive or transmit.'

As for civilizations vastly in advance of our own, Dr Sagan writes: 'Civilizations hundreds or thousands or millions of years beyond us should have sciences and technologies so far beyond our present capabilities as to be indistinguishable from magic. It is not that what they can do violates the laws of physics; it is that we will not understand how they are able to do what they do.'

Messages may be coming to us all the time, perhaps by radio waves, but also perhaps from 'X-ray stars, gravity waves, neutrinos, or transmission channels that no one on Earth will dream of for centuries'. On the other hand, they may be propelled earthwards by unimaginably sophisticated instruments – or even be here already in some everyday form of experience.

People worry that Earth might become enslaved by hostile advanced civilizations and advocate keeping the presence of this planet safely undetectable. But it is already too late: what Arthur C. Clarke (famous science fiction author of *2001: A Space Odyssey*) calls 'our electronic birthcries' have been radiating through space ever since the invention of radio broadcasting. However, the likelihood of hostility or aggression from more advanced civilizations may be a contradiction; more likely is a benevolent civilization waiting for this planet to 'grow up' and become a mature participant in a harmonious galactic culture.

A quite different means of extraterrestrial travel and communication may lie in an at-present hypothetical concept, the theory of 'black holes' in the universe. These are stars so massive (more than 2·5 times as massive as our sun) that even photons cannot escape; thus they are dark, and because no light emanates from them they cannot be seen directly. Existing gravitationally, they are optically absent. The first black hole, Cygnus X–1, has been tentatively located a few thousand light-years from Earth, but it is also speculated that our universe could be a black hole.

According to various postulations, there would be no way for matter to get out of these black holes, so that in a sense they are separate universes. They may be openings to other galaxies, and if plunged into by a spacecraft, provide 'short-cuts through space and time'. Travellers might re-emerge from a black hole in what Dr Sagan wryly calls 'elsewhere and elsewhen'.

In furthest speculation, he sees black holes (there could be one in every hundred stars) as providing a 'rapid-transit system established by a federation of societies in the Galaxy'. Spacecraft would travel in the space-time continuum through 'an interlaced network of black holes'. The whole universe would be made accessible to life, and ' – in the last deep sense – unifying the cosmos'.

There is yet another possibility for cosmic communication – with the mind itself, in body-free 'astral projection'. As evidence gathers of the ability of some persons to project their consciousness for considerable distances at will, this might become what Edgar Mitchell has described as 'a perfectly valid form of intergalactic travel, and a lot safer probably than space flight'.

And, in a more democratic and inclusive form of communication than science as such can prove, all barriers to cosmic unification could come from thought-travel, the language of ESP.

In a recent experiment at Stanford Research Institute conducted by the physicists Harold Puthoff and Russell Targ with Ingo Swann and Harold Sherman (famous sensitive and parapsychologist), an attempt was made to probe Jupiter psychically. The object was for these two men to project their minds to that planet and record their impressions of the conditions both on it and around it. The impressions were later to be compared with the instrumental and photographic findings of *Pioneer 10*. There is already evidence that Ingo Swann and Harold Sherman have scored some 'hits', and further results will be of undoubted interest to all concerned.

6

The pattern that emerges

COMING to the end of this attempted spectrum, I am regretfully aware of valuable people and work I may have overlooked, and of the fact that I may have given some projects and theories too much room, others too little.

Also, like the scientist who pronounced a new hypothesis 'absurd' only to find it soundly verified soon after, any use of the term 'breakthrough' risks embarrassment in the swift current of progress among the subjects dealt with. Support, however, may be provided by the inevitable time-lag between establishment of new ideas and their general infiltration, let alone acceptance. Quite possibly, the very concept of 'mindpower' will remain 'far-out' for some time to come, even though it is already considerably further 'in' than when this writing was begun.

My object in presenting these subjects was to set them out in coherent form for the reader's information and evaluation. When it comes to evaluating them myself, in terms of an over-all pattern, my appraisal has no more authority than that of any discerning reader, except that I have been a long time immersed and absorbed in the research and writing, which may have some advantages in supplying perspective.

In any case, it is impossible to avoid or escape personal bias and the colouring of evidence with individual opinion – as it is said in both quantum theory and Vedanta philosophy – that which is observed cannot be separated from the mind of the observer.

And so what follows can only be offered as a point of view, for what it's worth, of the possibilities, meanings and substance of the parts and the whole.

As I see it, for instance, the growing interest in parapsychology will not now die out, but gather force. Parapsychology will continue to have its difficulties, not least of which will be lingering residues of occult association and suspicion, the shortage of serious, trained researchers, and especially, funds for more ambitious experiments.

But now that it has become a part of science and the world of education, as well as an area of investigation for military intelligence, the general public will gradually gain a more informed and thereby more open-minded attitude, which will in turn help to support its progress. As Arthur Koestler has said in his book *The Roots of Coincidence*,[72] 'One can almost foresee the time when ESP will be the fashionable craze in science . . . the dock for the accused might be changing into a bandwagon'.

Psychic research, I believe, will benefit greatly from its increasingly multidisciplinary approach. Out of a synthesis of the sciences will emerge the principle of psychic function. I, personally, feel sure it will be found to be 'innersensory' rather than 'extrasensory' (e.g., inextricable as a sense separable by any category): I can understand how awareness of our sensory equipment can increase to include the mechanism of subconscious communication or picturing, but cannot see how it could possibly be 'extra' or 'another'. Surely all our senses are sensible from within; take away the vehicle of sense, and what is sense?

More and more, I think, psychic researchers will focus experiment on the psychological aspects of spontaneous ESP, where the conscious direction of thinking is lifted off, put in abeyance, lulled, numbed or otherwise diverted or distracted, and a sensory area normally 'drowned out' can flash or float through into awareness. In other words, altered states of consciousness will become the vital arena of investigation.

It is said that Hindu philosophy has names for 165 different states of consciousness; we have perhaps thirty at the moment, with more becoming known all the time. In fact, Charles Musès says, 'there is really no such thing as an ordinary state of consciousness . . . the world is run by trance states, focused on this subject or that, by this means or that, to this depth and intensity or that. So – acculturation is slow hypnosis, as is all conditioning and behaviouristic manipulation.'

Ways will be found to amass evidence of the states of mind in which psi experiences occurred and to analyse by computer the circumstances and emotions in common. From the resulting data will come the laws involved and the models for more effective experiments, as well as means to develop psi ability and increase its use.

Of the two theories, that ESP was once our only method of communication, pre-dating language, or that it is a new evolutionary stage of our development, I prefer the former. It seems more logical to me that something spoken of so often in history and claimed by the mystics to be an integral part of spiritual development has been smothered and almost lost in technological civilization, than that we are now coming to it for the first time. We are coming to it, yes, but surely in forced recognition of the failure and sterility of an outwardly-oriented world, because we are tuning to our inner-spaces generally, including the dormant potential of psi.

Many people cannot foresee how psychic abilities could be used for the benefit of mankind, thereby dismissing the worth of parapsychology. If, however, one considers increased self-understanding, increased knowledge of human capabilities as a positive advantage, then parapsychology may contribute much to our advancement. In an article entitled '2001 – A Psychic Odyssey', in *Psychic* magazine, Alan Vaughan (its co-editor) has predicted some ways in which the use of psi could become valuable:

He foresees 'the development of ESP Chambers to electronically modify the biological energies of a person so that his ESP ability becomes enhanced and more under conscious control'. This might be used to accelerate the rate of healing of a person inside, particularly in mental illness where it would produce a feeling of tranquillity and well-being without the side-effects of drugs. The 'parapsychiatrist' might use ESP to 'probe a patient's mind for clues to repressed traumas and roots of neurotic behaviour, could accomplish in days what now takes years', and perhaps 'implant in the patient's mind constructive patterns to replace the destructive, neurotic patterns.

'Historians,' he continues, 'will use ESP to pick up impressions from the past, to get clues to more fully understand the thought-processes and cultures of bygone days . . . archaeologists will utilize ESP to discover new facts about past civilizations; it may tell them where to dig for ancient artifacts . . . and, ancient, undeciphered languages may be "cracked",' their mystery logically clarified.

Alan Vaughan, himself a psychic and author of *Patterns of Prophecy*,[166] predicts that scientists will use ESP in deciding which line of research will be the most fruitful, which of a hundred time-consuming possible experiments is the one that will give the answer. ESP ability will be a regular adjunct of medical diagnosis and will go hand-in-hand with psychic healing. ESP will be commonly used, he foresees, in all forms of inter-personal communication. Nor does he fear the misuse of psi ability, for the meditation exercises necessary for developing ESP 'tend to produce as a side-effect an ethical disavowal of violence'. He has 'never met a psychic who has attempted to injure another person through his psychic gift'; if the powers are genuine, and are slowly, naturally developed, the psychic not only understands abuse as a two-edged sword, but is refined and uplifted by the process of his own development.

How deep, how far, how wide and high might the psychic potential of mankind extend? Russians are working on 'eyeless sight', and Dr Thelma Moss has presented on television a young blind woman who can 'read' colours with her fingers, sensing their different frequencies or vibrations. Are we, then, able to see, hear, taste, touch, smell, communicate, move about, look forward or backward in time, create, meld and mingle with all humanity, all life, at a bodiless level as well as within a body? Are we totally free through the process of imagination, are we never really confined at all by the seeming organism through which we express our individuality?

Are we siphoning the intelligence of one universal creative mind in which, in non-spatial terms, we are merely variations of a life-theme? Thomas Troward, an English judge and lecturer in metaphysics, put this question in his book *The Creative Process in the Individual*:[159] 'Why does matter exist?' and answers, 'if the form were not expressed in solid substance, things would be perpetually flowing into each other so that no identity could be maintained for a single moment. The will which holds it together in concrete form is not individual but cosmic . . . without a common factor binding us to one particular mode of recognition, no intercourse between individuals would be possible – then, without the consciousness of relation to other individuals the consciousness of our own individuality would be lost, and so we would cease to have any conscious existence at all.'

Many scientists find the concepts of modern physics and parapsychology tantalizingly near-yet-far. Werner Heisenberg, whose great contribution to physics was his 'Principle of Uncertainty', has said: 'When we get down to the atomic level, the objective world in space and time no longer exists, and the mathematical symbols of theoretical physics refer merely to possibilities, not to facts'. And Dr Henry Margenau, professor of physics at Yale University, sums up this impossible-possible relationship, saying '. . . Interestingly and perhaps amusingly the physicist's *psi* has a certain abstractness and vagueness of interpretation in common with the parapsychologist's *psi* – these interactions are wholly non-material, yet they are described by the most important and the most basic equations of present-day quantum mechanics'.

I believe that the thin veil described here will be torn aside any time now, at any moment within the next few years – perhaps by those physicists who are driven by their own personal experience of what they genuinely believe was psychic. As Dr Gina Cerminara, psychologist and author of *Many Mansions*[27] (the story of Edgar Cayce) has put it: 'He (the scientist) is a convert, but split between the scientific point of view and the non-material proof of his experience. He knows, but he cannot prove. Perhaps he is worse off than those who have no science.

'On the other hand,' she continues, 'the scientist who has had psychic experience is the best hope for the production of a new paradigm in which the two (psi and physics) can meet.'

Meanwhile, through the growing number of visionary pioneers in a world I see as mentally awakening (just beginning to rub its eyes, I admit), wonderfully down-to-earth and applicable help has already come to us in the form of meditation, biofeedback and other forms of mind-control of our bodies and inward states. I, myself, meditate, and find it even more permanently harmonizing to body, mind and spirit than is claimed and described in the recent scientific research. I feel that its benefits cannot be over-stated (properly practised), and its revelations change one profoundly, self-recognizably and irrevocably for the better.

If the Maharishi's plan for meditation at the school level continues to go forward (as it seems to be doing), I foresee a gentled world (one must actually practise TM to fully understand this) in which the moral values, the spiritual insights of advanced thinkers and 'saints' are grasped in principle and as a result practised naturally by all mankind. It may not happen as fast as Maharishi Mahesh Yogi envisions ('in one generation'), but it could, I believe, and certainly in two. Despite all the seeming contradictions of violent events and shoddy non-ethics which appear to dominate the societies of the earth, I believe the discoveries and work depicted in this book illustrate that evil is showing itself as ignorance, that wars and man's inhumanity to man generally is being globally highlighted in all its futility and error. For instance, if all people everywhere meditated, they would no longer feel greed, the lust for power, the justification to kill for any reason whatever. Conversely, they would feel compassion, friendship, the desire to share, to nurture, to live as affectionate members of one family, the human species.

Biofeedback is, in our very own time, leading us to new power over our health. Already, for instance, merely through learning about alpha for this book and practising it on myself, I can send blood to my feet, regularize my heartbeat when it has accelerated, and bring on calmness at any given moment I need it. To take it further, into altered states and higher levels of consciousness, will of course, require a great deal more study and concentrated time, though I've made a start, already.

Here, then, is the common element in these advancing techniques of mind control – *time*; every small success takes persistence, patience, and tenacious application to achieve. Researchers and their subjects (particularly, perhaps, in ESP) make their headway through dedication of purpose and time. How many of us, individually, have the will to follow suit, and how much is left undiscovered in ourselves because we have not? Without so doing, however, is it possible to judge or even have an opinion on the validity of mental power? If all of us put the concentration of a Madam Kulagina into moving objects, for instance, who knows how many of us could do the same? It is a matter of interest, of choice; most of us would rather just watch and pass comment.

In realms of non-medical healing other than biofeedback techniques, the common denominator, the holistic pattern, it seems to me, is *attunement*. Whatever form the healing takes, from the laying-on-of-hands to so-called psychic surgery, there is a blending of mind and body energy in the healer that creates an accelerated force of repair, of *harmonizing* of the cells (which have responding intelligence). To my way of thinking this happens first in the mind of the healer, whether we heal another or ourselves. It doesn't much matter how the energy is evoked, with what belief, or faith or technique; if the thoughts and feelings of the healer are totally convinced of a perfect principle of being underlying imperfection, this conviction becomes the healing force. If, as often happens, the conviction is more in the mind of the one to be healed than the healer, then it works just the same.

I believe this power to heal will emerge as the greatest discovery of the century (or rediscovery – there was a carpenter of Nazareth . . .), and will not exist in a separate context to science and medicine, but as integral to both. Its nature will be understood, and ill health will become a new kind of embarrassment, pointing to an inward state in need of therapy.

In my view, one need never mention the word God, or even, if it offends, religion, for the human race to stumble upon the scientific precision of a 'mind-stuff' principle. It will simply manifest naturally from the inner intelligence unfolding in meditation, from probing further into the physical structures that emerge somehow from an invisible life-essence that creates endless forms of itself, out of itself, by its own laws.

In final analysis, I see all the parts of the subject-matter adding up to one grand whole, a unity of the absolute and the relative in action, a pattern of man at the crossroads of his own evolutionary growth into a finer, more mature species with unlimited possibilities for a more truthful and beautiful experience of living stretched ahead.

Bibliography

THIS bibliography includes books read by the author for thematic content, but not directly quoted in the text.

1. *Acupuncture* (Special report from the Editors of Enterprise Science; UDP, New York, 1972)
2. *American Society for Psychical Research Newsletter*, New York: Nos. 5 and 6, 1970; Nos. 12, 13, 14, 1972; No. 16, 1973; Nos. 21, 22, 1974; No. 24, 1975
2a. Association of Research and Enlightenment (ARE): Literature from Headquarters, Virginia Beach, Va, USA
3. *Auroville*. Auropublication, Auroville, Pondicherry, India, 1974 Auroville Literature

4. BACKSTER, C. Taped talk at Science of Mind Symposium (Ernest Holmes Research Foundation, California, 1973)
   Evidence of Primary Perception in Plant Life, *Int. J. of Parapsychology*, vol. 10, No. 4, 1968.
5. BAILEY, A. A. *The Unfinished Autobiography* (New York: Lucis Publishing, 1951. London: Lucis Press, 1951)
6. BASTIN, E. W. Lecture, Healing Conference (Health for the New Age, London, 1974)
   Taped interview, London, 1973.
7. BELOFF, J. (Ed.) *New Directions in Parapsychology* (London: Elek, 1974. USA: Int. Publications Service, 1974)
8. BENDER, H. The Rosenheim Poltergeist Case (*S.P.R. Journal*, vol. 46, Dec. 1970; and Sept. 1971)
9. BENNETT, J. G. *The Dramatic Universe, A Spiritual Psychology* (London: Hodder, 3 vols.)
10. *Bhagavad Gita*, Translated by Juan Mascaro (London and New York: Penguin Books, 1962)
11. BOHM, D. *Fragmentation and Wholeness* (New York: Humanistic Press, 1973)
    The Implicate and Enfolded Order (Monograph)
12. BOLEN, J. S. Meditation and Psychotherapy in the Treatment of Cancer. USA: *Psychic*, August 1973

13. BORISOV, O. Are we Robinsons in the Universe, *Int. J. of Paraphysics* 1973, vol. 7, pp. 123–6. (UK)

14. BRADLEY, R. A. *The Varieties of Healing Experience*, Academy of Parapsychology and Medicine 1971 Symposium, Los Altos, California, USA

15. BRO, H. H. *Edgar Cayce on Religion and Psychic Experience* (New York: Coronet, 1970)

16. BROWN, B. B. *New Mind, New Body* (New York: Harper & Row, 1974)
    The Biofeedback Syllabus (Ed.)
    The Alpha Syllabus (with J. Klug)

17. BROWNING, N. L. *The Psychic World of Peter Hurkos* (New York: Doubleday 1970. London: Muller, 1972)

18. BUCKE, R. M. *Cosmic Consciousness* (1901) (UK: Olympia Press, rev. ed. 1972. USA: Causeway, 1974)

19. BURR, H. S. *Blueprint for Immortality* (London: Neville Spearman, 1972)

20. CADE, C. M. Electrometric Arousal Measurement in the Management of Clinical Hypnosis. *Brit. J. of Clinical Hypnosis*, 1972, vol. 3, pp. 108–17

21. CADE, C. M. and WOOLLEY-HART, A. Psychophysiological Studies of Hypnotic Phenomenon. *Brit. J. of Clinical Hypnosis*, 1974, vol. 5, pp. 14–25

22. CALDER, N. *Mind of Man* (London: BBC Publications, 1970. USA: British Book Centre)

23. CAMPBELL, A. *Seven States of Consciousness* (London: Victor Gollancz, 1973. New York: Harper & Row, 1974)

24. CARLSON, R. J. (ed.) *The Frontiers of Science and Medicine*. 1975 May Lectures (London: Wildwood House)

25. CASTANEDA, C. *Journey to Ixtlan* (New York: Simon & Schuster, 1972. London: Bodley Head, 1973)

26. *Century of Christian Science Healing* (Boston: Christian Science Publishing Soc., 1966)

27. CERMINARA, G. *Many Mansions* (London: Spearman, 1967. New York: The New American Library, 1967)

28. CLARKE, A. C. *Childhood's End* (London: Sidgewick, 1964. New York: Ballantine, 1972)

29. *Cloud of Unknowing* (Ed.) Evelyn Underhill (London: Stuart & Watkins, 1970)

30. COOPER, J. C. *Taoism: The Way of the Mystic* (London: The Aquarian Press, 1972. USA: Weiser)

31. COX, W. E. Psychokinesis, ASPR Newsletter, 1972, No. 13
32. *Creative Intelligence*, London: SRM Foundation, Nos. 1, 2 and 3
33. CUTTEN, J. Instrumentation in Parapsychology, USA: *Parapsychology Review*, 1973, vol. 4, No. 4

34. DAY, L. and DE LA WARR, G. *Matter in the Making* (London: Vincent Stuart, 1966)
35. DEAN, D. and MIHALASKY, J. *Executive ESP* (USA: Prentice Hall, 1974)
    ASPR Newsletter, Spring, 1972
    Radiation Field Photography (*Osteopathic Physician*, New York, Oct. 1972)
36. DILLAWAY, N. *The Gospel of Emerson* (Missouri: Unity Books)
37. DUNBAR, H.F. *Emotions and Bodily Changes* (New York: Columbia Univ. Press, 1954)
    Mind and Body: Psychosomatic Medicine (New York: Random House, 1947–55)

38. EISENBUD, J. *The World of Ted Serios* (New York: Morrow, 1967. London: Cape, 1968)

39. FIRSOFF, V. A. Life and Quantum Physics, USA: *Parapsychology Review* 1974, vol. 5, No. 6
40. FOREM, J. *Transcendental Meditation* (New York: Dutton, 1973)
41. FRIEDLANDER, I. *Year One Catalog* (New York: Harper & Row, 1972)
42. FROMM, E. *You Shall be as Gods* (New York: Holt Rinehart & Winston, 1966. London: Cape, 1967)
43. FULLER, J. G. *Arigo—Surgeon of the Rusty Knife* (New York: Crowell, 1974)

44. GARRETT, E. J. *Many Voices* (New York: Putnam's 1968)
45. GELLER, U. Interview in *Psychic*, USA, June 1973
46. GODWIN, J. *Occult America* (New York: Doubleday, 1972)
47. GRAD, B. Laboratory Evidence of the Laying on of Hands, *Dimensions of Healing*, Academy of Parapsychology and Medicine, 1972 Symposium, USA.
    A Telekinetic Effect on Plant Growth, No. 2, *Int. J. of Parapsychology*, 1964, vol. 6.
48. GREEN, C. *Out-of-the-Body Experiences* (London: Hamilton, 1968. New York: Ballantine Books, 1973)
49. GREEN, E. *The Varieties of Healing Experience*, Academy of Para-

psychology and Medicine, 1971 Symposium, Los Altos, Calif, USA
May Lectures, London, 1974

50. HAMMOND, S. *We are all Healers* (New York: Harper & Row, 1973. London: Turnstone Books: 1973)

51. HARDY, A. *The Living Stream* (London: Collins, 1965. New York: Harper & Row, 1967)
Biology of God (London: Cape, 1975)
Science and an Experimental Faith, *Religious Experience Research Unit*, Pamphlet, Manchester College, Oxford, 1968
Research into the Spirit of Man (USA: *Psychic*, Sept. 1972)
Taped Interview, London, 1972.

52. HARDY, A., HARVIE, R. and KOESTLER, A. *The Challenge of Chance* (London: Hutchinson, 1973. USA: Random, 1974)

53. HASTED, J. B,. BOHM, D. J., BASTIN, E. W. and O'REGAN, B. *The Many Worlds Interpretation of Quantum Mechanics*, ed. Dewitt, D. S. and Graham, N. (New Jersey: Princeton U. Press, 1973)
Taped interview, 1974
Article on metal bending (no title) (UK: *Nature*, vol. 254, pp. 470–2, April 1975)

54. Health for the New Age, Ltd. 1974 (1a, Addison Crescent, London W14 8JP)
Newsletter, 1974

55. HERBERT, B. Report on Nina Kulagina, USA: *Parapsychology Review*, 1972, vol. 3, No. 6
Kulagina Revisited, USA: *Parapsychology Review*, 1973, vol. 4, No. 4
International Congress at Prague (1973). *Int. J. of Paraphysics*, vol. 7, pp. 136–44, 1973 (UK)
PK Force Measurement, *Int. J. of Paraphysics*, vol. 7, pp. 102–5, 1973 (UK)

56. HILLS, C. B. *Nuclear Evolution: A Guide to Cosmic Enlightenment* (London: Centre Community Publications, 1968. USA: University of Trees, 1968)

57. HOLLAND, J. H. *The Varieties of Healing Experience*, Academy of Parapsychology and Medicine, 1971 Symposium, Los Altos, Calif, USA

58. HOLMES, E. *The Science of Mind* (New York: Dodd, Mead, 1938. London: Fowler)

59. HONORTON, C. Creativity and Precognition Scoring Level, *J. of Parapsychology*, vol. 31, pp. 29–42, 1967

    Relationship Between EEG Alpha Activity and ESP Card-Guessing Performance. Paper presented to the Twelfth Annual Convention of the Parapsychological Association, New York, Sept. 1969

    Effects of Feedback on Discrimination Between Correct and Incorrect ESP Responses. *J. of the ASPR*, vol. 64, pp. 404–10, 1970

    HONORTON, C., STUMP, J. A Preliminary Study of Hypnotically induced Clairvoyant Dreams. *J. of the ASPR*, vol. 63, 1969

60. HONORTON, C., DAVIDSON, R. and BINDLER, P. Feedback Augmented EEG Alpha Shifts in Subjective State and ESP Card-Guessing Performance. *J. of the ASPR*, vol. 65, pp. 308–23, 1971

61. HUMPHREYS, C. *Buddhism* (London: Penguin Books, 1951. USA: Penguin)

62. HUXLEY, A. *The Perennial Philosophy* (London: Chatto & Windus, 1969. New York: Harper & Row, 1970)

    Doors of Perception and Heaven & Hell (London: Chatto 1968. New York: Harper, 1956)

63. *International Journal of Paraphysics*, 1972, vol. 6, No. 5; 1973, vol. 7, No. 2. Paraphysical Laboratory, Downton, Wilts, England

64. JAMES, W. *The Varieties of Religious Experience* (London: Collins, 1960; USA: New American Library)

65. *Journal of American Society for Psychical Research*, vol. 63, pp. 69–82 and 167–84; 1969; vol. 66, pp. 86–102, 369–74, and 408–14, 1972

66. *Journal of Parapsychology*, USA: Vol. 30, pp. 172–83, 1966

67. *Journal for the Study of Consciousness*, USA: Vol. 5, Nos. 1 and 2, 1972–3

68. JUNG, C. G. *Memories, Dreams, Reflections* (London: Collins and Routledge & Kegan Paul, 1963. USA: Random)

69. KARAGULLA, S. *Breakthrough to Creativity* (USA: De Vorss, 1967) Interview in *Psychic*, USA: August 1973

70. KARGER, S. and ZICHA, G. *Psychical Investigation of Psychokinetic Phenomenon in Rosenheim, Germany*. 1967. Proc. of the Parapsychology Association, No. 5, pp. 33–5

71. KINNEAR, W. *Spiritual Healing* (Los Angeles, USA: Science of Mind Publications, 1973)

72. KOESTLER, A. *The Roots of Coincidence* (London: Hutchinson, 1972. USA: Random, 1972)
The Act of Creation (London: Hutchinson, 1964. New York: Dell, 1966)

73. KRIPPNER, S. An Experimental Study in Hypnosis and Telepathy *The American Journal of Clinical Hypnosis*, 1968, vol. 11, pp. 45–54
Experimentally Induced Telepathic Effects in Hypnosis and Non-Hypnosis Groups, *J. of the ASPR*, vol. 62, pp. 387–98, 1968
(Ed. with Rubin, D.) *Galaxies of Life: Human Aura in Acupuncture and Kirlian Photography* (New York: Gordon & Breach, 1973)

74. KRIPPNER, S. and HUBBARD, C. C. Clairvoyance and Alterations in Consciousness evoked by Electrosone 50 and other Devices. *International Journal of Paraphysics*, vol. 7, pp. 5–17, 1973

75. KRIPPNER, S. and ULLMAN, M. Experimentally Induced Paranormal Effects in Dreams. *International Journal of Paraphysics*, vol. 7, pp. 147–61, 1973

76. KRIPPNER, S. and VAUGHAN, A. *Dream Telepathy* (New York: Macmillan, 1973; London: Turnstone Press, 1973)

77. KRIPPNER, S. and DAVIDSON, R. *Parapsychology in the USSR* (New York, Saturday Review, March 1972)

78. KRISHNA, G. *The Biological Basis of Religion and Genius* (New York: Harper Row, 1972. London: Turnstone Press, 1973)
The True Aim of Yoga, USA: *Psychic*, February 1973

79. KRISHNAMURTI. *The First and Last Freedom* (London: Victor Gollancz 1954, USA: Theos. Publishing House, 1968)

80. KUHLMAN, K. *I believe in Miracles* (New York: Prentice Hall 1962 and New York: Pyramid, 1969)

81. LESHAN, L. *The Medium, the Mystic and the Physicist* (London: Turnstone Press, 1974. New York: Viking Press, 1974)
Physicists and Mystics: Similarities in World View, *Journal of Transpersonal Psychology*, vol. 1, No. 2, pp. 1–16, 1969
Toward a General Theory of the Paranormal. *Parapsychology Monograph*, No. 9, p. 112. New York: Parapsychology Foundation

82. LEWIS, H. R. and M. E. *Psychosomatics* (New York: Viking Press, 1972)

83. LILLY, J. C. *The Center of the Cyclone* (New York: Julian Press, 1972. London: Calder, 1973)

Man and Dolphin (New York: Julian Press, 1961. London: Gollancz, 1962)

The Mind of the Dolphin (New York: Doubleday, 1967 and Avon, 1969)

Programming and Metaprogramming in the Human Biocomputer (Menlo Park, Calif, USA: Whole Earth Catalog, 1968)

84. LILLEY, R. K. *The Varieties of Healing Experience*, Academy of Parapsychology and Medicine, 1971 Symposium, Los Altos, Calif, USA

85. LOEHR, F. *The Power of Prayer on Plants* (New York, New American Library, 1969)

86. MANN, F. *Acupuncture: Cure of Many Diseases* (London: Heinemann Medical Books, 1971. USA: Random, 1973)

The Meridians of Acupuncture (London: Heinemann Medical Books, 1964)

The Treatment of Disease by Acupuncture (London: Heinemann Medical Books, 1963)

87. MARGENAU, H. ESP in the Framework of Modern Science, *J. of ASPR*, vol. 60, pp. 198–228, 1966

88. MASTERS, R. E. L. and HOUSTON, J. *The Varieties of Psychedelic Experience* (New York: Dell, 1966. London: Turnstone Press, 1973)

Mind Games (New York: Viking, 1972. London: Turnstone Press, 1973)

89. MAY, A. A Yogic Cure for Diabetes? USA: *Psychic*, August 1973

90. MAYNE, A. J. Theoretical and Philosophical Aspects of Psychical Research, *The Soc. of Metaphysicians Ltd.*, Research Journal of Philosophy and Social Sciences (Borderline Series, No. 9) (UK)

91. MCCARTNEY, J. *Yoga—The Key to Life* (London: Rider, 1969. New York: Dutton)

92. MCCAREY, W. A. *The Varieties of Healing Experience*. Academy of Parapsychology and Medicine, 1971 Symposium, Los Altos, Calif, USA

93. MCCAUSLAND, M. Firsthand report on Psychic Surgery in the Philippines (Health for the New Age, 1973)

94. MEEK, G. W. and HARRIS, B. *From Seance to Science* (London and New York: Regency Press, 1973)

95. MIHALASKY, J. The Role of Proscopy in Managerial Decision Making. *Int. J. of Paraphysics*, vol. 7, No. 1, pp. 19–34, 1973 (UK)

How Extrasensory Perception Can Play a Role in Idea Generation, *Int. J. of Paraphysics*, vol. 7, No. 5, pp. 194–200, 1973 (UK)

96. MIHALASKY, J. and DEAN, D. Bio-Communication, *Int. J. of Paraphysics*, vol. 7, No. 3, pp. 105–13, 1973 (UK)

97. MITCHELL, E. D. (Ed.) *Psychic Exploration* (New York: Putnam, 1974)
An Adventure in Consciousness, USA: *Psychic*, December 1972
Noetics: The Emerging Science of Consciousness, USA: *Psychic*, April 1973
Papers of The Institute of Noetic Sciences (California, 1974)

98. MILLER, R. N. The Positive Effect of Prayer on Plants, USA: *Psychic*, April 1972
Taped talk, with Olga Worrall, *Scientific methods for the Detection and Measurement of Healing Energies* (Science of Mind Symposium, 'Thought as Energy', California, 1975)

99. MONKS OF THE RAMAKRISHNA ORDER, *Meditation* (London: Ramakrishna Vedanta Centre, 1972)

100. MONROE, R. A. *Journeys out of the Body* (New York: Doubleday, 1971. London: Souvenir Press, 1972)

101. MORRIS, R. L. Animals and ESP, USA *Psychic*, October 1973

102. MOSS, T. and GENGERELLI, J. A. ESP Effects Generated by Affective States, *J. of Parapsychology*, vol. 32, 1968

103. MOSS, T., CHANG, A. F. and LEVITT, M. *Journal of Abnormal Psychology*, vol. 76, 1970
and JOHNSON, K. Radiation Field Photography—report, *Psychic* July 1972
Tape, Science of Mind Symposium, 'Thought as Energy', California, 1975

104. MUSÈS, C. and YOUNG, A. M. (Ed.) *Consciousness and Reality* (New York: E. P. Dutton, 1972, Avon/Discus, 1974)

105. NARANJO, C. *The One Quest* (New York: The Viking Press, 1972)

106. *National Enquirer*, New York: 1975

107. NEEDLEMAN, J. *The New Religions* (New York: Doubleday, 1970. London: Lane, 1972)

108. *Newsweek*, 29 April 1974

109. ORNSTEIN, R. *The Psychology of Consciousness* (New York: Viking, 1972. London: Freeman, 1973)
The Brain's Other Half (London: *New Scientist*, 6 June 1974)

110. OSIS, K. Out-of-Body Research at the ASPR, USA: *ASPR Newsletter*, No. 22, 1974

New ASPR Research on Out-of-the-Body Experiences, USA: *ASPR Newsletter*, No. 14, 1972

111. OSIS, K. and BOKERT, E. ESP and Changed States of Consciousness Induced by Meditation. *J. of the ASPR*, vol. 65, pp. 18–65, 1971

112. OSTRANDER, S. and SCHROEDER, L. *Psychic Discoveries Behind the Iron Curtain* (New York: Prentice Hall, 1970)

113. OUSPENSKY, P. D. *The Fourth Way* (London: Routledge & Kegan Paul, 1957. USA: Random, 1971)

114. PANATI, C. Supersenses: *Our Potential for Parasensory Experience* (New York: New York Times Book Co., 1974)
Quantum Physics and Parapsychology (USA: *Parapsychology Review*, vol. 5:6. 1974)

115. *Parapsychology Review*, Vol. 3:6, Vol. 4:1, 2, 3, 4, 5, and 6; vol. 5:6; vol. 6:1, 2, 3. Parapsychology Foundation, New York, 1972–5

116. PEARCE, J. C. *The Crack in the Cosmic Egg* (New York: Julian Press, 1971. London: Lyrebird, 1973)

117. PERLS, F. S., HEFFERLINE, R. F. and GOODMAN, P. *Gestalt Therapy* (New York: Dell, 1965. London: Souvenir Press, 1972)

118. PETERSON, S. *A Catalog of Ways People Grow* (New York: Ballantine, 1973)

119. PIERRAKOS, J. *The Energy Field in Man and Nature* (Institute of Bioenergetic Analysis, New York, 1971: originally published as a series of articles in the Journal of Bioenergetic Research, England)

120. PRATT, J. G. *Parapsychology* (New York: E. P. Dutton, 1966)

121. *Psychic*, Calif, USA: February, April, September, December 1972; February, April, June, August, October 1973; June 1974

122. PUHARICH, A. *Uri* (London: W. H. Allen, 1974. New York: Doubleday, 1974)
The Varieties of Healing Experience, Academy of Parapsychology and Medicine, 1971 Symposium, Los Altos, Calif, USA

123. RAMACHARAKA, *Yogi Philosophy and Oriental Occultism* (London: Fowler, 1964)

124. RANDALL, J. L. Experiments to detect the Psi Effect with Small Animals, *J. of SPR*, No. 46, pp. 31–9, 1971
Group Experiments with Schoolboys, *Journal of Parapsychology*, vol. 36, June 1972
Psi Experiments with Gerbils. *J. of SPR*, No. 46, pp. 22–30, 1972

125. RAY, M. B. *Doctors of the Mind* (New York: Little, Brown, 1942)
126. RHINE, J. B. *Extra-Sensory Perception* (1934) (USA: Brandon, Rev. ed., 1971)
    New Frontiers of the Mind (1937), (USA: Greenwood, reprint 1972)
    Extrasensory Perception after Sixty Years (1940), (USA: Brandon reprint, 1965)
127. RHINE, L. E. *Mind Over Matter* (New York: Macmillan, 1970. London: Collier-Macmillan, 1972)
128. ROLL, W. G. *The Poltergeist* (USA: New American Library, 1974)
    Science Looks at the Occult, USA: *Psychic*, June 1973
129. ROLL, W. G. and MORRIS, R. L. (Ed.) *Research in Parapsychology*, 1972/3. Abstracts and papers from the 15th and 16th Annual Conventions of the Parapsychology Association (London and Los Angeles: Scarecrow, 1973 and 1974)
130. RUSSELL, E. *Design for Destiny* (London: Neville Spearman, 1971. New York: Ballantine, 1973)
131. RYZL, M. *Parapsychology: a Scientific Approach* (New York: Hawthorn, 1970)

132. SAGAN, C. *The Cosmic Connection: An Extraterrestrial Perspective* (New York: Doubleday, 1973. London: Hodder & Stoughton, 1974)
133. *Science of Mind Magazine.* Ernest Holmes, Los Angeles, Calif, USA
    Science of Mind Annual—Thought as Energy, Calif, USA, 1975
134. SCHMEIDLER, G. R. (Ed.) *Extrasensory Perception* (New York: Atherton, 1969)
    Interview in *Psychic*, USA, February 1972
    Hints to Aspiring Parapsychologists, USA: *ASPR Newsletter* No. 12, 1972
    The Focusing Effect, USA: *ASPR Newsletter*, No. 5, 1970
135. SCHMIDT, H. PK Test with a High Speed Random Number Generator, *J. of Parapsychology*, vol. 37, 1973. USA
    Psychic Exploration (Ed. Edgar Mitchell, New York, Putnam 1974)
136. SCHUTZ, W. C. *Joy—Expanding Human Awareness* (USA: Grove 1967. London: Souvenir Press, 1971)
137. SCOTT ROGO, D. The Academic Status of Parapsychology, *Parapsychology Review*, vol. 4:6, 1973 (USA)

Parapsychology, A Century of Inquiry (New York: Taplinger, 1975)

Out-of-the-Body Experiences, USA: *Psychic*, April 1973

138. SHAH, I. *Caravan of Dreams* (London: Octogon Press, 1968. USA: Penguin, 1972)

139. SHASTRI, H. P. *Meditation—its Theory and Practice* (London: Shanti, 1971)

140. SIMEONS, A. T. W. *Man's Presumptuous Brain* (New York: E. P. Dutton, 1962)

141. SIMONTON, C. O. Taped Lectures, Science of Mind Symposium, Calif. 1973

Meditation and Psychotherapy with the Treatment of Cancer, *Psychic*, July 1973

May Lectures, London, 1974

142. SLATER, W. *Hatha Yoga* (London: Theosophical Publishing House, 1966)

143. SMITH, J. Paranormal Effects on Enzyme Activity, *Int. J. of Parapsychology*, vol. 32, p. 281, 1968

144. SOAL, S. G. and BATEMAN, F. *Modern Experiments in Telepathy* (London: Faber, 1954. USA: Yale)

145. *Spiritual Frontiers Fellowship*, SFF literature (Headquarters, New York)

146. STANFORD, R. G. Psi in Everyday Life, USA: *ASPR Newsletter*, No. 16, 1973

147. STEVENSON, I. and PRATT, J. G. Explanatory Investigations of the Psychic Photography of Ted Serios, *J. of the ASPR*, vol. 62, pp. 104–29, 1968

148. STRACHAN, F. *Aquarian Guide* (UK)

149. SUGRUE, T. *There is a River: The Story of Edgar Cayce* (New York: Holt, Rinehart & Winston, 1945, Dell, 1972)

150. SWANN, I. Cosmic Art, USA: *Psychic*, February 1973

Interview in *Psychic*, USA, April 1973

ASPR Newsletter (Summer 1972)

Investigation of Psychoenergetic Phenomena, Stanford Research Institute, October 1974

Research Viewing of Natural Targets, *Parapsychology Review*, vol. 6, No. 1, 1975

151. TARG, R. and PUTHOFF, H. *Investigation of Psychoenergetic Phenomena*—Final Report, Stanford Research Institute, 1974

Remote Viewing of Natural Targets, USA: *Parapsychology Review*, vol. 6, No. 1, 1975

152. TART, C. T. (Ed.) *Altered States of Consciousness* (New York: Wiley, 1969. London: Wiley, 1969)
Interview in *Psychic,* USA, February 1973

153. TAYLOR, J. *Superminds: An Enquiry into the Paranormal* (London: Macmillan, 1975)
Article on metal bending (no title), UK: *Nature*, vol. 254, pp. 472–3, April 1975

154. TEILHARD DE CHARDIN, P. *The Phenomenon of Man* (Paris: Editions du Senil, 1955. London: William Collins, 1959. New York: Harper, 1959)
Let me Explain (London: Collins, 1970. New York: Harper & Row, 1972)

155. THOULESS, R. H. *From Anecdote to Experiment in Psychical Research* (London and Boston: Routledge & Kegan Paul, 1972)

156. TILLER, W. A. *The Varieties of Healing Experience*, Academy of Parapsychology and Medicine, 1971 Symposium, Los Altos, Calif, USA
The Transformation of Man; Monograph USA, 1970

157. TOMPKINS, P. and BIRD, C. *The Secret Life of Plants* (London: Allen Lane, 1974)

158. Transcendental Meditation, Information and Literature, available from SRM, 32 Cranbourn Street, London WC2H 7EY
Talks given at the Religious Science Church at Palo Alto, Calif, USA

159. TROWARD, T. *The Creative Process in the Individual* (1910) (London: Fowler, rev. ed. 1956. USA: Dodd, rev. ed.)
The Edinburgh Lectures on Mental Science (1904) (Fowler: London, rev. ed. 1956. USA: Dodd)

160. ULLMAN, M., KRIPPNER, S. and VAUGHAN, A. *Dream Telepathy* (New York: Macmillan, 1973. London: Turnstone, 1973)

161. ULLMAN, M., and KRIPPNER, S. A. Review of the Maimonides Dream ESP Experiments, 1964–1969. USA: *Psychophysiological.* No. 7

162. UNDERHILL, E. *Mysticism* (London: Methuen, 1904. New York: New American Library, 1955)

163. VALENTINE, T. *Psychic Surgery* (New York: Henry Regnery, 1973)

164. *Varieties of Healing Experience*, Academy of Parapsychology and Medicine, 1971 Symposium, Los Altos, Calif, USA

165. VASILIEV, L. *Experiments in Mental Suggestion*, Institute for the Study of Mental Images, Church Crookham, England, 1962

166. VAUGHAN, A. In Pursuit of the Whole. USA: *Psychic*, April 1972
2001—A Psychic Odyssey. USA: *Psychic*, September 1972
Unorthodox Healing—an Overview. USA: *Psychic*, August 1973
Patterns of Prophecy (USA: Hawthorn, 1973. London: Turnstone, 1974)

167. VOGEL, M. Taped Talk at Science of Mind Symposium (Ernest Holmes Research Foundation, Calif, 1973)
May lectures, London, 1974

168. WALLACE, R. K. *The Physiological Effects of Transcendental Meditation* (UK: Science, No. 222, 1970)

169. WALKER, E. H. *Foundations of Paraphysical & Parapsychological Phenomena* (An abstract paper, 1972)

170. WATSON, L. *Supernature* (London: Hodder, 1973. New York: Doubleday, 1973)
Romeo Error (London: Hodder, 1974. New York: Doubleday, 1975)

171. WENTZ, W. Y. E. (Ed.) *The Tibetan Book of the Dead* (London and New York: Oxford University Press, 1968)

172. WHITE, J. (Ed.) *The Highest State of Consciousness* (New York: Doubleday, 1972)
Plants, Polygraphs and Paraphysics, USA; *Psychic*, December 1972
Exobiology, the Study of Extraterrestrial Life. USA: *Psychic*, April 1973

173. WILSON, C. *The Occult* (London: Hodder, 1971. USA: Random, 1973)

174. WOLF, F. A., TOBEN, B. and SARGATTI, J. *Space, Time and Beyond* (New York: Dutton, 1975)
Taped interview, London, 1975

175. WORRALL, A. and O. Interview in *Psychic*, April 1972. USA
The Miracle Healers (New American Library, 1968)
Explore Your Psychic World (New World: Harper & Row, 1970)

176. WORSLEY, J. *Acupuncture* (Taped lecture; Big Sur recordings, Calif, 1972)
Interview in *Psychic*, July 1972

Organizations and centres concerned with mindpower research

THE following list of organizations and bodies where information about subjects in this book can be obtained, or interest in them furthered, is only partial. Although most of the main ones have been given, that is not to discount many others of value throughout the world. There are a great number of centres and brotherhoods promoting new ways of life based on mind and spirit, as well as educational bodies concerned with mindpower and the growth of consciousness within the curriculum. More complete lists, including college courses (with or without credits) can be obtained through pertinent addresses provided here.

Academy of Parapsychology and Medicine
314A Second Street,
Los Altos, California 94022
USA
Created in 1971 for the purpose of focusing lay and professional attention on interdisciplinary research in the realm of paranormal and unorthodox healing practices throughout the world. Publishes typescripts of symposia.

Acupuncture Association
34 Alderney Street
London SW 1 V 4 EU
England

American Metapsychiatric Association
2121 North Bayshore Drive
Miami, Florida 33137
USA

Director: Stanley Dean, M.D.

American Society for Psychical Research
5 West 73rd Street
New York, NY 10023
USA
Publishes newsletter and journal of proceedings and has an educational information service.

Association for Transpersonal Psychology
Box 3049
Stanford, California 94305
USA

Auroville
Pondicherry
India

or **Auroville International**
82 Bell Street
London NW 1 6 SP
England

An international 'township' of about 15 square miles in southern India, established in 1967 with approval of Government of India and commendation of UNESCO, in honour of Sri Aurbindo, and providing a 'New Age' spiritually-oriented mode of existence for all who choose to come there and espouse it. Publishes UK newsletter.

Backster Research Foundation, Inc.
1356 Seventh Avenue
San Diego, California 92101
USA
Director: Cleve Backster

The California Institute of Asian Studies
3494 Twenty-first Street
San Francisco, California 94110
USA
Graduate school for convergence of East-West cultures and comparative studies, to build a bridge of East-West spiritual-cultural understanding.

Churches' Fellowship for Psychical and Spiritual Studies
St. Mary's Abchurch
Abchurch Lane
London EC4N 7BA
England
Publishes quarterly review.

College of Psychic Studies
16 Queensberry Place
London SW7 2EB
England

Department of Psychology and Parapsychology
Andhra University
Waltair, Visakhapatnam 3
India

Director: K. Ramakrishna Rao

Division of Parapsychology
Department of Psychiatry
School of Medicine
University of Virginia
Charlottesville, Virginia 22901
USA

Division of Parapsychology and Psychophysics
Maimonides Medical Center
Department of Psychiatry
4802 Tenth Avenue
Brooklyn NY 11219
USA

The Educational Centre
Brockwood Park
Bramdean, Alresford, Hampshire
SO 24 OLQ England
Krishnamurti philosophy taught.

Energy Research Group
Institute for Bioenergetic Analysis
144 East 36th Street
New York, NY 10016
USA
Director: John Pierrakos

Ernest Holmes Research Foundation
Science of Mind
P.O. Box 75127
Los Angeles, California 90075
USA

Esalen Institute
1793 Union Street
San Francisco, California 94123
USA

Foundation of Mind Research
P.O. Box 600
Pomona NY 10970
USA

Foundation for Parasensory Investigation
1 West 81st Street – Suite 5D

New York, NY 10024
USA
Director: Judith Skutch

**Foundation for Research on
    the Nature of Man**
402 Buchanan Boulevard
Durham, North Carolina 27708
USA
Director: Joseph B. Rhine
Publishes *Journal of Parapsychology*

**Franklin School of
    Contemporary Studies**
43 Adelaide Road
London NW 3 3 QB
England
A full range of mind- and
    consciousness-expanding
    subjects are taught here.

**Group for Psychotronic
    Investigations**
Zdenek Rejdak
V Chaloupkach 59
Praha 9 – Hloubetin
Czechoslovakia

Health for the New Age
1a Addison Crescent
London W 14 8JP
England
Director: Marcus McCausland
'Holistic' Healing Trust and
    source of world-wide informa-
    tion on healing work and
    organizations.

**Higher Sense Perception
    Research Foundation**
8668½ Wilshire Boulevard
Beverly Hills, California 90211
USA
Director: Shafica Karagulla

Human Dimensions Institute
at Rosary Hill College
4380 Main Street
Buffalo, NY 14226

USA
Publishes *Human Dimensions*.

**Indian Institute of
    Parapsychology**
Jamuna Prasad
28 Hamilton Road
Allahabad
India

**Information Sources for Psi
    Education**
P.O. Box 2221
New York, NY 10001
USA
Directors: Parimal Das
    Marian Nester
Publishes *Psi News*.

**Institut für Grenzgebiete der
    Psychologie und
    Psychohygiene**
Eichhalde 12
D78 Freiburg im Bresgau
West Germany
Director: Hans Bender

**Institut Métapsychique
    International**
1 Place Wagram
75017 Paris
France

**Institute of Mystical and
    Parapsychological Studies**
John F. Kennedy University
Martinez, California 94553
USA

Institute of Noetic Sciences
575 Middlefield Road
Palo Alto, California 94301
USA
Publishes *Noetic News*

**Institute of Suggestology and
    Parapsychology**
9 Budapest Street
Sofia
Bulgaria

**Instituto Brazileiro de
Pesquisas Psicobiofisicas**
Hernani Andrades
Rua Dr Diago de Faria No. 239
Vila Clementino
04037 Sao Paulo
Brazil
Director: Hernani Andrades

**International Association for
Psychotronic Research**
Box 107
Cotati, California 94928
USA
Director in US: Stanley Krippner

**International Society for
Religion and Parapsychology**
No. 181, 4-11-7 Inokashira,
Mitaki-shi, Tokyo
Japan
Director: Hiroshi Motoyama

**Jersey Society of
Parapsychology Inc.**
P.O. Box 2071
Morristown, NJ 07960, USA

**Kundalini Research
Foundation**
10 East Thirty-Ninth Street
New York, NY 10016, USA
Based on work of Gope Krishna.

**Maharishi International
University (MIU)**
Fairfield, Iowa, USA

**Mankind Research Unlimited,
Inc.**
1143 New Hampshire Ave. N.W.
Washington, DC 20037, USA

Mind Science Foundation
102 Rector Street, 209 San
Antonio, Texas 78216, USA

**National Federation of
Spiritual Healers**
Shortacres, Church Hill

Loughton, Essex IG10 1LG
England

**New Horizons Research
Foundation**
P.O. Box 427, Station F
(10 North Sherbourne Street)
Toronto, Ontario M4Y 2L8
Canada

**New York University School
of Continuing Education**
2 University Place
New York, NY 10003
USA

Paraphysical laboratory,
Privett Farm,
Downton,
Salisbury,
Wiltshire SP 5 3 QL
England
Director: Benson Herbert
Publishes *Journal of Paraphysics.*

Parapsychological Association
(no registered address)
President: (as of 1974) Robert L.
Morris, University of
California, Santa Barbara,
California, USA
Vice-President: Gertrude R.
Schmeidler, City College, New
York
Secretary: Helmut Schmidt,
Institute of Parapsychology
(FRNM)
Treasurer: Robert L. Van de
Castle, University of Virginia
Medical Center

Parapsychology Division
Psychologisch Laboratorium der
Rijksuniversiteit
Varkenmarkt 2
Utrecht
Netherlands
Director: Martin Johnson
Publishes *Research Letter.*

Parapsychology Foundation
29 West 57th Street
New York, NY 10019
USA
President: Eileen Coly
Publishes *Parapsychology Review*;
proceedings of annual
conferences and
Parapsychological Monograph
series.

Parascience Research Unit
Institute of Parascience
Sprytown, Lifton
Devon PL16 0AY
England
Director: Peter Maddock
Publishes *Parascience*.

Psi Communications Project
Newark College of Engineering
323 High Street
Newark, NJ 07102
USA
Director: Douglas Dean

Psychical Research Foundation
Duke Station
Durham, North Carolina 27706
USA
Director: William G. Roll
Publishes *Theta*.

Psychosynthesis Institute
150 Doherty Way
Redwood City, California 94062
USA
A mind-body approach developed
by Roberto Assagioli.

**Religious Experience Research
Unit** (RERU)
Manchester College
Oxford OX1 3TD
England
Director: Sir Alister Hardy

**R. M. Bucke Memorial
Society**

4453 Maisonneuve Boulevard
West
Montreal 215
Canada
Explores states of mystical
illumination as described in
his book *Cosmic Consciousness*

**Schweizer Parapsychologische
Gesellschaft**
Fraumunsterstrasse 8
8001 Zürich
Switzerland
Publishes *Parapsychika*.

**Society for Psychical
Research** (SPR)
1 Adam & Eve Mews
London W8 6UQ
England

**Spiritual Frontiers
Fellowship** (SFF)
800 Custer Avenue
Evanston, Illinois 60202
USA
and 701 Seventh Avenue –
Suite 1010
New York, NY 10036
USA
Membership open to public.

**Spiritualist Association of
Great Britain** (SAGB)
33 Belgrave Square
London SW1X 8QB
England

Stanford Research Institute
333 Ravenswood Avenue
Menlo Park, California 94025
USA

Transcendental Meditation
(Spiritual Regeneration
Movement, SRM; Students
International Meditation
Society, SIMS; Maharishi
International University, MIU;

Science of Creative
Intelligence, SCI)
32 Cranbourn Street
London WC2 7EY
England
Centres in 60 countries
Roydon Hall Rd,
East Peckham,
Tonbridge, Kent
TN 12 5NH
England
All subjects are taught in the
light of the Science of Creative

Intelligence (SCI), the practical
aspect of which is
Transcendental Meditation.

**World Federation of
Healers**
Shortacres
Church Hill
Loughton, Essex IG 10 1 LG
England
First organization of its kind;
est. 1975.

Index

Acuometer, 157
Acupuncture, 154–60
  American investigation, 154–5
  basic premise, 156
  physiological correlation of
    meridians, 207
  point detection, 201
  point measurement, 157–8
  points related to etheric form, 204
  Russian approach, 157
  treatments for deafness and for
    mental illness, 159
Adam, Sigmund, 52
Adamenko, Victor, 157, 162
Aggression in adolescents, 53
Agpaoa, Tony, 184–5, 186–9
Alcohol effect on coronas, 165
Alexander, Charles, 132
Alpha waves, 79–81, 96, 216, 241
  self-controlled, 97–8
  training for mind control, 98–
    100
Altered states of consciousness, 76
American Association for the
    Advancement of Science, 10
  Parapsychological Association
    affiliated, 23–5
American Foundation of Religion
    and Psychiatry, 136–7
American Society for Psychical
    Research, 18
Anand, B. K., 80
Anandanand, Swami, 178, 180
Anderson, Gilbert, 175–7
Andhra University, 70
Antares (lunar module), 58
Aquarian Guide, 228
Arigo, *see* de Freitas, Jose Pedro
Asana, 179
Aserinsky, Eugene, 78
Association of Research and
    Enlightenment, 132, 133
Auras, 146
  description, 150–53

possible scientific explanation,
  162
see also Coronas; Higher sense
  perception
Autogenic Feedback Training,
  101
Autohypnotic state, 78

Backster, Cleve, 59, 190–96
Barshay, Marshall, 166
Bastin E. W., 45, 209
Beloff, John, 31
Bender, Hans, 52–3
Bennette, G., 174
Benson, Herbert, 83
  relaxation therapy, 90
Berendzen, Richard, 230
Berger, Hans, 78
Bessent, Michael, 95
Beta waves, 79, 80, 102
Bioenergetics, 36, 61
Biofeedback, 11, 34, 101–103,
    169–70, 216, 241
Bio-plasma, 160, 162, 199
Black holes, 234
Blance 185–6
Blind-matching experiments, 31
Bohm, David, 212–13
Bokert, Edwin, 91
Bonn, J. A., 86
Bose, Sir Jagadis C., 191–2
Boyers, David, 167
Brain
  structure, 103
  use of individual hemispheres,
    216–18
Brainwaves
  cycles, 78–80
  self-controlled, 97
Brazilian psychic surgery, 181–3
Breakthrough to Creativity, 147
Broad, C. D., 22
Brown, Barbara B., 99, 107
Bucke, Richard M., 209

Burbank, Luther, 197
Burr, Harold Saxton, 151–2, 160, 194

Cade, C. Maxwell, 112–16
Cancer
  detection, 162
  influence of mind state, 169–77
  National Federation of Spiritual Healers' inquiry, 173–4
  personality traits, 172
  psychic surgery, 182
  spontaneous remissions, 174
  triggering immune response, 195
Cassirer, Manfred, 41, 43
A Catalog of Ways People Grow, 228
Cayce, Edgar, 132–3, 146, 240
The Center of the Cyclone, 126
Cerebral cortex, 216
Cerminara, Gina, 240
Chakras, 204–5
  physiological correlation, 207
Chen, Norbu, 132
Chhina, G. S., 80
Chiang, Han Twu, 156–7
Children with psychokinetic ability, 48–51
Chinese health care, 160
Christian Science, 135
Circadian rhythms, 158
Clairvoyance, 10
  in diagnosis of illness, 137–8
  scepticism, 18
  travelling, 65
Clarke, Arthur C., 234
Clergy counsellors 136–7
Cloud chambers, 139–40
College courses, 70–71
  see also Education
Colours
  frequencies, 239
  sensitivity, 149
Consciousness, 207–18
  altered states, 76
  cosmic, 209
  working hypothesis, 208
Coronas, 164–5
The Cosmic Connection, 233
Cosmic consciousness, 209
Cox, W. E., 38–9

The Creative Process in the Individual, 239
Crime rate, 88–9
Cutten, John, 69
Cygnus X-1, 234

Darwin, Charles, 197
Deafness treated by acupuncture, 159
Dean, E. Douglas, 24, 60, 166–7
Deathbed observations, 121
Decision-making, 60–61
Deep relaxation, 62
de Freitas, Jose Pedro, 181–3
DeLoach, Ethel, 166–7
Delphi Method, 60
Delta waves, 79, 102
Dermatone, 158
Diabetes, 177–80
Dice tests, 38
Dimbleby, David, 47
Dolphins, 125
Domash, Lawrence, 90
Doust, John Lovatt, 174
Drawings reproduced telepathically, 46–7
Dream Telepathy, 34
Dreams, 92–5
  electroencephalograph monitoring, 32–3
  telepathy, 32–4
Drugs
  abuse, 11, 76–7
  use of transcendental meditation in rehabilitation, 86
  electrical skin resistance of users, 115
  related to extrasensory perception, 91
Dubrov, Alexander, 200
Dunbar, Helen Flanders, 130, 172

Ecsomatic experiences, 121
Eddington, Sir Arthur, 66
Education, 70–75
Edwards, Harry, 11, 173, 175
Einstein, Albert, 190
  on religion, 218
  use of cerebral hemispheres, 217–18

Eisenbud, Jule, 54
Electrical force fields
    around Madam Kulagina, 39–43
    during rotation of object 49–50
    see also Energy fields
Electrical potential of skin, 157
Electrical skin resistance, 113
Electro-dynamic fields, 151–2
Electroencephalograph
    invented by Berger, 78
    tests for telepathic reception,
        37–8
    use in dream monitoring, 32–3
Electrography, 160–62
Electrosone, 95–6
Emotions
    effect on extrasensory perception,
        29
    in long-distance extrasensory
        perception, 31–2
Emotions and Bodily Changes, 130
Endocrine glands, 204–5
Energy fields
    Kirlian photographs, 160–62
    see also Auras; Electrical force
        fields; Magnetic fields
Energy streams, 12
    in acupuncture, 156
Enlightenment, 227–8
Enzyme activity, 144–5
Epilepsy, 216
Epley, David, 134
Estebany, Oskar, 141–5
Eternal state, 203
Evolution not Revolution, 202
Executive ESP, 60
Exobiology, 12, 229
Experiments
    blind-matching, 31
    current trends, 62–9
    see also Tests
Experiments in Mental Suggestion, 35
Extrasensory perception, 11, 222
    alternative terminology, 61
    as pre-language communication,
        238
    drug-induced, 91
    tests: Schmidt's machine, 56–7
        to discover controlling
        factors 21–2
    see also Psi

Extrasensory Perception, 20
*Extrasensory Perception after Sixty
    Years*, 21
Extraterrestrial life, *see* Exobiology
Eysenck Personality Inventory
    (EPI), 30
Faith healing, 11, 130–8
    see also Healing; Psychic surgery
Faraday Chambers, 36
Focusing effect, 28
Forwald, Haakon, 39, 66
Foundation for Research into the
    Nature of Man, 23
Freud, Sigmund, 17
Frustration, 174

Gaikin, Mikhail, 167
Galaxies of Life, 166
Garrett, Eileen J., 19
Gaussmeters, 64
    in psychokinesis tests, 46
Geiger counters, 48
Geller, Uri, 43–51, 63–4, 212
Gengerelli, J. A., 29
Goitre development test on mice,
    141–2
Grad, Bernard, 140–44
Gravitational effect, 66
Green, Alyce, 100–101, 105
Green, Elmer, 100–106, 136, 169
Gurus, 226–8
Guthrie, Malcolm, 31

Hardy, Sir Alister, 31, 218–20, 222
Hasted, John, 211–12
Hatha Yoga, 204
Healing, 129–38, 242
    ability found in Japanese
        children, 51
    alteration in coronas, 165–6
    biological effect of laying-on-of-
        hands, 140–44
    cancer, 170–77
    compared to magnetic fields, 145
    increased emanations, 167
    light emanations from hands, 162
    mental state of healer, 145
    psychic surgery, 181–9
Heartbeat regulation, 105
Heat production, 41–2
Heisenberg, Werner, 240

Herbert, Benson, 41–3, 201
Higher sense perception (HSP), 146–53
Hippocrates, 129
Hirai, Tomio, 79
Hoagland, Hudson, 152
Holmes, Alex, 134
Holmes, Ernest, 136
Holmes, Ernest, Research Foundation, 139f
Holograms, 212–13
Honorton, Charles, 63, 73, 93
Houston, Jean, 91, 94–5, 108
Humanistic psychology, 128
Huxley, Aldous, 77
Hydrometer used to test psychokinesis, 42
Hypernumbers, 214–15
Hypnagogic state, 78, 102
Hypnopompic state, 78
Hypnosis, 11, 78, 108–15
    applied to dreams, 93–4
    autohypnotic state, 78
    effect on extrasensory perception, 34
    effect on paralysis, 36
    physiological correlates, 112–13
    used to develop extrasensory perception, 27
Hypnotherapy, 108

Ichazo, Oscar, 128
Ideas and Opinions, 218
Imich, A., 207
Information exchange, 74
Inner Space, 59
Insomnia, 85
Institute for Border Areas of Psychology, 70
Institute of Noetic Sciences, 59
Institute of Parapsychology, 23
Instrumentation, 205–6
    see also Gaussmeters; Geiger counters; Polygraphs; Radiometers
Investigation of Psychoenergetic Phenomena, 47
Inyushin, V., 162
Isthula vyayam, 179

James, William, 180, 218

Jeans, Sir James, 66
Johnson, Kendall R., 157, 163, 164
Johnson, Martin, 69
Journeys Out of the Body, 120
Jouvet, Michel, 113
Jupiter, 235

Ka, 160
Kamensky, Yuri, 37
Kamiya, Joe, 97–8, 169
Karagulla, Shafica, 146–50, 166, 205
Karger, Friedbert, 44, 53, 188
Kasamatsu, Akira, 79
Kidney disease, 166
Kirlian, Semyon and Valentina, 160–63, 167–8, 201
Kirlian photography, 160–63, 167–8, 201
Kleuter, H. H., 138
Kline, Milton V., 111
Koestler, Arthur, 237
Konecci, Eugene B., 35
Krippner, Stanley, 32–4, 91, 94, 162
Krishna, Gopi, 225–6
Krivorotov, Alexei, 162
Kuhlman, Kathryn, 11, 131
Kulagina, Ninel, 38, 39–43, 63
Kunjel kriya, 178–9

L-fields, 151–3, 160, 194
LSD, 125–6
Leaves, *see* Plants
Leggett, D. M. A., 222
LeShan, Lawrence, 222–5
Lewis, Howard R. and Martha E., 172
Lie detectors, *see* Polygraphs
Lilly, John, 125–8
Loehr, Franklin, 138
Long-distance telepathy, 31–2
    Moon-Earth, 58
    Moscow-Siberia, 36–7
Love, 215
Lowen, Alexander, 150
Ludwig, Arnold M., 76

MacBain, William, 61
McDougall, William, 19

Magnetic fields, 145
  see also Electrical force fields;
    Energy fields
Maharishi International University,
    86–7
Mahesh Yogi, Maharishi, 81–3,
    86–7, 241
Man and Dolphins, 125
Mana, 160
Mandus, Brother, 135
Mann, Felix, 158–9
Man's Presumptuous Brain, 172
Margenau, Henry, 51, 240
Mariner 10 spacecraft, 232
Masters, Robert, 91, 94–5, 108
Maxey, E. S., 188
Mayne, Alan, 209
Mead, Margaret, 24
Meditation, 11–12, 62, 77–92, 206–7
  no electrical skin resistance
    changes, 115
  physiological monitoring, 79–81,
    84–5
  see also Transcendental
    meditation
Meditative state, 78
*The Medium, the Mystic and the
    Physicist*, 223
Meerloo, Joost, 174
Memory improvement, 102
Menninger Foundation, 32
Mental illness, 216
  acupuncture treatment, 159
  influencing incidence of cancer,
    174–5
  use of parapsychiatry, 238
Mercado, 185
Meridians in acupuncture, 156
Mesmer, Franz Anton, 17
Metabolism
  effect of meditation, 81
  effect of transcendental
    meditation, 84–5
Metal-mind interactions, 43–51
Mihalasky, John, 60
Mikhailova, Nelya, *see* Kulagina,
    Ninel
Miller, Robert N., 138–9, 195
Milner, Dennis, 164
Mind expansion, 11
Mind games, 108–12

The Mind of the Dolphin, 125
Mitchell, Edgar, 57–9, 136
  astral projection, 234
Mitchell, Janet, 122
Monroe, Robert, 116–21
Morris, Robert, 64
Moss, Thelma, 29, 157, 162–7, 169,
    239
  college courses, 71
  long-distance extrasensory
    perception, 31
Motoyama, Hiroshi, 207
Murphy, Gardner, 32, 74, 78,
    101
Musès, Charles, 214–15, 237
Mystics, 222–5

Nadis, 207
Naranjo, Claudio, 228
National Federation of Spiritual
    Healers, 173–4
Nautilus (US submarine), 35
Needleman, Jacob, 226
Neisser, Ulric, 34
New Frontiers of the Mind, 20
New Mind, New Body, 107
The New Religions, 226
New Thought Movement, 135
Nikolaiev, Karl, 37
Northrup, F. S. C., 151

Ogilvie, Sir Heneage, 175
Organization, 210
Ornstein, Robert, 216–18
Osis, Karlis, 58, 74, 91
Out-of-the-body experiences, 10, 62,
    116–28
  physiological monitoring, 119–20
    122
Out-of-body perception, 121
Ovulation period, 153
O'Wellen, Richard, 131

P M I R, *see* Psi-mediated
    instrumental response
Paralysis affected by hypnosis, 36
Paraphysical Laboratory, 41
Parapsychological Association
  affiliated to American Association
    for the Advancement of
    Science, 23–5

Parapsychological, *cont.*
  Convention (1973), 62–3
  established, 23
Parapsychology, 238
  academic attitudes, 71–2
  college courses, 10
  routes to qualification, 74
  subjects included in term, 10
  term established in use, 21
*Parapsychology: a Scientific
  Approach*, 28
Parapsychology Foundation, 19
Parise, Felicia, 63
Patterns of Prophecy, 239
Pavlita, Robert, 200–201
Pavlova, Lutsia, 37
Peale, Norman Vincent, 136
Pentecostal Church, 135
Philippine psychic surgery, 183–9
Photography
  Kirlian, 160–63, 167–8, 201
  psychic, 54–6
  radiation, 163
Pierrakos, John, 150–51
Pioneer 10 spacecraft, 231–2
  comparison with psychic probe,
    235
Pioneer 11 spacecraft, 232
Placement technique, 39
Plants
  effect of prayer on growth, 138–9
  healing tests, 142–3
  hybridization, 197
  influence of thought, 197–8
  Kirlian/radiation photography,
    161, 163–4
  polygraph recordings, 191–6
Poltergeists, 52–4, 212
Polygraphs, 190–96, 205
Prana, 160, 164
Pratt, J. Gaither, 28, 30, 55, 162
Precognition, 10
  regarded septically, 18
  test, 59–60
Price, Patrick, 123–4
Problem solving, 216
Project Viking, 233
Psi
  definition, 26
  research, 63
  see also Extrasensory perception

The Psi Communication Project,
  59
Psi-mediated instrumental response,
  67–9
  limitations and misuses, 68–9
Psychedelic drugs, 91
Psychiatry, 17–18, 129
Psychic photography, 54–6
Psychic surgery, 181–9
  see also Faith healing; Healing
Psychoenergetics, 202–6
Psychokinesis, 10, 38–51 63–4
  in psychic surgery, 188
  negative effects, 57
  physical strain, 40
  regarded sceptically, 18
  see also Psi
Psychometry, 147
Psychosomatic illness, 130
Psychosomatics, 172
Psychotronics, 61, 200
Puharich, Andrija, 43–4, 51
  interest in psychic surgery, 181–2
Pulse rate, 40
Purification processes in Yoga,
  178–9
Puryear, Herbert, 162
Puthoff, Harold, 46, 63, 235
  remote viewing tests, 123–5

Qi, 156, 158, 160, 167
Quantum events, 211–12
Quantum mechanics, 207, 211,
  212
*Quantum Physics and
  Parapsychology* (conference),
  215
Quasi-sensory communication, 61

Radiation photography, 163–4,
  201, 205
Radiation treatment, 170
Radio telescopes, 231
Radiometers, 42
Rama, Swami, 103, 105–6
Ramakrishna Rao, K., 70
Randall, John, 30
Random events, 211
Rapid-eye-movements (R E M),
  32
  noted by Aserinsky, 78

Rassidakis, N. C., 175
'Ratchet' effect, 203–4
Ravitz, Leonard J., 153
Reich, Wilhelm, 150
Reinhart, Philip B., 139
Rejdak, Zdenek, 200
Relaxation
  deep, 62
  therapy, 90
Religions, 218–25
  Eastern, 225–8
  search by young people, 225
Religions of the East, 228
Religious Experience Research
    Unit, 218
Religious experiences, 218–22
Religious philosophies, 77
Religious Science, 135–6, 139,
    140
Remote viewing tests, 123–5
Rhine, Joseph Banks, 19–23, 26, 30,
    38, 58, 60, 70, 74
  views on hypnosis, 94
Rhine, Louisa, 19, 26
Rigby, Byron, 86
Risk analysis, 60
Rogo, D. Scott, 71, 72
Roll, W. G., 53, 206
The Roots of Coincidence, 237
Rosenheim Case, 52–3
Russia
  government-sponsored research,
    10
  research into telepathy, 23, 35–8
Ryzl, Milan, 27–8, 73
  college courses, 71

Sagan, Carl, 233, 234
Sasaki, Shigemi, 50
Schaberl, Annemarie, 53–4
Schmeidler, Gertrude, 22, 30–31,
    73–4, 123
Schmidt, Helmut, 56–7, 69, 74
Schultz, Johannes, 100
Schwarz, Berthold Eric, 33
The Science of Creative Intelligence,
    90
Science of Mind, 135–6, 139, 140
Sclerosis, 177
Scudder, John, 132
Séances, 18–19

Selkirk College, 71
Sensory deprivation, 62, 96
  as treatment for illness, 113
  effect on extrasensory perception,
    34
Sensory overload, 94–6
  effect on extrasensory perception,
    34
Sergeyev, Genady, 37, 40, 42
Serios, Ted, 54–6
Seutemann, Edwin and Sigrun,
    188–9
Shackleton, Basil, 22
Shankh-prachalan, 179
Shat karama, 178–9
Sherman, Harold, 235
Silva, Jose, 100
Simeon, A. T. W., 172
Simonton, Carl, 136, 169–72, 175
Singh, B. Baldev, 80
Smith, Ivan, 174
Smith, Sister Justa, 144–6
Soal, S. G., 22
Society for Psychical Research, 18
Sonopuncture, 158
Space-time continuum, 234
Spacecraft, 231–2
Sperry, Roger, 216
Spinal troubles, 177
Spinelli, Ernesto, 50
Spiritual Frontiers Fellowship, 134
Spiritual healing, *see* Faith healing;
    Healing
Stanford, Rex, 66–7, 69
Stepanek, Pavel, 27–8
Stevenson, Ian, 55
Stress diseases, 130, 171–2
Stump, John P., 54, 93
Suggestion, 62
Sukshyan vyayam, 179
Surgery, *see* Psychic surgery
Surrey University, 71
Swann, Ingo, 122–3, 235
  remote viewing ability, 124

Targ, Russell, 46, 235
  remote viewing tests, 123, 124
Tart, Charles T., 119–21
Taylor, Alfred, 210–11
Taylor, John, 47–50
Teilhard de Chardin, Pierre, 66

Telepathy, 10
  dream, 32–4
  long-distance, 31–2, 36–8
    Moon-Earth, 57–8
    Moscow-Siberia, 36–8
  regarded sceptically, 18
  Russian research, 35–8
  thematic, 94–5
  use of electroencephalograph,
    37–8
Temporal state, 203, 204
Terletsky, Dr Ya, 39
Terte, Eleuterio, 183
Tests
  effect of meditation on
    extrasensory perception,
    91–2
  for precognition, 59–60
  of extrasensory perception, 19–23
  on children, 30
  to discover factors controlling
    extrasensory perception, 21
  see also Experiments
Theta waves, 79, 80, 102
Thought influence on plants, 198
Thouless, Robert H., 65
Tiller, William, 136, 162, 167, 168,
    202
  leaf healing, 164
Ting, Ching Yuen, 155
Tkach, Walter, 154
Tobioscopes, 157
Trances, 62
Transcendental meditation, 81–91,
    241
  effect on crime rate, 88–9
  use in rehabilitation of
    drugtakers, 86
  see also Meditation
Tropisms, 215
Troward, Thomas, 239
Trypsin, *see* Enzyme activity
Tyrrell, G. N. N., 65

Ullman, Montague, 32–4, 74, 162
The Ultimate Mystery, 59
Underhill, Evelyn, 223
United Churches of Religious
    Science, 135, 136
University of . . ., *see* under place
    name

Uri, 44
Utrecht University, 70

Van de Castle, Robert, 34, 73
Varandani, Narain, 179
*The Varieties of Psychedelic
    Experience*, 91
*The Varieties of Religious
    Experience*, 218
Vasiliev, Leonid L., 23, 35–6
Vaughan, Alan, 34, 238–9
Virgilio, 186
Vogel, Marcel, 196–9
Voluntary control of alpha waves,
    98–102
Voluntary Control Project, 100

Walker, Evan Harris, 207–9
Wallace, Robert Keith, 83
Watson, Bernard, 207
Webb, C. C. J., 220
West, D. J., 91
Wigner, Eugene P., 209
Wolf, Fred Alan, 213–14
Woolley-Hart, Ann, 112–15, 176
World Healing Crusade, 134–5
The World of Ted Serios, 55
Worrall, Ambrose, 137, 138, 139,
    195
Worrall, Olga, 137–8, 139–40,
    195
Worsley, J. R., 158

Yang, 154, 155, 158
Year One Catalog, 228
Yin, 154, 155, 158
Yoga, 77–81
  Hatha Yoga, 204
  healing applications, 178–80
  meditation, 81
  seven principles in man, 204
Young, A. M., 65–6

Zazen meditation, 79–80
Zen, 77, 79
Zener cards, 19, 20, 27
  in Moon-Earth experiment,
    58
Zheu Jiu, *see* Acupuncture
Zicha, G., 53
Zimmerman, Robert A., 150